PERUVIAN DREAM

Lani Imhof

Lahuanta Publishing

First published in 2014
Uptaded February 2015

Lahuanta publishing

62 Coconut Drive
North Nowra NSW 2541

Phone: (61 2) 4421 2584
Email: laniimhof@gmail.com

National Library of Australia Cataloguing-in-Publication Entry

ISBN 978-1-876779-98-6
Imhof, Lani, author
Peruvian Dream / Lani Imhof
Imhof, Lani – Relations with Quechua
Smith, Michael – Relations with Quechua
Carbajal Moreira Family
Travellers – Biography
Social networks
Interpersonal Relations
Peru Biography
Austrlalia Biography

910.92

Cover photo: Margot, Nélida and Carmen sorting Pacay

Cover design: Gillian Souter

All profits from the sale of this book will be donated So They Can' – www.sotheycan.org

To the Carbajal Moreira family
Without whom there would be no story to tell
And especially to Margot in her fight
to regain her health

A la familia Carbajal Moreira
Sin ellos no habría ninguna historia que contar
Y sobre todo a Margot en su lucha
por recuperar su salud

"Son las dos únicas personas que tienen un alma muy pura y es el ángel de nosotros y de muchos más porque gracias a ti, nosotros nos alimentamos y estudiamos y seguimos adelante. Pues para nosotros no hay nada y nadie que iguale su amor. Te amamos muchoooooooooo y mucho para nosotros es como el aire como el agua y como el sol y la naturaleza que nos ilumina. Te amo Michael y te amo Lani. De toda la familia que tienes en Perú. Te amoooooooos."

"You are the only two people who have such a pure soul and you are our angels and angels for many others because thanks to you, we eat, study and progress. For us, there is nothing and no-one that equals your love. We love you lots and lots. For us you are like water, sun and the nature that illuminates us. I love you Michael and I love you Lani. From all the family that you have in Peru, we love you."

Mariluz Carbajal Moreyra

COLOMBIA
ECUADOR
PERU
BRAZIL
CHILE
SOUTH
PACIFIC
OCEAN
Equator
Santo Domingo
de los Colorados
Quito
Manta
Quevedo
Portoviejo
Ambato
Riobamba
Guayaquil
Cuenca
Machala
Tumbes
Loja
Macará
Talara
Sullana
Paita
Piura
Puerto
Leguízamo
Nuevo
Rocafuerte
Pantoja
Puerto
Santander
La Pedrera
Leticia
Tabatinga
Iquitos
Nauta
Yurimaguas
Moyobamba
Tarapoto
Chachapoyas
Chiclayo
Cajamarca
Cruzeiro
do Sul
Trujillo
Salaverry
Santa
Lucia
Pucallpa
Chimbote
Tingo
Maria
Huaraz
Huánuco
Goyllarisquizga
Cerro
de Pasco
Atalaya
Huacho
La Oroya
Tarma
Lima
Callao
Huancayo
Sivia
Huancavelica
Huanta
Ayacucho
Quillabamba
Machupicchu
(ruins)
Cuzco
Manú
Puerto
Maldonado
Assis Brasil
Iñapari
Cobija
Chincha
Alta
Pisco
San Martín
Ica
Abancay
Andahuaylas
Nazca
Pan-American Highway
Juliaca
Puno
Lago
Titicaca
Arequipa
Desaguadero
Matarani
Moquegua
Toquepala
Ilo
Tacna
Arica
Río Napo
Río Putumayo
Río Caquetá
Río Pastaza
Río Santiago
Río Marañón
Río Ucayali
Río Huallaga
Río Mantaro
Río Apurímac
Río Urubamba
Río Yavari
Río Javari
Río Juruá
Río Alto Purús
Amazon
0 100 200 Kilometers
0 100 200 Miles
COLOMBIA
ECUADOR
BRAZIL
PERU
BOLIVIA
CHILE
ARGENTINA

PREFACE

I had no intention of writing a book. I'd never particularly enjoyed writing and found it quite difficult. It was my oldest and dearest friend, Kathy Thieben, who put me up to the task. While Michael and I were with the Carbajal Moreiras (who we consider our adopted Peruvian family) in 2010, we sent a group email telling our friends and family back home about our stay and how everyone was doing. Kathy, who knew the story from our first meeting with the family nine years before, replied to the email suggesting I write a book. When I read the suggestion I just laughed and thought "*as if*." "*As if* I had enough material for a book. *As if* I had the patience to sit at a computer typing away when I'd prefer to be off riding my bike. *As if* I could possibly ever write a publishable book. Sure, I had written short and fun articles for magazines. Sure, I'd written thousands of words in emails back home from our travels, but that was different. That wasn't a whole book.

I thought no more of writing a book. Then, after we arrived home I began to think about our amazing travels in South America. I thought of all of our experiences with our most wonderful and beautiful Peruvian family and the overwhelming pride Michael and I have in their achievements. I began to think maybe, just maybe, I could write a book. After all, we love telling everyone who will listen to us about our family and what they have achieved with limited means. Why not try to tell more people about the Carbajal Moreira family to demonstrate how a little support can go a long way? So I started and, four long years later, here is the finished product.

It has been painstaking, enjoyable, and at times an emotional journey as I trawled through emails and letters back and forth from the family. I'm so glad that I saved all those emails over the years even though I'm usually quick with the 'Delete' button. For someone who is not a natural writer the writing of this book has been a long and arduous process, but pales into insignificance as compared with the efforts put in by the Carbajal Moreira family to improve their future prospects.

The process of writing this book has been personally rewarding and if I have inspired one individual or family to support one needy child or family then it will have been worthwhile.

~~~~~~

NOTES ON SPANISH USAGE

I have used many Spanish terms in the book and where the meaning is not obvious, I have given the English meaning the first time a word appears. There is a glossary at the end of the book.

On pronunciation – In Spanish the letter 'H' is not pronounced. Hence the Spanish word *'hola'*, meaning hello is actually pronounced 'ola'. And the town of Huanta is pronounced 'one ta'.

As for the letter 'J', it is more like a guttural H sound. Hence the name *'Carbajal'* is pronounced Carbahal with the last syllable coming from the back of the throat.

~~~~~~

DISCLAIMER

I apologise to the Carbajal Moreira Family for any errors or omissions, due to either my recall of events or misunderstandings due to my less than perfect Spanish. There were times when Michael and I thought we were getting conflicting information from one or other family member, but it was more likely to be a misunderstanding of the language.

CONTENTS

PROLOGUE

April 2010, Huanta, Peru

I feel sick. I have diarrhoea. I hate having to wade through the mud to go to the outdoor squat hole-in-the-ground dunny in the pouring rain. I'm fed up with sharing my bed with fleas. I'm tired of the fly bites all over my legs which itch like crazy. I've had enough of the dogs barking all night... I just want to go home.

It is week nine of a twelve-week holiday in South America. After spending the first seven weeks on a wonderful adventure, cycling through Patagonia in southern Chile and Argentina, my husband Michael and I are in Huanta in the Peruvian Highlands, staying in the home of the Carbajal Moreiras, our adopted Peruvian family. Our plan was to stay with the family for three weeks and now, after only five days, I am homesick and ready to leave.

I know leaving now is not an option; the main reason we have returned to South America is to spend time with our much-loved family. Each of the eight family members had been begging us for many years to return to Peru and they had all been impatiently counting down the days until we arrived. So had we.

Maybe if I'd listened to them in the first place, I wouldn't have become ill. While harvesting peas at the back of their house, I had started eating them straight out of the pod. They told me I shouldn't be doing that as it would make me sick. I, the all-knowing *gringo,* laughed and told them that I always eat raw peas at home and they are delicious. Maybe I should have listened when they told me the little red capsicum I had been given in the markets was actually a hot chilli. Maybe if I hadn't gorged myself on the *pacay* (a strange legume) we were harvesting, I wouldn't have got sick. Maybe, maybe, maybe ... it was too late now. I was sick and I had to deal with it.

We *will* stay for the full three weeks and I know I will again become accustomed to the harsh living conditions. It's just that I am a spoilt *gringa* who is not used to living this way. Yet I only have to endure these basic conditions for three weeks and then I can go back to the luxury of living in a developed country. The Carbajal

Moreira family does not have this option. This is their home and, moreover, it is a vast improvement on how they used to live. They now have water and electricity.

It is an unfair world. By the luck of the draw, Michael and I were born in Australia, the 'lucky country', to middle-class parents. We had easy and carefree childhoods, without the need to worry about our next meal. If we were sick, our parents could afford to take us to the doctor; if it was cold at night, we had sufficient blankets to keep us warm. We were well educated and could choose to receive a tertiary education if and when we wished.

For the Carbajal Moreira family, these basics could not be taken for granted. Life for them was often a struggle for survival. All the family members had dreams for their futures, but not the means to achieve them.

We lived in two worlds on the one planet until, on a fateful day in July 2001, our paths crossed while Michael and I were half way through a ten-month journey across Latin America. At the time, we could never have envisioned the close bond that would develop between our two families over the ensuing years.

Our journey had begun as a predominantly trekking holiday in relatively westernised Chile. However, as we travelled northward into the more impoverished countries of the high Andes, we were to see and experience things that would test us to the core and help shape who we have become. We emerged stronger than before and with the determination to try to help others less fortunate than ourselves. Perhaps it was this gradual maturation that led us to meet the Carbajal Moreira family; perhaps it was pure chance, although the matriarch of this family indeed believes that some divine intervention was involved. Whatever the reason and despite the many other inspirational people on our journey, it was the *Familia Carbajal Moreira* who stole our hearts and ensured our return to Peru two more times over the next decade.

CHAPTER ONE It's Love

March 1993

'Will you marry me?' Michael asks me while kayaking down a gnarly rapid on the Shoalhaven River. I promptly capsize. My roll works perfectly and I pop up with a mile-wide grin. 'Yes,' I blubber, tears of joy rolling down my face.

Michael and I met in 1992. It was on a white-water kayaking trip on the Murrumbidgee River, near Canberra. I was 26 years old and had never been in a relationship that lasted more than a few months, and couldn't imagine that I'd ever meet someone who I could spend the rest of my life with. Michael was 28, and had been in several long-term relationships. At this stage in his life, he was not wishing to get deeply involved with a woman, especially not one who shared his love of kayaking. Kayaking was Michael's true passion, his escape – he didn't want a woman intruding on his most precious time.

On that first trip together I was mesmerized by Michael's kayaking skills and the stories of the big water he had paddled. I was impressed by his gentlemanly acts of assisting all the women on the trip with the necessary portages – passing the kayaks down the rocks beside the rapids that were too big for the novice paddlers. I was a bit miffed, however, that when it was my turn to pass my kayak down he had already moved on, leaving me to wrestle the ungainly beast on my own.

On the drive back to Sydney, we talked and talked and sang (or I should say 'yelled') to the beat of Roxanne, oblivious to the other passengers in the car. The others were dropped off first, and then it was just Michael and me in the car. Now he would surely ask me out. We arrived at his place, where I'd left my car for the weekend. He stopped the car. We kept talking. My inner voice was screaming at him to ask me out. He didn't.

As we were just about to part company, and with no sign from Michael that he was going to take the situation any further, I took the bull by the horns and asked him if he would like to see a movie the following week. His eyes lit up. 'Yes.'

It was a whirlwind romance. Within two weeks I'd told my sister that Michael was the man I was going to marry. She reminded me that I was the one who had always maintained that you needed to live with a man for a couple of years before you could contemplate marriage.

From our first date, Michael and I spent many of our evenings and most weekends together, usually on some adventure or other. On our first overnight bushwalk, Michael cursed the day we met. I had planned a lovely circuit in the Blue Mountains but had omitted to tell him about the rock climb at the end. Half way up the chains and spikes on the vertical Carlon's Head I found out about Michael's fear of heights. Unbeknown to me, he was having second thoughts about the relationship. How could he remain with a woman who seemed intent on killing him? He kept those thoughts to himself and managed to climb to the top in order to impress that same woman. However, he did curse me later, not only about the climb but also because I'd advised him to wear Dunlop Volleys (as all good bushwalkers did in those days) and his feet were aching by the time we'd completed the long road trudge at the end of the walk.

I later found out why I was the only woman he hadn't helped on that first weekend on the river. 'Oh, you came across as just so independent that I didn't think you'd want any help.'

~~~~

Within a year we were engaged, had bought a town house in West Ryde and moved in together. Six months later we were married, in a lovely ceremony in the bush overlooking Middle Harbour in Castle Cove.

We continued our active outdoors life, going away for weekends out in the bush, usually with one or other outdoor club we were members of. Life was rosy for me. I was married to a wonderful man, had a job I loved, outdoor activities most weekends and family and friends close by. Michael, however, became increasingly unhappy.
~~~~

He had grown up in the Blue Mountains and although he was living in Sydney when we met, he was never really happy there and was already harbouring a desire to leave the city. While in theory I didn't have a problem with moving to the country, I wasn't yet ready to leave Sydney and my job. How could I leave a job where I was paid to have fun with a great bunch of people? I was co-ordinating a recreation program for young people with intellectual disabilities. The members of the group were great company and I had a wonderful team of staff and volunteers to work with. I organised a range of indoor and outdoor activities as well as camps and holidays away, and I would let nothing stand in the way of the young people experiencing everything that life had to offer. My working hours were filled with laughter, and seeing the young people growing in their independence and life skills was hugely gratifying. I thought I had the best job in the world.

When I first met Michael, he had been working as a gardener for a pharmaceutical company, being a horticulturalist by trade. He found the job a bit mundane and was envious of the way I would come home from work animated and enthused and with lots of great stories about the day's activity and the achievements of the group members. He decided to look for something a little more rewarding and found a job as a trainer of long-term unemployed youth. He was given a group of 15 troubled young people to prepare for work in the natural environment. He now also came home with great stories about his youths' activities for the day, although not always so positive.

At the completion of his group's six-month course, Michael was accepted into an environmental science degree, which he began in 1996. After graduation, he got a part-time job at Warringah Council and did casual work for another company as a bush regenerator. Although he enjoyed both jobs, he was finding it increasingly difficult to face the long commutes. Living in West Ryde at the time, it took him up to an hour and a half to get to Warringah and anywhere from half to one hour to get to his bush regeneration locations spread all around Sydney.

The commuting and city life wore him down and after a year Michael was suffering from bouts of depression. Something had to give. It did.

Peruvian Dream

Pinned to my wall at home was a photo of Mount Fitz Roy, a series of sheer jagged granite peaks, in the Southern Patagonian Ice Field in Argentina. It had beckoned me every day for years. Over those years friends had regaled me with stories of their South American adventures and their picturesque photos of the Andean highlands, the local people in their colourful costumes and the women with their ubiquitous bowler hats offered more enticements. It was a part of the world I longed to experience for myself. Then Michael found an irresistible carrot to dangle before my eyes: an extended trip to South America.

His proposal would mean a painful resignation from my job, but the trip suggestion was a great incentive and I knew Michael definitely needed to get out of the city. We began learning Spanish while enjoying the new millennium celebrations, then later in the year the thrill of the Sydney Olympics. We then packed our possessions into storage and sold the car in preparation to leave in 2001. We were on a high right through the year.

Our rough plan was to spend about seven months in South America, starting in the south of Chile and gradually working our way northward through Argentina, Bolivia, Peru and Ecuador, doing many treks along the way. After South America we would visit my sister, Aviva, in California and then finish our travels in Central America.

CHAPTER 2 The Journey Begins

January 2001

We touched down in Santiago de Chile on a hot summer's day. The frenetic energy of the airport swirled around us unintelligibly and although many people offered their assistance, we understood very little, despite a year and a half of Spanish lessons.

We spent just enough time in Santiago to gather maps and information, before taking a flight to Punta Arenas in the far south of the country to begin our trekking journey northward. I had expected to be immersed into a markedly different culture but was surprised that Chile seemed remarkably similar to Australia, albeit a 1980s Australia. Perhaps from all those friends' photos, I had anticipated unique dress and food sold at street markets. But we found ourselves in Punta Arenas walking the aisles of a modern *supermercado* and lining up to pay the cashier behind people dressed much the same as Australians, in jeans and shirts.

With the help of some Chilean students we met on the plane, we were initiated into a fantastic type of accommodation – *hospedajes* - family homes that are opened up for tourists during the busy summer months. They proved to be a wonderful way to meet the locals and learn about their lives.

Our initial efforts to communicate with Chileans were rather frustrating because the language didn't sound like the Spanish we had learnt at home from our Peruvian teacher. We soon learned that Chileans speak Spanish like Australians speak English: they cut off half the word endings and they use a lot of slang. They also speak incredibly fast. And they don't bother to pronounce the letter 'S'. For example the classic Spanish saying of '*más o menos*', meaning 'more or less' becomes '*ma o mé*' in Chile speak and to buy a box of matches we had to ask for '*fóforo*' instead of the correct Spanish word, *fósforos.*

Our three new student friends laughed good-naturedly at our pitiful attempts in Spanish, and answered us in good English. We had many questions for them, but they had several for us as well. They wanted to know why a couple in their mid-thirties didn't have children. My answer that we had decided not to have children astounded them. They had never heard of people who *choose* not to have children, and were unable to comprehend my explanation that we believed there were already too many people in the world and that for selfish reasons we had opted for a life of freedom.

This was an oft-repeated question throughout our journey in Latin America. The first question most local people asked when meeting us was 'where are your children?' followed with incredulous looks when we explained that we didn't have any. The next question was always 'Why?' to which Michael often cheekily answered in Spanglish, '*Me no funciona*'. I don't work. This usually had the desired effect of causing the questioner to laugh and ask no more questions. Perhaps the reason we were asked this question with such monotonous regularity was that throughout the countries in which we travelled, the people were predominantly Catholic and couldn't fathom why anyone would not have children. We later found out that even the indigenous peoples of countries such as Bolivia and Peru practised Catholicism, sometimes mixed with their own traditional religions.

Michael and I eased into new routines and way of life as we spent the next three months in the far south of the continent in Chilean and Argentinean Patagonia. Much of our time was spent trekking through verdant forest, green foothills and soaring mountains. Mount Fitz Roy lived up to all my expectations with its huge granite domes and towers rearing above its ice and rock surrounds. The sunrise after a huge storm was especially magical with the towers taking on a burnished hue as they were struck by the sun's rays.

Between treks we stayed in *hospedajes*, trying to familiarise ourselves both with Chilean Spanish and the people.

In one such *hospedaje*, in the southern city of Coihaique, we spent several days in the home of a wonderful old couple. *Señor* Robinson was lots of fun and sprightly for his 74 years. He laughed at everything and anything and told us fantastic stories in rapid Spanish that in Michael's words 'had him nearly wetting his pants'.

He also told us much about the awful Pinochet era, when thousands of people were incarcerated and suffered horrendous torture for having anything to do with the Communist/Socialist party or for being under suspicion of having leftist leanings. This period started on September 11, 1973 when the military, headed by General Augusto Pinochet, staged a coup d'état, overthrowing President Salvador Allende's democratically elected Socialist Party. General Pinochet assumed power and established a military dictatorship that ruled Chile until 1990.

'It was an awful period,' *Señor* Robinson told us. 'I was incarcerated and tortured by the Pinochet regime. You know, the torturers were really good at their jobs because they had learned their skills from Hitler's men. After the Second World War, many Nazis and their families migrated to Chile and other South American countries. Some of them hadn't had enough of torturing and killing and they taught Pinochet's men how to inflict severe pain on people without leaving scars. I don't like talking about this time, but it taught me to be strong.'

It amazed us that *Señor* Robinson was able to come through this ghastly period with his sense of humour and zest for life intact.

He suggested we take a ferry heading north, through a beautiful archipelago of heavily rain-forested islands. Taking his advice, we booked onto the ferry which was supposed to be a 36 hour trip involving several stops en route to small fishing villages whose only access to the outside world was by water. The 36 hour trip turned into 62 hours and became a comedy of errors.

The ferry stopped at several small fishing villages to let people alight and to board. Most of these villages didn't have a boat ramp; the ferry would dock onto some rocks, or put anchor out close by, and little motor-boats would come out to meet the ferry.

We never saw much of the beautiful scenery as it rained torrentially almost the entire time, and as the ferry became more and more crowded, we were squeezed in closer together, making it difficult to even find space to lie down on the floor.

On our second night we docked at one of the larger ports at three o'clock in the morning, and by sunrise we still hadn't moved. It transpired that the ferry had docked at the boat ramp, the tide had dropped and we were then stuck on a sandbar until the tide came back in.

The next planned stop was on an island. The boat needed to dock on a narrow road ending, but the strong wind kept blowing it sideways, making it impossible for the Captain to land. He then tried to find somewhere calm enough to anchor, which proved unsuccessful as when the anchor was lowered, it was lost. We then spent several hours cruising around in circles waiting for the rough weather to abate until he finally managed to pull in to the port.

That morning Michael and I had been joking that we would be spending a third night aboard, and that joke turned into reality. During our third night on the boat, things got worse or better, depending upon your perspective. The seas became very rough – we were now in more open water and were going through a storm – and gradually the inside of the boat emptied out as people went out on deck to vomit. At this point I got a bench to myself! A cheerful smiling *Chileno* wandered through the cabin, big black garbage bag in hand, calling out '*vomitar, vomitar*'. Michael only just managed to hold in his dinner!

When we arrived at the port of Quellón on *Isla* Chiloé at 3 am it was still pouring. There was an announcement that everyone must disembark, but after many complaints from passengers, we were informed that we could stay on board until 6 am. When we did finally prepare to leave, we walked onto the outside deck of the boat and stared at the cascade of water pouring off the wharf. The town was in flood and we had to wade through cold water up to our knees to disembark.

The thing that amazed us on this 'cruise' was how well the Chileans accepted their lot with patience, good humour and resignation. Chileans must be used to things not going according to plan or to timetable because none of the locals ever tried to find out what was happening and why the boat was continually being delayed. There were seven *gringos* on board, one of whom kept going up to the Captain to enquire about our progress. We would then relay the news to the Chileans, who seemed only mildly interested and were resigned to the fact that we would get there eventually.

It was also interesting to note the different safety standards – or lack thereof. There was a sign inside the boat that said the maximum capacity was 200 passengers. By the end of the trip there must have been at least double that figure on board. If this was how it was to travel in the better off and more Westernised Chile, Michael and I wondered how bad things would get once we got to Peru and the poorest country on the continent, Bolivia. With only two toilets it could have been horrendous, but somehow the hard working crew kept the toilets in a reasonable state of cleanliness for the most part. Hot meals could be bought on board and there seemed to be sufficient food, even with the extended delays.

After drying out on *Isla* Chiloé, one of the poorer regions of Chile and which charmingly seemed to be 30 years behind the rest of the country, we did a few more treks before returning to Santiago in April. We'd just spent two and a half wonderful months in Patagonia. As the bus approached the outskirts of the metropolis of Santiago, Michael and I were horrified to see hundreds of families alongside the highway, living in squalor under pieces of corrugated iron, cardboard and even in wrecks of cars. We found it hard to comprehend how a relatively Westernised country such as Chile could have so many of its people living in such appalling conditions.

From Santiago we did a trip to nearby Valparaiso – Santiago's port city, about one and a half hours away. It's an old city with many colonial buildings in the centre, but most of the dwellings, many of which are ramshackle, are built into the exceedingly steep hills around the city centre and are tightly crammed together. Despite its historic buildings and interesting features, the city was run-down and decrepit. The streets were crowded and dirty, and full of vendors calling out their wares in an effort to make a meagre living. There were people rifling through the rubbish bins, taking out glass and cardboard, just to make a few pesos. There were beggars on the streets and poverty was everywhere.

Ten kilometres away from Valparaiso is the modern and ritzy city of Viña del Mar and the contrast between old and new, and rich and poor, made the two places seem worlds apart. *Viña* (as it is affectionately called) was obviously the playground of the rich and famous with its spotlessly clean contemporary buildings and an impressively clean and modern bus station. The contrasts between rich and poor could not have been more stark, or more overt.

Michael and I discussed the fact that although there is also a huge gap between the 'haves' and 'have-nots' in Australia, at least in Australia there is social welfare for those who need it. We also knew that we would experience a much greater degree of poverty once we began travelling in Bolivia and Peru.

From Santiago, Michael and I flew to Arica, Chile's northern-most city. This coastal city once belonged to Peru, until its defeat in the War of the Pacific in the early 1880s, still a sore point to the Peruvians. Arica is situated in the Atacama Desert, one of the driest regions of the world. With its endless sand dunes devoid of all vegetation, it is such a contrast to the lush green of southern Chile. From here we were heading to the high *altiplano*. As the bus wound its way up through the barren sand hills, climbing ever higher into the thin air, sparse vegetation began to appear. First there were cactus and grasses, and as we ascended further more plant life began to appear. After four hours, we arrived at Putre (3500m) and were surprised to find that the only trees there were eucalyptus – originally imported from Australia!

We stopped at Putre for two days to acclimatise before heading higher towards the Bolivian border. Even at this altitude we both had headaches and found ourselves breathless while walking even short distances. This was to be the start of our acclimatisation for the rest of our trip through Bolivia and Peru where we would spend much time at altitudes above 4,000m.

In Putre we met indigenous Chileans for the first time, many of whom were wearing traditional colourful Aymaran clothing. The Aymaran people are of an older civilisation than the Incas who dominated this central part of South America during the hundred years prior to the Spanish conquest in the sixteenth century. Unusually for the times, the dominating Incas (of whom the Quechuan people are direct descendants) allowed the Aymarans to keep their own language and culture. Although they speak a completely different language, there are some similarities with the Quechuan language, as we later found out from the Carbajal Moreiras. They told us that although Quechuan speakers can understand some words of Aymara, they can't really have a conversation with Aymara people.

~~~~

After travelling in Chile for over three months, Michael and I departed from San Pedro de Atacama (south of Arica) on a three-day four-wheel drive tour across the desert and salt plains to Uyuni in Bolivia, looking forward to a new country and culture.
~~~~

CHAPTER 3 Misadventure in Bolivia

May 2001

Along with five other *gringos*, Michael and I were met at the Bolivian border by our tour guide cum driver. In a laconic drawl, Ibán introduced himself. *'Mi .. nombre .. es .. Ibán.'* My name is Ibán. And this was the speed at which he talked for the entire three-day tour, causing great amusement as we recalled what several Chileans had told us deprecatingly about Bolivians. 'They are simple people who talk *very* slowly.' It was great for us as we had no trouble understanding his Spanish.

Worryingly, Ibán seemed to be half asleep when he met us at the border, and we soon found out why. He had been driving for twelve hours straight to meet us and then, without a break, he'd begun our tour. Michael sat up front and had to nudge him a few times to keep him awake.

The seven of us were squeezed tightly into an old Toyota Landcruiser for the incredible three day journey across the desert, to finish in Uyuni. For two days we drove through desolate but strikingly beautiful red sandy desert, punctuated with bizarrely-shaped sculptured rocks and coloured lakes in varying hues, ranging from reds to greens to blues, many filled with resident flocks of pink flamingos.

The final day involved a drive across the *Salar de Uyuni,* an immense white shimmering salt plain, from where all of Bolivia's salt originates. It was covered by about twenty centimetres of water which, Ibán told us, was quite unusual. The workers had an unenviable job. All day they stood in the ankle-deep salt water, shovelling salt. Due to the glare, we *gringos* were unable to look at the *salar* without wearing sunglasses, and could only imagine the pain endured by the Bolivian workers with their unprotected eyes and the damage caused.

From Uyuni Michael and I took a bus to Potosí, one of the poorest cities in Bolivia. It was an eye-opening journey. We spent seven hours being thoroughly shaken on the rough roads while feeling sick due to a lack of circulating air. The bus broke down several times, necessitating roadside repairs. At least while the driver was on his back under the bus performing the repairs, we could escape its stifling heat.

The real revelation for us, however, was to see the position accorded to Bolivia's indigenous peoples (who comprise 80 percent of the population) by those in authority, and the lack of respect shown to them by the other *gringo* tourists. The bus was half full of *gringo*s, and the other half comprised local people, most of whom appeared to be indigenous. All the *gringos* had seats, while many of the indigenous women were standing.

After a couple of hours, Michael and I offered our seats to some older women, who took them, none too gratefully. Sometime later the bus conductor, having noticed us standing, came to ask the women tersely if these were indeed their seats. He was clearly surprised that we were standing and they were sitting. The women squirmed and I assured him that we had freely given up our seats. It shocked us that none of the other *gringo* travellers (most of whom were younger than us) had offered their seats to women who could have been the same age as their grandmothers.

Although the women were reluctant to talk with us *gringos,* one of them responded after I made a concerted effort to make friendly conversation. She was dressed in traditional clothing – layers of voluminous coloured skirts, numerous jumpers and the ubiquitous bowler hat – and told us she lived in a tiny village of about twenty people, two hours from Uyuni.

'My living comes from my 200 llamas. I weave their wool and sell the animals for meat. My first language is Quechuan. I don't like speaking Spanish, my second language.' With a sigh she then told us that her five children all wear western clothing, prefer to speak Spanish and had moved to the city. We were later to hear similar comments from other indigenous Bolivians lamenting the loss of the old ways.

After an excruciatingly long trip, we finally arrived in Potosí and found ourselves a hostel.

Potosí became one of the largest cities in South America and one of the richest in the world during the sixteenth and seventeenth centuries, when it was heavily mined for its silver ore. Nowadays mining continues to be its mainstay, but the city is extremely poor.

Back in the early days, when the Spanish had operated the mines, they had used the slave labour of the indigenous peoples. These slaves were forced to work underground for four months at a time, without coming to the surface. If they survived their first four months, they were given a two month break, and then sent back for another four months. Very few survived their second spell underground. Children as young as thirteen were sent into the mines.

While Michael spent most of the following day on the hostel toilet, his first dose of 'Bolivia's Revenge', I did a tour of the mines and was shocked by the harsh working conditions which the miners had to endure, even in modern times. The labour is entirely by hand. The men can be in the mines for eight, sixteen or even twenty-four hour shifts. They use large amounts of dynamite to blast their way underground, the air is fetid and they are unable to afford face masks or other 'luxuries' such as gloves. Their life expectancy is short. Many miners have been killed by cave-ins, and some have become lost underground and died. I was told that 'if the miner doesn´t die from an accident he will die at a young age of lung disease'. One miner I spoke with said he only had six months to live – he was coughing up blood.

The dead miners' widows work on the surface, chipping away at rocks with a hammer and their bare hands, looking for remnants of tin, silver, lead and any other metal. The paltry amount they earn from this has to feed and support their typically large families, there being no workers' compensation or social security in Bolivia.

From Potosí Michael and I headed to La Paz, the administrative capital of Bolivia and at 3660 metres above sea level, the highest capital city in the world. *Paz* means 'peace' in Spanish, but it was anything but peaceful. The city is a madhouse; the roads and pavements are full of people trying to sell anything and everything, their wares spread out for all to see, from fruit and vegetables to handicrafts and dried llama foetuses (a good luck charm). Men labour, back bent, under heavy sacks of produce or whole carcasses, blood still dripping, while colourfully dressed indigenous women, bowler hats perched on their heads, sit cross-legged on the pavement, hawking their produce. To walk around the city you need to negotiate all of this while avoiding stepping on to the road where the traffic crawls along creating choking fumes, with drivers honking their horns and bus boys hanging out of the mini-van buses, yelling out their destination. The smell of urine is everywhere.

We were glad to escape the city.

Our first Bolivian trek, the Taquesi Trail, started on the outskirts of La Paz. We were accompanied for the first part of the walk by two twelve-year old school-boys who told us they walk one and a half hours downhill to school in the morning and then have to retrace their steps uphill in the afternoon. The boys cheerfully chatted with us and said they enjoyed going to school, despite the long walk. As we approached the boys' village, young children appeared with their hands out: *'Regálame!'* Give me a present, or *'Dame dulces!'* Give me sweets. Instead of handing anything out, I pulled out my well-thumbed photo album of Australiana and our families and chatted with them about Australia. They forgot about requesting presents and took delight in the photos and talk of a far away land.

Soon the vehicle track turned into a walking trail, an ancient Inca pathway still used by the local people. We followed this trail for four days and the *campesinos* (peasant farmers), wearing sandals made from old car tyres and travelling by foot, donkey or mule, greeted us with a nod as they passed us by. We felt blessed to be witnessing this ancient way of life, seemingly untouched by the twentieth century.

After this trek we returned to La Paz where we spent a couple of days before catching a bus to Sorata, a popular tourist location from which there are many trails into the mountains. As the trail we selected was to be a tough seven-day hike at high altitude, we hired a local guide with two mules. We were surprised when Constancio showed up in sandals but he assured us he would be fine. Our first night was spent camped on his family's property at over 4,000 metres of altitude and we wondered how they withstood the cold. As soon as the sun went down at 6 pm, we were forced into our tent and sleeping bags for warmth.

After leaving the family property, the next six days were spent walking through largely uninhabited country above the tree-line. The landscape was stark and barren, with soaring peaks and steep river valleys and we had many high passes to negotiate. When the mules escaped one afternoon, Constancio chased after them, with

Michael hot on his heels. Michael discovered how difficult it is to run at altitude, and was doubled over trying to catch his breath after only a short distance. Needless to say, Constancio caught the mules.

On the final night we experienced an unseasonal snow storm, when camped at 5,000 metres. While our good quality tent withstood the conditions, we awoke to find Constancio and his son (who had joined us for the last part of the hike) huddled under their cheap worn-out nylon tent, which had collapsed around them. They hadn't been able to sleep at all as they were too wet and cold. It angered and saddened us that our Bolivian guide should have to suffer from such inadequate equipment while we rich Westerners could afford quality gear.

Once back in Sorata we found the town to be unusually devoid of *gringos*. Then we heard the news that a road block was being set up by the *campesinos* in the neighbouring village. This was the only route out of Sorata. Most of the *gringos* had already left town, and we were told to leave as soon as we could as nobody knew for how long the protest would last. If we didn't leave before the roadblock was completed, we could be stuck there anywhere from a few days to three months. We found out that roadblocks are a common form of protest in both Bolivia and Peru.

That night, along with an Austrian and a Czech couple, Michael, Anja (a German friend who had hiked with us) and I talked to local people, looking for someone who had a *camioneta* (ute) and who would be prepared to drive us out. Everyone was asking an exorbitantly high price as they would run the risk of having rocks thrown at their vehicle. We finally found a fellow who said he knew of back roads to get us past the road block and to the village of Huarina, from where we could get transport to La Paz.

The following morning we seven *gringos* jumped in the back of the ute and were promptly joined by another seven Bolivians for an adventurous drive on rough roads, past villages with people yelling at us to stop, and past piles of rocks on the road, forcing us to go bush. After three hours we came to a village with a group of men, armed with rocks and slingshots, standing threateningly on the road. The vehicle could go no further, but our driver told us that we were only about two to three hours walk away from Huarina. He assured us that on foot we would experience no problems with the locals. The *campesinos'* issues were not with us *gringos* but with their Government, and it was only vehicles they were aiming to prevent from travelling.

A local man appeared with a tricycle equipped with a carrying tray, and we negotiated a price for him to carry our backpacks while we walked alongside. Walking with us seven *gringos* were a Bolivian couple with a baby and a young Bolivian lad. The road was strewn with rocks of all sizes, wire and glass, but the tricycle was able to wind its way through the maze of debris. After about six kilometres, not far from a small town, we encountered our first full road block with hundreds of *campesinos*. Our driver, being a bit scared, told us we should take our packs and walk through while he went back country. Once past the road block, our driver reappeared and we re-loaded our packs onto the tricycle and continued.

A little further along we encountered a series of groups of *campesinos,* each of which had to be bribed to allow our passage. After another two hours of walking, one of the tricycle tyres punctured and the driver, becoming afraid, refused to go any further. He told us it was only '*media hora más.*' Half an hour more to Huarina. So we shouldered our 20kg plus packs and continued walking.

The young Bolivian lad and the couple with the baby were still with us. We continued walking for more than an hour with no sign of the town. The young Bolivian then told us he knew a shortcut – 'only *media hora más.*' So we foolishly followed him through the countryside, up and down hills, with our heavy loads, wondering if he really did know where he was going. An hour later he once again told us, '*media hora más.*'

The sun was setting and it was getting cold. We reached a dirt road and asked a *campesino* for directions.

'Ah, Huarina, '*media hora más,*' he told us pointing down the road, and then on further questioning admitted that it may take us over an hour to get there.

By this stage we realised that Bolivians lacked any real sense of time and it suddenly dawned on us that the young Bolivian lad had purposely been leading us astray and was heading straight towards La Paz. He wanted to use us *gringos* as protection. After a few choice words were said to him, we seven *gringos* headed off towards Huarina in the dark.

At about 8 pm we finally saw the lights of the town twinkling away beneath us. We met an old couple on the road who told us it would be dangerous for us to go into Huarina as the town was full of drunken *campesinos* and the army had been there firing tear gas. They offered us their basement to sleep in. Having walked over thirty kilometres, we were relieved to stop.

The following morning we walked down to Huarina and found that there was no transport available. The vehicle owners were all too frightened to go out. We had no choice but to shoulder the packs and continue walking towards La Paz, seventy kilometres away.

Following back country dirt roads, we encountered groups of *campesinos*, all of whom were friendly and thought it a huge joke that we *gringos* had to walk to La Paz. At times other tracks crossed ours, and on asking local farmers if we were heading the right way, we were often given conflicting information. We found that Bolivians like to give you some sort of answer, even if they don't know the correct answer themselves.

After four hours of walking we got to the small village of Peñas. At this stage we were all exhausted - especially me. The Austrians and Czechs decided to continue on but I was unable to carry my pack any further. Michael, Anja and I walked around the town looking for vehicles in yards, hoping to convince someone to drive us to the main road – anywhere between one and three hours walk away, depending who you spoke to.

Once again, people were too scared to take their cars out and there was no petrol available. A friendly young man, Claudio, offered us the floor of his house on which to sleep. That night he filled us in on the reasons for the strikes and road blocks, which were being extended into other regions. The *campesinos* were protesting the Government's lack of action on basic needs such as clean water, regular electricity and good roads, all of which were seriously lacking in many villages. There were numerous other issues as well. During the seven weeks we'd just spent in Bolivia, there had been strikes and protests by miners, teachers, doctors, transport workers, coca growers and farmers, all complaining about their wages and working conditions.

After a good night's sleep, Claudio kindly walked with us to the intersection with the main highway to La Paz, wheeling his bicycle with two of our packs strapped on.

During the two and a half hour walk, Claudio, who was of mixed Spanish and indigenous blood, told us much about life in Bolivia and how tough survival can be when living hand to mouth in the cold and thin air of the high *altiplano*. He related stories about the poor working conditions for workers and complained about the lack of infrastructure throughout the country. I mentioned that most of the indigenous Bolivians we'd met were rather cold towards us, and he explained why:

'The indigenous people dislike and distrust white people because when the Spanish conquistadores arrived they plundered the country and over the following years sent all their mineral wealth back to Spain. Ever since Bolivia gained its independence from Spain in 1825, the members of the Government of Bolivia have been predominantly white. The Government has always been corrupt and ensures the wealth stays in the hands of the white minority.'

(nb. With the election of the indigenous Evo Morales in 2005 the make-up of the Bolivian Government has changed dramatically).

Claudio thought that on the main highway we, being tourists, would be able to get a lift back with the army. There being no sign of any vehicles, we thanked Claudio, shouldered our packs and continued walking towards La Paz. The road, still littered with rocks and debris, was busy with *campesinos* travelling on foot. Some of them had been walking for several days in atrocious footwear, while a handful of the more fortunate travellers were riding bicycles.

After over an hour of walking we heard gunshots and were told by people coming the other way that the army was ahead, firing teargas. We stopped with other *campesinos,* far enough away to keep out of trouble, then watched in horror as the army fired shots at the protesting crowd.

The army trucks then approached, clearing the rocks from the road as they went. This was our chance. Walking up to the first truck, I asked for the *jefe*.

'Could you give us a lift back to La Paz?' I enquired.

'No problem,' answered the boss, 'jump in the back. But we are going to Huarina first.'

So we sat in the open-tray back of the vehicle with a few young soldiers and their guns and drove, in a couple of hours, the distance we had walked in the last two days.

Michael, Anja and I certainly felt like traitors as our sympathies lay with the *campesinos* rather than the army, but we were relieved to be getting a lift. As we drove back towards La Paz some older people tried to jump on the back of the truck with us. The young soldiers yelled out, '*No campesinos!*', making us feel even worse. As one old barefooted man reached up to us in the truck, we instinctively pulled him in. He was clearly suffering, and once in the vehicle, the soldiers allowed him to stay, and didn't complain as we pulled in another old woman.

Most of the young army recruits came from *campesino* families themselves and must have felt compromised in the situation in which they found themselves. They told us they had been firing rubber bullets as well as tear gas, and we found out later that one person had been killed and another six injured at the protest we had witnessed.

The army drove us as far as El Alto which sits on the *altiplano* at an altitude of 4,100m, on the rim of the canyon above La Paz. It is home to almost two million people, mostly Aymarans. After being dropped off, we had to wend our way through mobs of angry people to find transport back to the city centre.

After our little adventure, Michael and I were ready to leave Bolivia and head for Peru. We had to fly out of La Paz as it was unknown for how long the roads out of the country would remain blocked. We booked on a flight bound for Cuzco.

CHAPTER 4 Peru

June 2001

Michael and I had been fearful of going to Peru. We thought Bolivia had been dangerous enough and from what we'd heard from other travellers, many *gringos* had been robbed in Peru, some of them violently.

One story in particular, told to us by a Japanese cycle tourist we had met some months earlier, worried us. Ichiro had been dining in a restaurant in the city of Arequipa in southern Peru. After dinner he had hailed a 'taxi' and requested to be taken back to his hotel. But he never made it. Instead, he found himself being driven out of town to a quiet backstreet, where he was dragged out of the car, strangled until he passed out, and then left lying on the road dressed only in his underclothes, everything else having been taken.

Ichiro's story terrified us and had caused us to question whether or not we would travel in Peru. However, on asking his favourite South American country, we were surprised to hear his answer was Peru, and his favourite city, Arequipa. 'How this could be possible after such an awful experience?' we asked, and he replied that after the robbery he had met so many wonderful people who helped and looked after him, that it left him with fond memories.

Despite our reservations, we flew to Cuzco to continue our travels. We began our exploration in the *plaza de armas*, the town square. The plaza is the central feature of almost every village, town and city in Latin America and most main roads radiate from it. Walking around Cuzco's *plaza de armas* and the surrounding streets, we were amazed at the order and cleanliness, in stark contrast to the filth of La Paz. And unlike in Bolivia where, as tourists, we were largely ignored, in Cuzco we were approached by a continuous stream of locals trying to sell us postcards, paintings, clay models, artefacts or any number of other articles. If they weren't trying to sell us something, they wanted to shine our shoes, even when I pointed to the sandals on my feet. If we walked past a restaurant, a young person out the front would try to entice us in. There was a constant procession of tour touts approaching us and asking us if we wanted to walk the Inca Trail, or visit the Sacred Valley, or take a white-water rafting trip.

At first we held onto our belongings tightly and mistrusted everyone who approached, but gradually I was able to relax and started to enjoy talking with the salespeople, although Michael continued to be guarded, being quite travel weary by this stage. Even when we declined their goods or services, the local people were generally eager to have a chat and ask us about our country and travels, and many were keen to practise their English.

I relished the opportunity to talk to so many different people and further improve my Spanish. By this stage of our travels I had a reasonable command of Spanish and could happily talk to people for ages. Michael, however, became frustrated at not being able to keep up with, or comprehend, enough of the conversation and wasn't coping well with being in such a tourist city. So we immediately organised our trek on the *Camino Inca* to the world famous Machu Picchu.

The four day Inca trail was spectacular, as we traversed ancient pathways built and used by the Incas. Much of the trail was through beautiful lush green cloud forest and en-route were many impressive Inca ruins, in stunning locations. There were three high passes to negotiate, all with incredible views of the steep mountainous countryside. The highest pass, Warmiwañusca, or Dead Woman's Pass, at 4,200m offered 360 degree views of jagged mountain ranges and deep valleys.

On the last morning, we began walking before dawn to get to the Sun Gate at the top entrance to Machu Picchu to view the sunrise. As the sun's rays illuminated the surrounding mountains and then beamed straight onto the archaeological site, nestled in the mountains, we were completely overawed. As we walked closer to the ruins, the sheer size of the site, thought to have been a secret hideaway for the Incas, was breathtaking.

As spectacular as the Inca Trail was, and although still a wonderful experience, it was somewhat marred for us by the crowds of tourists and the rubbish left behind. We couldn't help but compare it with the many other amazing hikes we had done, in less popular areas, some of which had also utilised old Inca built trails.

On finishing the *Camino Inca*, we were forced to spend several more days in Cuzco in order for me to recover from the flu, which had started on our last day on the trail. During this time Michael became increasingly fed up with the constant hassling by the tourist touts, so we decided to escape the hordes of tourists and leave the recognised *gringo* trail. We would head into the Central Highlands, for a chance to see a more traditional way of life.

This proved to be a fateful decision, and one which was to become a defining moment in our lives. We were heading for the Andean city of Ayacucho, a journey which would take three days.

From Cuzco we caught a bus to Abancay, a beautiful town with friendly townsfolk. After booking into a cheap but clean hotel, Michael and I set off to explore the town. On the outskirts, we were mobbed by a group of soccer-playing children who wanted to talk to us. As we headed back to the town centre, they followed us, and as we walked the entourage grew, with other kids and some adults joining us. They all wanted to find out about our life in Australia. Once again my trusty little photo album was pulled out and proved to be popular. We spent the rest of the afternoon answering innumerable questions about Australia.

Michael and I then realised one of the advantages of visiting less touristy towns – the local people were genuinely interested in us, without wanting to sell us anything. We were amazed that many of the questions asked by the youngsters (and some adults as well) were in relation to how much things cost in Australia. To them we must have oozed wealth as they wanted to know how much we'd paid for our airfares, how much we earned in Australia, and what was the cost of each piece of our equipment. This was quite embarrassing when we realised we were possibly talking about more money than they would ever be likely to earn in a lifetime.

From Abancay, it was a five-hour bus trip up and down tortuous mountain roads, going from lush green and warm river valleys at less than 2000m of altitude to freezing mountain passes above 4000m, to get to the town of Andahuaylas. Here we ended up in a dirty and dilapidated hotel, mould climbing the walls and a putrid bathroom. Michael angrily vented about the state of the hotel. He'd had enough of travelling and staying in cheap and dingy accommodation. I reminded him that this hotel was one of only a handful of awful places in which we'd stayed, but promised I would be happy to pay more, if necessary, to get decent accommodation in the future.

Michael and I had started having more frequent arguments once we began travelling in the less developed countries of Bolivia and Peru. Things had been fine earlier on in the trip when we'd been trekking in Chile and Argentina and didn't have to deal with difficult situations. Michael was always happiest while out in the wilderness and had taken good care of me when I found the going tough. I was not always so patient and understanding with Michael when he had trouble coping with the different types of challenging situations we encountered in more populated areas. He was not coping now.

~~~~

Despite the spectacular mountainous scenery, the following day was a long, gruelling day of ascents over several more high passes and steep descents into river valleys on rough winding dirt roads to get to Ayacucho. The trip was interminable and, after a few hours without a break, I was in need of a toilet. I approached the bus driver several times and each time was told '*media hora más*' or '*pronto*'. Soon. After another hour I was becoming quite desperate and eventually resorted to threatening the driver:

'If you don't stop *AHORA MISMO,* RIGHT NOW, I will urinate right here,' pointing to the platform beside him. This had the desired effect, and within five minutes the driver stopped the bus and there followed a mad panic by all the other passengers to get off and use the facilities, fetid as they were. None of the predominantly indigenous passengers had asked the driver to stop, but the relief on the faces of most of the women and children was clear.

Our first impressions of Ayacucho weren't favourable. Looking out the bus windows on the outskirts of the city, our senses were assailed by scenes of abject poverty. The narrow streets had never been constructed to take such a large bus so progress was slow, giving us time to view the living conditions. The inhabitants lived in small, half-finished hovels of mud-brick, all
~~~~

crammed closely together, with what appeared to be open sewers nearby. There was dust and dirt everywhere and not a blade of grass in sight. The children looked sickly, while mangy-looking dogs roamed around guarding their territories. I could sense Michael's discomfort and worried that he would want to go home straight away.

As we pulled into the bus station, Michael and I wondered what sort of lodging we might find in Ayacucho and he reminded me of my promise to him the night before. A young boy approached and asked if we were looking for accommodation.

'Yes we are,' I told him, 'is it clean and quiet?'

'Yes,' he replied, 'it's a brand new hostel and is *muy limpio y muy seguro'* (very clean and very safe) and quoted a ridiculously low price. Michael baulked at the price, thinking that such a cheap hostel would be another filthy unpleasant place. I suggested we take a look, and Michael grudgingly agreed.

We followed the young boy to '*Hospedaje Mi Casa'* – 'my house' – and were shown into the spotlessly clean white tiled lobby. The friendly owner greeted us and asked us if we'd like to see the room. As promised, the room was clean, bright and airy, and with an en-suite bathroom with hot water. Providence was shining upon us when we needed it.

After a good night's sleep, and in better spirits, we set off the following day to explore Ayacucho, and found it to be a vastly different place from our initial observations. The city centre was vibrant and, like Cuzco, the *plaza de armas* was surrounded by churches and colonial buildings from the sixteenth century. Although more unkempt than Cuzco, it had more of a 'lived in' feel to it. Apart from the shoe-shine boys, who are ubiquitous in South America, we were not pestered by any vendors trying to extract money from us. People were busily going about their own lives and not too interested in the strange *gringos.*

Michael began to relax as we looked around the city and said he was up to the challenge of visiting the jail the following day. Our hostel owner had told us about the *artesanía* (handicraft) markets at the jail, on the outskirts of town. The prisoners hand-craft the products and then sell them at their weekly markets.

To get to the jail, we boarded the crowded *colectivo* mini-bus Number 13. I was motioned to the back of the van by two men, one of whom was rather fat. They indicated that I could fit in between them on the back seat and I thought it kind of them to have squeezed over to offer me a seat. A short time later, one of the men called *baja* (the call to ask the driver to stop), then they both stood up simultaneously, pushing me around as they did so. I remember saying something to them like 'careful, one at a time'. They alighted and the bus continued, and I was pleased to have more space. A few minutes later an elderly woman asked me if I had lost anything out of my pocket. Patting my pocket, I felt the blood drain from my face when I discovered it was empty. That's when I realised that all the pushing and shoving I had experienced as the two men jostled to get past me, was actually their unzipping my pocket and removing my wallet. I'd been so cleverly pick-pocketed that I wasn't even aware that it had taken place. Michael and I never made it to the jail but, somewhat ironically, spent the rest of the afternoon at the police station making a report.

After the formalities at the police station, we visited the tourist office to find out what else was of interest around Ayacucho. Picking up a brochure of events, I noticed a *fiesta* (festival) in Quinrapa, a town not mentioned in our guidebook. It was in two days time. Pointing it out to Michael, he agreed that it could be fun and even more appealing because Quinrapa didn't rate a mention in our guidebook so there were unlikely to be many, if any, other tourists, and after my little incident we were keen to escape the city.

That afternoon I recounted the tale of my pick-pocketing adventure to the shopkeepers in the small general store near our hostel. The shopkeepers invited us to sit down with them for a chat. The first thing they wanted to know was if the *ratero* (thief) was a *gordo* (fat man) and whether he was well-dressed.

Each new customer that entered the store was told our story and they all commiserated with us, laughed with us and tried to help. Several other customers also queried whether our man was a *gordo*. He was apparently well known around town. The shopkeepers freely offered their advice and assistance in the necessities – such as the cancelling of credit cards, and the use of their telephone. While spending a good part of the afternoon chatting to these wonderful Peruvians I thought back to Ichiro and his statement that Peru was his favourite country, even after his awful strangulation experience. We could now understand.

On the evening before our departure for Quinrapa, I received a bizarre phone call at *Hospedaje Mi Casa*, from the driver of *colectivo* 13 – from which I had been pick pocketed. The driver told me that he had my wallet and that I must meet him at a certain church so that he could return it. This sounded very strange – if he had my wallet why didn't he just return it to me at the hostel, where he knew we were staying? I was intrigued but also a bit wary and unsure of what to do, so I asked our hostel owner his opinion. He suggested we should go to meet the driver, but to be safe we should take a police officer with us.

'Where can we find a police officer prepared to accompany us?' I asked.

'My son will escort you,' he replied.

So Michael and I went off with the owner's ten year old son. He took us to a nearby bus station where there was a plain-clothed police officer on duty and we told him our tale. Sounding both intrigued and bemused by my story, he agreed to accompany us. We thanked the son, sending him back home, and then hailed a *moto-taxi* – a 3-wheeled motorbike with a cabin on the back to take passengers. During the trip to the appointed church, we filled the police officer in on the details of the pick-pocketing.

On arrival, the bus driver immediately spotted us and approached.

'Who is he?' he asked nodding towards the police officer.

I explained that he was a police officer and that we had requested him to accompany us for our own security.

'*Bueno*' (good), he replied, sounding as if he had expected us to appear with a policeman.

'Do you really have my wallet?' I asked the driver.

No, he didn't have the wallet but he knew where it was. He indicated a group of men standing about a hundred metres away. '*Gordo* (fatty) over there has your wallet.'

This was all getting weirder and more confusing by the minute.

'But you told me you had my wallet.' I said to the driver.

'I just needed to get you here,' he replied.

The police officer then accompanied us to confront the group of men, while the driver remained at a discreet distance, not wanting the men to know that he was involved in their arrest.

The police officer lined up the three men and asked if we could identify any of them as the thief. Michael and I looked at each other, but neither of us could be sure whether or not we had the right '*gordo*'. Not wanting to indict an innocent man, we told the policeman that we couldn't be sure, so the policemen told the men they could leave.

The three men raced off and our fuming driver ran over to us.

'What are you doing?' He asked sharply, '*Gordo* is definitely the man who stole your wallet.'

I told him that I could not be certain and explained that I thought the man who robbed me was even fatter. The driver was so sure that he was 'our man' that the police officer chased after the three men and brought them back for us to have a second look.

Michael and I studied the mens' faces again but we were still unsure; even though they all looked like shifty characters, I couldn't make an accusation of which I was not absolutely sure.

The *colectivo* driver was furious. 'He is *definitely* the *gordo* who robbed you.'

'Sorry,' I replied, 'but I can't be sure.'

The driver angrily told us I could never expect to get my wallet back and stormed off. We hailed another *moto-taxi* and took the amused policeman back to the bus station; he laughed and joked with us the whole way back and teased Michael.

'So where were you when your wife was being robbed? You should have been protecting your wife, what sort of a husband are you?' Michael just shrugged and laughed along with the policeman.

Back at the hostel Michael and I recounted our tale of intrigue and adventure to the owner and packed our gear ready to head to Huanta and Quinrapa the next day.

CHAPTER 5

Meeting the Carbajal Moreira Family

July 2001

Following the directions we'd been given, Michael and I found the mini-bus terminus for Huanta. As we drew near, a man beckoned and pointing to a van, instructed us to get in.

'*Sí, Sí*, it's going to Huanta. *Pronto! Pronto!*'

We were informed by other passengers that these *combi* vans don't run to any timetable. The driver waits until he has a full vehicle and then he waits a bit longer to cram in a few more bodies. The more passengers he has, the more he earns. We had a seat but were squeezed in with other passengers virtually sitting on us. It was a fun trip, nevertheless, as the other passengers, all locals, were interested to know why two *gringos* would want to go to Huanta. *Gringos never* go to Huanta.

Two ladies seated opposite started chatting to us and soon many other passengers joined in the conversation. By the time we got to Huanta we had made friends with virtually everyone on the bus.

'*Pruébelo, pruébelo,*' Try it, said one of the women thrusting an interesting looking steaming parcel towards us, '*Es rico.*' She told us that the food she was offering was a *humita*, a typical Peruvian dish, made from crushed sweet corn with various spices, wrapped up and cooked in its own husk. She was right, it was delicious.

On arrival at Huanta, we were given directions on how to walk to the *fiesta,* although many in the bus had thought it too far to walk. Apart from the scare given to us on the way by a drunken *campesino,* propping himself up against his front gate with gun in hand, we made it to Quinrapa in about half an hour, without any problems.

The *fiesta* was akin to an agricultural show and as well as being an excuse to get drunk and party, like all good South American *fiestas* appeared to be, it aimed to showcase and market some of the local agricultural products.

As we were looking around and wondering where to start, two teenage girls approached and introduced themselves as Karina and Martha. They told us that they were part of a youth tourist guiding group called *Explore Razuillca* and asked if they could show us around. We were immediately drawn to the girls, in particular to Karina who was confident and bubbly, so we readily agreed and enjoyed the next couple of hours being taken to the different stalls and being informed about the local produce. Michael and I were (as we had expected) the only *gringos* at the *fiesta* and we thoroughly enjoyed the special treatment given to us.

Karina and Martha, obviously enjoying playing the role of tour guides, told all the stall owners that Michael and I were *very* important tourists from overseas and that they must let us taste their produce. Although we initially felt a bit uncomfortable with this introduction, we played along with the girls and made sure we purchased some of the exotic produce such as the fruit called *tuna* (pronounced toona). It turned out to be the fruit from the prickly pear cactus plant and is deliciously sweet and juicy, as is the ice-cream made from it. The *lúcuma* fruit, a Peruvian specialty, has the size and appearance of a nashi pear. It has a distinctive sweet flavour, like vanilla, but with an unpleasant floury texture. The products made from the *lúcuma*, however, such as the *lúcuma* flavoured ice-creams, are delicious. After Michael scoffed three ice-creams, I had to remind him that there were still many more unusual and different foods to be tasted.

We were also offered a variety of *chichas*. These fermented drinks are generally made from maize, but can also be made from different fruits. The chichas offered to us were mostly non-alcoholic, and to me they all tasted quite bitter and reminiscent of beer. We were a bit wary of trying the *chichas*, unsure about the quality of water used, but the girls assured us they were safe to drink, as the fermenting process involved boiling the water. What they omitted to tell us at the time is that *chicha* is traditionally made by the *campesinos* chewing the ground maize. Once it is well mixed with their saliva, they spit it out, add water and leave it all to ferment.

The youth in *Explore Razuillca* were preparing a '*pachamanca*'. This is a bit like a New Zealand Maori *hangi* where the meat and vegetables are roasted underground in a dug-out pit. Karina and Martha invited us to join the group later on for their *pachamanca* feast. 'But first,' they told us, 'you absolutely must go to the afternoon bull fight to be held in the make-shift ring.'

I was horrified that there was going to be a bullfight, but the girls assured us that in this bull fight the bulls were not harmed. They told us that the townspeople were too poor to want to kill their bulls and all livestock was considered valuable. So, somewhat reluctantly, we agreed to go to our first bull fight.

The bulls were led into the ring, one at a time, to face beer-drinking locals armed with rags, hats and old jumpers. One 'matador', who was not very coordinated, kept hanging his rag in front of himself so he was continually butted front and back by the bull and yet he continued coming out for more.

There were two hay-stuffed dummies in the middle of the ring and these were often the bulls' first target. They would race up to a dummy and butt it, lifting it high into the air. A couple of bulls did this, and then when they noticed the hay stuffing falling out of its casing, they casually proceeded to eat. No amount of coaxing by the 'matadors' could convince these bulls to 'fight'.

As the afternoon wore on, more and more alcohol was consumed and, fuelled by a drunken bravado, more and more local men entered the ring. At one point two drunken 'friends' tried to annoy the bull and ended up knocking each other over. This turned into a fight between the two men, with the bullfight suddenly forgotten, as the crowd cheered and laughed at the two drunks. Some other 'matadors' came to break up the fight and then the bull wandered over to see what all the commotion was about. One of the drunks then walked towards the bull indicating to it that he should charge his 'mate'. The bull just looked on with a bemused expression on his face as the drunk was thrown over the fence by another 'matador'. Not to be outdone by his *compañeros* (comrades), yet another drunken 'matador' entered the ring, against the wishes of his wife. The crowd cheered madly as the wife, bending down over the railing, pulled her husband out of the ring while giving him a good thrashing on the behind with a stick. By now, 30 or 40 'matadors' were milling in the ring and the score when we left the fight was Bulls 23, Matadors 0. We later heard that one of the tormented bulls escaped, ran through the streets, and injured one of the matadors to the point of his needing an ambulance. One more for the bulls!

As we walked from the bullfight to the *pachamanca*, we asked Karina to tell us a bit about her family.

'I'm 14 years old and I have an older sister and brother, and three younger sisters. My father is very sick and can't work, so my sisters and I have to take care of him because our mother spends a lot of time away, working in the jungle. I'd love to go to university to study, but I won't be able to because my family doesn't have enough money.'

While the *pachamanca* was cooking, she introduced us to some of the other young people who were part of the youth guiding project. Among them was Karina's older sister, 18 year-old Mariluz, who explained that the aim of *Explore Razuillca* was to give young people confidence and experience in guiding tourists and to put Huanta on the tourist map, both for Peruvian tourists and for foreigners.

Mariluz, who had finished her schooling, offered to take us to a nearby village the next day.

As I'm a vegetarian, we decided not to stay for the *pachamanca* feast, and we also wanted to get back to Huanta before it got too late. Karina showed us where we could get a *colectivo* back to Huanta, telling us it was too dangerous to walk back in the dark.

The hostel we had booked into, the best of a bad bunch, didn't seem much safer than the road. It was noisy, the paint peeling off the grimy walls and then in the middle of the night we were woken in alarm, our hearts thumping, by someone trying to break into our room. Neither of us slept well after this and we couldn't wait to get out of there in the morning.

We met Mariluz in the *plaza de armas*. She wanted to take us to the nearby township of Luricocha, about an hour and a half walk away. She asked if we'd like to go by *moto-taxi* and looked pleased when we assured her we preferred to walk. She also enjoyed walking, she told us.

One of the things that had immediately struck us about Mariluz was that her two front teeth were missing, and she only ever smiled with her mouth firmly closed. It seemed such a shame that an attractive young woman should have lost her teeth so young and clearly couldn't afford dentures. We later found out why she'd lost her teeth. Mariluz told us that when she was young her family didn't know about the importance of teeth-brushing, and they didn't have an understanding of, nor could they have afforded, a balanced diet. They ate what they could harvest from their *chacra* (small farm). Hence she and her brother each lost some teeth at an early age.

The rural road we followed had small mud brick houses spaced out along its length. Most of the houses were surrounded by fruit trees, and other crops were growing on the land behind the houses. Mariluz explained that the homes in this rural area all had *chacras*, which are home orchards or small farms. The air smelt fresher than it had in Huanta, away from the strong smell of urine that is omnipresent in most Bolivian and Peruvian towns and cities. As we walked, Mariluz gave us a running commentary in slow and clear Spanish that we could both easily understand. She was an excellent guide, as she pointed out the many different and unusual fruit trees such as numerous varieties of avocado, *lúcuma*, and *cherimoya* (custard apple), to name a few.

Nearing Luricocha, the vegetation changed and began to look greener and lusher. Mariluz pointed out that the Luricocha Valley sits at a slightly lower elevation than Huanta, and is an important fruit growing area for the region.

From Luricocha, Mariluz guided us back via a waterfall and a couple of small typical communities. The mud brick houses, many of which were double-storied, directly fronted the narrow, rough earthen streets. We watched as mud bricks were made by hand for a new house, the bricks all laid out in neat rows in the sun to dry. Quechuan women in their large traditional colourful skirts carried huge bundles on their backs. The bundles, wrapped up in a colourful *manta* (large cloth), were either of wood for the cooking fires or alfalfa to feed the '*cuy*' (guinea pigs). Mariluz explained to us that *cuy* are a delicacy in Peru.

'Really?' Michael asked, 'I used to have guinea pigs as pets.'

Mariluz looked amazed. 'We don't keep them as pets in Peru; they're too wild and vicious.'

Mariluz told us more about the financial troubles her family faced because of her father's inability to work.

'There is no social security in Peru, so if you don't work then there is no money for food or education. I am always worrying about my family and what will become of us. My mother spends long periods of time away from us, working in the jungle. She earns only a little, not enough to feed, clothe and educate us. I am looking for work, but it's really difficult to find, and when I've had jobs, I've always been exploited. I really want to study and become a professional, but how can I when we have no money and I have to look after my father and my sisters and brother?'

Once back in Huanta, Mariluz told us that Karina had asked that we come back to their house, about three kilometres from town, to meet her and the rest of the family after school. We travelled to their house in a *moto-taxi.* Travelling up the main road from Huanta's town centre, the surroundings soon took on a rural appearance. The houses fronting the road were predominantly mud brick with roofs of corrugated iron. Behind all the houses, which were fairly close together, was agricultural land. Crops were visible on some of the land, while other areas were sparsely vegetated with shrubs, grasses, cactus and small trees.

From the outside, the Carbajal Moreira house seemed fairly typical. Mariluz guided us through the corrugated iron gate, which led into the brown sun-baked dirt back yard. We were greeted by their father, Celestino, with a toothless smile, tousled dark hair and several days' growth of beard. Celestino did not look like a healthy man, with a definite yellow tinge to his skin. Also present was Celestino's mother (the children's *abuela* – grandmother), who was a traditional Quechuan woman with dark weathered skin and a voluminous coloured skirt; and a gaggle of children, all excited to have exotic *gringos* in their house.

Two straight-backed wooden chairs were provided for the guests of honour and placed in the middle of the yard. We were instructed to take a seat, while the family all stood around us. The children all crowded in close and wanted to touch us. We were the first *gringos* they had ever met.

We took in our surroundings; there were chooks running around pecking on food scraps and the yard had an earthy smell. The house was in an L-shape and looked to be part mud brick, and part concrete. It was topped with a rusty corrugated iron roof and had an unfinished look about it.

Abuela waddled off and came back a few minutes later with a bagful of bread rolls and a small bottle of *Inca cola* (a popular soft drink). Realising this was a big outlay for the family; we politely ate a bread roll each and insisted on sharing the remainder with the family.

Karina excitedly introduced *her gringos* to the family and then introduced us to all her sisters: Marleni (11), Margot (9), and Nélida (7), and a couple of young cousins. They told us that their mother, Carmen, was away working in the *selva* (jungle) and brother, Wilbur (16), was at school.

The younger kids were eager to show us their home *chacra* and excitedly raced off up the back into the fields behind the house, dragging us with them. They climbed up trees to pick fruit and insisted we try all the varieties, despite our concern as to the cleanliness of their hands. We tried *granadillas* (a type of passionfruit), *níspero* (like a small plum) and many other fruits we didn't recognise. They all talked at once and we didn't understand much, but that didn't matter as we could feel their excitement and happiness.

Back in the yard, we continued talking with Celestino and the older girls. 'It's an honour to have you in my house.' Celestino told us while apologising for his dishevelled appearance. 'I am very ill and unable to work, and it's a constant struggle to care for and educate all of my children. My wife Carmen is working in the *selva* (jungle) on our *chacra.* It's hard work for a woman, but it's the only income we have now.'

During the conversation, I dropped several hints that I would like to have a look inside their house. Michael squirmed in embarrassment at my subtle hints, but they were either not understood, or ignored, and we weren't invited inside.

I took some photos of the family and promised to send them copies when we returned to Australia. I asked for their address and was greeted with blank stares. A noisy family discussion then ensued as to how the photos could be sent to them, as they didn't actually have a mailing address and had never received mail before. Mariluz suggested we send the letter to the post office in Huanta. I asked her how she would know when it had arrived and she assured me she would go and ask. I told her that Michael and I may not be home for another six months, so it would be quite some time before the letter arrived. How would she know when to go and ask? Karina then had the idea to send it to the address of *Explore Razuillca*, and wrote down the address for us, while Michael also scribbled down our contact details for them.

After about an hour with the family, it was time for us to depart as we had a bus booked that night from Ayacucho to Lima. The kids were all hanging on to us and begging us not to leave. Indeed, we found it very hard to leave. The children had, in a very short time, touched our hearts deeply, freely giving their affection and sharing whatever they had. We gave Mariluz a donation of 50 soles (about $20) for *Explore Razuillca* and thanked her for the day.

That night on the bus to Lima, all we could think about was the family and how wonderful they were. Although obviously poor, they were willing to share whatever they had and asked for nothing in return. The older girls clearly adored their father and took great care of him, without resentment. They also took the time to volunteer their services to *Explore Razuillca* to improve themselves and their community.

They had really struck us as a special family and we both felt that we'd have liked more time to spend with them. Michael summed up my feelings in an email sent home: 'The highlight of the day was meeting the family in their home. A lovely family of six kids, father and grandma and Lani now wants to adopt a few Peruvian children!'

We left Huanta and continued on our travels, but we soon discovered the family had come with us. We found ourselves thinking about the Carbajal Moreira family, and talking about them for the remainder of our trip. We had spent such a few short hours with them, but we couldn't shake off our observations of how weighed down Karina and Mariluz were with the responsibility and concern for their entire family, and how happy and generous the younger siblings were, despite their dire circumstances. What would become of them all? Would they ever have the opportunity to get a tertiary education? It seemed so far-fetched a notion for people in their circumstances. As the weeks went by, we wondered if Mariluz had managed to find a job yet. We talked a great deal about Karina, who had initially attracted us with her bright sparkling personality and intelligence. We wondered how she was going at school. We wondered how she could reach her potential.

~~~~

We continued our journey further north in Peru.
~~~~

CHAPTER 6

Further Travels in Peru and Ecuador

July 2001

After the fateful meeting with the family in Huanta, Michael and I returned to Lima by bus. We then went directly to Huaraz in the *Cordillera Blanca* where we spent the next couple of weeks hiking in the magnificent mountain range.

Our favourite hike was the spectacular four-day Santa Cruz trek. We walked with two Spanish women and Victorino, a local mountain guide they had hired. Our Peruvian Spanish was so good by now that at times we had to interpret. Victorino had no idea what the women were talking about when they talked about the '*tienda*' and he told them there were no *tiendas* in the mountains. We explained to the Spaniards that in Peru the word *tienda* is a shop. (In Spain the word can be used for either a shop or a tent). In Peru a tent is known as a '*carpa*'.

It was satisfying to realise how much our Spanish had improved, which was to prove invaluable for our future relations with the Carbajal Moreira Family.

We headed up to northern Peru and visited several historical sites near the city of Trujillo. The huge ruin of Chan Chan, the largest adobe (clay brick) city in the world, and capital of the Chimu Empire, was built around AD 1300 and housed an estimated 60,000 inhabitants. The Incas conquered Chan Chan in 1471 but their dominance lasted less than a century. In 1532 the Spanish arrived and, with their superior weapons and horses, brutally conquered the Incan empire. The modern day Quechuan people are descendants of the Incas.

From Northern Peru, we continued on to Ecuador, leaving Peru with much sadness. Ironically, although we had initially been afraid of going there, we found we loved Peru for its friendly people, and the Carbajal Moriera family was always foremost in our minds.

In Central Ecuador, on an excursion to Baños, a touristy town at the foot of the active volcano Tungurahua, Michael and I did a walk onto the flanks of the puffing mountain which, with its huge billowing explosion, looked like the mushroom cloud of the atomic bomb. In the small *pueblo* of Runtun, a *campesino* took us onto the roof-top of his half finished house and told us about the volcano.

'The last major eruption was two years ago. The whole area was evacuated for five months and we were all sent to live near the town of Ambato, an hour away. The Government did not provide us with any food even though international aid agencies had donated money for the people. It was all sequestered by the leaders. After five months, we decided we would rather risk being killed by a volcanic eruption than starve to death, so we all came back. We fought the army and pushed through the blockade they had set up. When we got back to our homes we found that they had been plundered by the military.'

We were learning more and more about the deep-rooted corruption of many of the South American Governments, and felt for the local people just trying to eke out a living.

~~~~

Michael and I deliberated on whether or not to visit the Galapagos Islands. We had always intended going there, but our travels in South America had changed our way of thinking. It would be expensive, especially with our poor exchange rate. We had seen so much poverty in South America that we found it hard to justify spending the large sum of money required for an eight day trip, when that money could feed a Peruvian family for years.

After much soul searching, we made the decision to go. I harboured strong feelings of guilt over the amount we were spending and decided, in an attempt to allay these feelings, that I would give more money to needy people begging on the streets. I thought that if I could afford to go to the Galapagos, then I could afford to give more away. Michael was less enthusiastic about giving money to beggars as he thought this creates more problems than it solves. While I agreed with Michael, I was also keenly aware that in most South American countries many people would starve
~~~~

to death without begging. There was insufficient employment for all and no social security payments for the sick and unemployed.

Michael described our trip to the Galapagos as *'being inside a wildlife documentary'*. Every time we got off the boat onto an island, our welcoming committee consisted of numerous sea lions. Usually they were basking in the sun, lying all over each other cutely cuddling with their flippers. Swimming with them was a joy, as the females and youngsters frolicked and played with us humans in their environment. Snorkelling above giant sea turtles as they so gracefully and serenely moved their flippers, totally unbothered by our presence, was another highlight. In the Galapagos Islands the animals showed no fear of humans, allowing us to approach closely. We were witness to the highly entertaining mating antics of the Blue-footed Boobies, with their clownish electric-blue coloured feet, and the Waved Albatrosses clacking their beaks as if sword-fighting.

Neither of us regretted our decision to visit the Galapagos and we took comfort from the fact that the islands rely on tourism in order to protect their unique environment and to help ensure that they are not turned into a hunting and fishing playground.

~~~~

This was the final episode of our seven-month South American journey. From Quito in Ecuador, Michael and I flew to the USA to visit my sister in Berkeley, Northern California. Our three weeks there gave us the opportunity to take a break from travelling and reflect on the previous seven months of travel.
~~~~

CHAPTER 7 Chilling out in USA, Central America and Mexico

September 2001

The first thing that struck us, apart from the orderliness, was the beggars on the streets. We thought we had left the poverty of South America behind, for the wealthy USA, so were surprised that homelessness exists even in affluent Berkeley. However, after having seen the destitute in South America who had absolutely nothing, the Californian beggars, wearing their Nike shoes, appeared rich in comparison. They had shopping trolleys full of their belongings, including sleeping bags.

'Share some prosperity' was the slogan of a well-presented beggar, whom we heard every day as we walked to town. We stopped to talk.

'I used to have a job and live in a nice house,' he told us with a wistful sigh, 'but I lost my job, then my family broke up and now I'm living on the streets. I don't know how I'll be able to pull my life back together again, I've lost so much. Thanks for asking though.'

It seems that no place in the world is immune to having people living in poverty. The USA lacked adequate unemployment and sickness benefits, but in California there were non-profit organisations assisting the homeless, which is why the beggars we saw at least had decent clothing and footwear.

Another thing that struck Michael and me about Berkeley was that cars stopped for pedestrians. We had become accustomed to taking our life into our hands every time we crossed the road in South America, looking both ways quickly and then running when we saw a gap. In Berkeley, when trying to cross the road, we invariably caused a stand-off. We would see a car approaching, so would stop at the kerb; the car would then stop when the driver saw us and no-one dared to move. My sister, Aviva, later explained that in California a pedestrian has right of way – if a pedestrian is at the kerb the motorist is obliged to stop and allow the pedestrian to cross. How civilised!

When travelling in rural California, at times we had almost as much trouble making ourselves understood as we had in South America. Many locals struggled with our Australian accents and trying to order a vegetarian meal was equally difficult and very comical.

'Does this have meat in it?' I asked a waitress.

'Mayt, what's that?' replied the waitress.

I tried again, 'Does this have meat in it?'

Mayt? Ah don't know what you mean.'

So a third try, 'Does it have any dead animal in it, I'm vegetarian?'

'Ah you mean meeeeet,' replied the waitress, wha didn't you say so?'

Another time, while taking a dip in a swimming hole, a father and son overheard us talking.

'What language are you speaking?' the American teenager asked us.

'English,' I laughingly replied.

'Really? It doesn't sound like English.'

After a bit more chatting, he asked us where we were from.

'Australia' I said, to which the youngster replied, 'Wow, you speak really good English; what language do you speak in Australia?'

~~~~

Michael and I were in Berkeley when the 9/11 terrorist attacks happened. We were the only ones home when the telephone rang early in the morning. Answering it, I was surprised to find Aviva's flat mate's mum phoning from New York. 'The World Trade Centre has collapsed,' she told me, panic in her voice, 'turn on the TV, it's really bad.'

In my semi-conscious state I tried to show some concern, but in reality I wasn't too concerned about world trade and went back to bed. I thought she was talking about the stock exchange crashing. We were pretty dumbstruck, of course, when we did turn on the television and realised what had happened. We were then
~~~~

glued to the television for the next couple of days like the rest of the world.

The USA was a scary place after 9/11 and Michael and I were pleased to leave the country and continue our journey in Latin America.

~~~~

Our next port of call was Costa Rica, a country unlike most other Latin American countries. It doesn't have the same degree of poverty as the other countries, partly due to not having an army. As one of the oldest democracies in the Americas, it is politically and socially stable.

Working at one of the hotels we were staying at was José, a well presented, educated young man who told us his story:

'I was abandoned as a child and had a difficult childhood growing up, first in an orphanage and later in foster care. I was desperately keen to continue my studies, but my foster carers didn't have the means to support me. One of my school teachers, though, had heard about a foundation in the USA that supported disadvantaged children. She made an application on my behalf, and I was accepted to receive an all-expenses-paid university education.'

This act of goodwill changed José's prospects completely. He is forever grateful for the support of the foundation and to the family who had given him a home.

José's story resonated with Michael and me and over time we began to talk more about José, and then about Karina, who had so impressed us with her intelligence, charm and outgoing nature. Wouldn't it be wonderful if we could support Karina to attend university and give her a better future? This thought stayed with us for the remainder of our time in Costa Rica, but it would be another year before our vague thoughts were turned into action.

For now, Michael and I had a few personal matters to overcome. We had been travelling together for nine months and had had many ups and downs, which is bound to happen when travelling and living with someone night and day. Michael had been ready to come home after a few months of travel, but I had encouraged him to continue with me. Everything was fine when we were hiking in the mountains, but when we were just travelling, Michael became stressed and this led to many arguments.
~~~~

We had had a relaxing three week 'holiday' in the USA and I thought Michael would now be fine for another few months of travel. This was not to be. The final straw was the day we were bound for a beach somewhere on the Costa Rican Pacific coast. On the ferry, we started chatting to some of the other travellers. I liked our new found 'friends' and the place they were headed for sounded great, so I said to Michael 'let's go with them...' At this point Michael went into meltdown, as I had apparently changed my mind several times already that day. He reminded me that in the morning *I* had urged *him* to select our destination. I had conveniently forgotten this. As well as demonstrating my lack of concern for his needs, this situation highlighted our different travelling mentalities. Michael wanted to know in advance where he was going to sleep each night and for how long he was going to be travelling, whereas I would just go with the flow, trusting that things would work out. There had been many arguments and heated discussions throughout the trip around this theme.

Everyone said that travelling together is a great test for a relationship and they were certainly on target. This truly was a test and we were not passing with flying colours. Michael decided that he would return home after our three weeks in Costa Rica and I would continue alone on our planned route to Guatemala and Mexico, before returning home five weeks later.

~~~~

Arriving in Guatemala, I decided to work on improving my Spanish and signed up for a week-long Spanish school and home-stay program in the city of Quetzaltenango. With my improved Spanish, I travelled for a further two weeks in Guatemala before heading to Mexico for my final fortnight.

~~~~

In the city of Oaxaca (pronounced wahaca), I was befriended by Juan, a local indigenous young man, who invited me to share a meal. Juan came from a poor *campesino* family but, through sheer hard work and persistence, working numerous jobs, including guiding tourists through the museum where I met him, he had been getting himself educated. He was in his final year of architecture at university and his philosophy on life impressed me to such an extent that it changed my way of thinking.

'My basic philosophy is to help other people. Although I don't have much money and often struggle to make ends meet, if I find at the end of the week that I have more money than I need, then I will give money to people who are needier. Then at other times, if I have run out of money, there are shopkeepers who know me and will give me food, trusting that I will pay them back as soon as I can.'

This well and truly answered my question on what he thought about giving to beggars on the street. His communal way of thinking is representative of many of the indigenous people in Mexico, and indeed other indigenous cultures throughout Latin America. I began to question my own ethics. Why should I have money saved in the bank, when there are people who need that money to survive right now? Should I not be sharing more of my wealth around with those who have a greater need? I had many of my own difficult questions to answer.

~~~~

The end of my ten and a half month Latin American adventure was fast approaching. Arriving in Mexico City, I was dumbstruck by the size of the city, which at the time had a population of about 18 million. It made Sydney seem like a provincial town.

On my last day in Mexico, it took me two hours to pay my departure tax so that I could leave. In most countries where there is a departure tax, it is simply paid at the airport before leaving. Not in Mexico. In Mexico, it had to be paid at a bank and involved hours of queuing up in different lines and even in two different banks.

Having paid my departure tax, I was free to leave Mexico, and in fact the Americas. It had been an incredible journey, with memories and experiences that will stay with me for the rest of my life. Through the people I had met along the way, and through leaving the comforts of home behind, I had learned lessons far beyond those that could be learnt in any class room. I was going home an enriched person, who needed to find some way of helping others less fortunate than myself.
~~~~

CHAPTER 8

Home Sweet Home & New Contact with Peru

December 2001

I arrived home to a warm and sultry Sydney after over ten months away and was hit like a slap in the face by a huge dose of culture shock. It was in the days leading up to Christmas and I felt disgusted at all the bags full of plastic toys I saw Australian parents buying for their pampered children. Didn't these people realise that a child can have just as much fun with a bucket on a piece of string as with all these rubbishy toys? Didn't they realise that all around the globe there were people dying of starvation and malnutrition and here they were wasting so much money on presents for children who had too much junk anyway? There seemed to be so much wealth and waste in our Western society.

Interestingly, it seemed like I had a greater dose of culture shock on returning to Australia than when we had started our journey in Chile.

It was, of course, marvellous to be reunited with Michael after our five week separation, but we both had a lot of readjusting to do. We had to learn to live with one another again, while at the same time reconstructing our lives back in Australia and regaining some sort of normality. That is, 'normal' for life in the Western world – getting a job and having to think about what to wear that day instead of throwing on the same clothes, day in and day out.

Our original plan had been to travel for up to a year then return to Sydney and stay with either one of our parents while Michael searched for a job somewhere in the country. We'd had no plans to move back into our town house in West Ryde.

When Michael returned in November, he had moved in with my father in Waverton (near North Sydney) as he had been offered temporary work back at Warringah Council. Dad was happy to have Michael's company and they could talk sport for hours. When I returned five weeks later, my father had the dubious pleasure of having us both living with him in his unit. We only planned to stay there until Michael found permanent employment out of Sydney. What we hadn't factored in, or thought too much about, was just how long it might take to find that job.

We hadn't forgotten our promise to the Carbajal Moreira family and as soon as we had our photos developed and printed, we posted them, along with a letter, to the address they had given us for *Explore Razuillca.* The idea of continued support hadn't yet been cemented into our minds; however the family was certainly in our thoughts. Over time we wondered if they had received our mail, but had no way of knowing. We thought it such a shame that we had no other way of contacting them.

A few months later, when I turned on the computer one day after work I got a huge surprise to see, blinking in our inbox, an email from Mariluz, the eldest daughter. It was especially astonishing as I hadn't even remembered having left an email address with the family, as computers hadn't yet arrived in their town and they had never heard of email. I excitedly opened it and tried to decipher the not so well-written message. The gist of it was that the family had not heard from us and they were wondering why, and if we were okay. The letter with the photos had never arrived and they wondered if we had sent them. Mariluz went on to tell us about her family and how much they were suffering. She explained that her father was still sick as were two of her younger sisters, Marleni and Margot. They didn't have enough money for medicines or for sufficient food. Although Mariluz sounded very worried about her family, she didn't directly ask us for money.

Later, when we did finally meet Mariluz and her family again in 2004, she explained that she had written the email in desperation – not really to ask for money. At the time she felt she just needed to offload her problems and tell someone that she could trust.

Mariluz's message tore at our heartstrings and we realised we needed and wanted to help this family. It was great to now have email contact, although we couldn't work out from where Mariluz had sent the email. I replied straight away and told her that I had posted the photos some weeks earlier. I asked if she could give me an alternative address, along with asking her a torrent of other questions.

Answering my questions, Mariluz explained that she was now working in Ayacucho as a cleaner in an office building and she had befriended one of the office workers, Pedro, whom she referred to as *tío* (uncle). *Tío* is commonly used as a sign of respect for older people and those close to the family. Mariluz had confided in *tío* Pedro about her family and their health problems and told him about meeting two Australians whom she was desperate to contact. So Pedro had taught Mariluz to use the computer and to send emails. He'd helped her to set up a 'Hotmail' account, and allowed her to use his office computer to communicate with us.

Pedro thus opened up the electronic world to Mariluz, without which we probably would never have been able to reconnect and maintain contact with the family. He also let Mariluz use his home address to receive mail from us.

I posted off a parcel with photos and some small presents to Pedro's address in Ayacucho. A few weeks later we received an envelope in the post with heartfelt letters from each of the girls and from Celestino. They all thanked us very much for the presents and mentioned how happy they were to receive them. Marleni, who was 12 years old at the time, wrote:

'I am very sick with a urinary tract infection. I've had to stop attending school and this upsets me a lot. I wish my family had money to cure me. Please help me.'

A similar letter was written by ten year old Margot, saying she also had a urinary tract infection:

'I cry every day because I don't think I will ever recover. Every time I look at the photos of you I begin to cry because I don't think you will ever return to Peru. I will always remember you. Please don't forget me.'

The letter from seven year old Nélida was very cute, asking us to return to Peru, send her more games to play with and thanking us for the presents. She told us that her two sisters Marleni and Margot were sick and begged us to help them. She mentioned that she was in fourth grade at school and that she had passed the year as the first student in her class. At the end of the letter she asked us to take Mariluz to work in Australia so that she could make enough money to send home to cure Margot and Marleni.

Michael and I knew we had to get money to the family quickly. We still had some travellers' cheques left over from our trip, so we endorsed those and posted them immediately, with an explanation of how to cash them.

The cheques arrived promptly and Mariluz immediately took them to the bank. We then received an email from her explaining that out of the US$150 we had sent, the bank had taken US$18 in fees. She was very upset. This also annoyed us greatly and we thought there must be a better way to get money to them. Nevertheless, the family had some money to get them out of their immediate troubles.

Soon after, we received a long email from Karina, written at an internet café that had recently opened in Huanta. She wrote how grateful her whole family was for our support and said the money we sent was like a blessing from God. It arrived just when her family was experiencing extremely difficult times.

'*Your gift made everyone so happy and my family now considers you as a part of our family,*' she wrote.

Karina then surprised us by asking if Michael and I would consider becoming her *padrinos*. Godparents are vitally important to many Peruvians and Karina told us that her *padrino* had passed away some years earlier. The role of the *padrino* is to guide their *ahijada* (godchild) through their important life decisions and to ensure they are well looked after. We were touched that Karina had requested this of us, and gladly accepted. Michael was now called *padrino* (godfather) and I, *madrina* (godmother).

I continued to converse regularly via email with both Karina and Mariluz. In every email they thanked Michael and me profusely for the support we had given them and told us how much they loved and cared for us and that we were an important part of their family. They told us that they would be waiting for us with open arms if we could return to Peru. They also mentioned that we were the only family members that cared enough about them to help them financially.

It wasn't long before a desperate email from Karina arrived: '*Now in Huanta we are in a crisis situation and we don't even have enough food to eat.*'

We were spurred into action, but our second attempt to send money was even worse than the first. We asked Mariluz to open up a bank account so that we could do a telegraphic transfer directly from our bank account to hers. Once done we transferred US$150. For the privilege, our bank in Australia charged us A$27, and we thought that would be the end of it. Mariluz should now have $150 in her account.

When we received the next email from Mariluz, we were shocked and angered. Yes, $150 had been deposited into her account, but when she and Karina went to withdraw the money, they found that their bank had charged them US$36 in fees, leaving only $114 for them to withdraw. Mariluz and Karina had burst into tears right there in the bank. $36 was a huge amount of money for them, and money that they so desperately needed. The girls blamed it on the corruption that is rampant throughout Peru and explained that it is commonplace for poorer, less educated people to be exploited like this.

Michael and I were livid. We both worked hard for our money, and due to local fees and the corrupt Peruvian bank, we had just spent A$290 and the girls had only received the equivalent of A$200. We certainly had no intention of continuing to support the banks, but wondered how we were to get money to our desperate family.

We pondered this problem for a while and then suddenly I had a brainwave. How had we withdrawn cash when we had been travelling in South America? We had simply gone to the automatic teller machines, punched in our PIN numbers and taken the cash. Why couldn't the girls do the same? The solution was simple. Michael and I just needed to open a new bank account and post an ATM card to the girls. At least we now had a reliable address to which to send the card.

I emailed the girls asking them to check that there were ATMs in Ayacucho that were on the Maestro/Cirrus network, as we didn't want to give them a credit card. Once we received confirmation of this, we opened a savings account in both our names, giving us each an ATM card. We posted one card to Peru and kept the other card.

Once the girls received the card they were to email us and then I would email the PIN number, along with detailed instructions of how to use an ATM, as they had never before used one. This certainly challenged my Spanish to the max.

~~~~
~~~~

Meanwhile, the months were ticking by and our lives were beginning to gain some sort of normality.

I found work as a casual vocational trainer – training young people with disabilities to enter the workforce. Once again I was fortunate to find work that was rewarding and enjoyable, and an added bonus for me was that I already knew many of the young people as they were also members of my old recreation program.

Wishing to continue with our Spanish we both signed up for another TAFE course.

The weeks stretched into months – there were not many suitable jobs for which Michael was able to apply, and they were hotly contested. My work became permanent and Michael began to despair ever getting out of 'the big smoke'.

Six months after our return, our town house in West Ryde was vacated by the tenants so we moved back in. It was quite a shock to us to take everything out of the garage and see the huge pile of possessions we owned. Why did we need all this stuff when we had travelled for almost a year living solely out of a backpack? Did we really need it all?

In addition to Michael's three days per week at Warringah Council, he also began working at the Penrith white-water stadium, teaching kayaking and working in the office. Michael now had two jobs, both of which he loved, but at opposite ends of the city. Once again he began to suffer from depression. We had been overseas, moved back to Sydney and nothing had really changed. He was still stuck in Sydney and facing the tiring commutes to work and back. I had fallen on my feet and Michael was concerned that I was once again becoming too attached to my job.

~~~~

Not long after our move back to West Ryde, we received another big envelope from the family, and once again this contained letters written from the heart by each member of the family, along with some old photos of them and postcards from their town. Wilbur had written for the first time and expressed how sorry he was not to have met us when we first visited as he had been at school. Each of the children wrote that we were like a mother and father to them and thanked us profusely for our support. Mariluz had taken
~~~~

Margot and Marleni to Lima for treatment and they all wrote how our money had saved them from starvation as things were more expensive there than they'd realised. Carmen, the mother, wrote that she had been in the jungle when we had visited but she also felt we were like a mother and father to her as her parents had passed away.

By this stage we had been in regular email contact with Karina and Mariluz for over eight months and were aware that we were now committed to supporting the family for the long term. Initially our support was only covering medical expenses and food, but we wished for more than that. We thought back to José, the young man we had met in Costa Rica who had received a university education thanks to a grant from the US. This inspired us to want to do the same for Karina.

We had been able to ascertain, from our brief time with Karina in Huanta and from our email communications, that she was intelligent, and with her great drive, sparkling personality and maturity, we were confident that, given the opportunity, she would do well at university. We also hoped that if we could help Karina to get an education, she could then help the rest of her family.

Just before Christmas 2002, we received an email from Karina in which she had written about her high school graduation ceremony.

'You were present in my heart. I thank you from the bottom of my heart for being my padrinos for the rest of my life. My family is very, very thankful for the confidence that you have in us and we will never break that. You can trust us completely.'

So, at the end of 2002, at just under 16 years of age, Karina had finished high school.

Michael and I realised we needed to come to an agreement for an amount that we could give to the girls and their family each month. After asking them to work out their monthly living costs, we decided on US$140. We were hoping this would cover their costs for medicines, food and education.

With the assistance of *Tio* Pedro and my emailed instructions, Karina and Mariluz were able to withdraw the funds from the *cajero automatico* (ATM). This was a relief – it worked and the bank fees would only amount to $5 per month.

Thus, in January 2003, we began regular monthly support of *our* extended family, the *Familia Carbajal Moreira.*

Karina told us that she would be attending an academy in Huanta for six months in order to prepare to matriculate and gain entry to university.

At the same time, Margot and Marleni's ill health continued. Their symptoms were remarkably similar. They needed to urinate frequently, and several times during the night. It was a serious problem at school because their teachers would not let them leave the class-room as regularly as necessary. The family believes that their illnesses were caused by their school teachers not allowing them to go to the toilet during class, and a lack of adequate nutrition due to their poverty. The name the doctors gave to the girls' illness was 'hyperactive bladder'. After the family received our first amount of money, Margot and Marleni underwent many tests to investigate their problems, and were given various treatments which led to a gradual improvement, although Margot was never fully cured.

Mariluz got a job as a fee collector for the local council. She walked throughout the neighbourhood, door to door, collecting money for the residential electricity usage. Many people in Huanta, including the Carbajal Moreiras, didn't have an official connection to the electricity supply. They would simply run a wire into the main conductor nearby and tap into the town electricity and saw no reason why they should have to pay for their power usage. Mariluz's job was to inform these residents that they did have to pay, and to collect that money. She was paid on commission, depending on how much money she was able to collect. However, the majority of the residents flatly refused to pay anything and there was nothing Mariluz could do about this. This job ended up costing her more money in worn out shoes than she actually earned.

In March 2003 we received our first email from Celestino, hand-written at home and then later typed into the computer by Karina. This was the only way Celestino could converse with us because his illness was such that he was unable to leave the house.

'My dear Michael and Lani. I am sending you this message with a great appreciation and a lot of affection. I can never thank you enough for all the support you are offering my family. Words are not enough to express my sincere

gratitude... Your valuable advice strengthens me greatly and many thanks for the confidence that you have in us and thank you for your concern over my daughters... We value your advice because you are our true family and we love you sincerely...My home is your home and I hope you will come again soon to Peru...'

It was a heart-warming letter. The following month we received a beautifully written, though heart-wrenching email from Karina:

'My dear madrina and padrino. We are worried because you are so far from us and sometimes we think that we are no longer important to you and then my little sisters begin to cry. I hope that this is not the case. My father and mother beg you from the bottom of their hearts that you won't forget the family that loves you so much. For us you are like a mother and a father that will never abandon their children and who will always watch over them. We only pray to God that all goes well in your work, and with your families around you. Now we are very far from you and we can remember you by looking at the photos and waiting for your emails.

You know we feel very anxious about all the problems in our family. My father feels so bad and the truth is that it pains me a lot to see my father's health going downhill. We only can pray to God that it doesn't get any worse.

I'm sorry for giving you another worry but telling you is a way of relieving this grief that I am suffering. Thank you for all your support and to read what you have written me gives me a lot of strength to move forward...

My dear madrina and padrino I say good-bye with a strong hug and many kisses until the next time. Please never forget about us.

Your ahijada, Karina'

~~~~

We knew we would have to return to Peru as soon as we could but as we were still living in Sydney and looking for jobs in the country, we didn't know when this would possibly be.

~~~~

Finally in August 2003, after almost two years of searching and numerous job applications and interviews, Michael was successful in gaining the position of 'Threatened Species Officer' for Shoalhaven Council, based in Nowra, two and a half hours drive south of Sydney. The excitement was high. We found a house to rent and Michael started his new job three days before his 40th birthday.

After spending the first six weeks exploring our beautiful new area, I opted for a career change and became an Outdoor Guide and found casual work in the disability field at the same time. Thus I was able to combine my main passions.

In my quest to assist those less fortunate than myself, I joined the local Amnesty International group and began taking action on human rights issues all around the world.

~~~~

Michael and I continued to communicate regularly with Mariluz and Karina (although I did most of the writing as my Spanish was more usable) and they always asked when we were coming back to Peru. We received long emails from them every few days – so frequently it was hard to keep up the replies, as although my Spanish was reasonable, it did take me some time to comprehend and then write back.

We were getting to know the family through the numerous emails. They explained more about the family's *chacra* in the *selva*, where Carmen spent months at a time working, usually alone. During school holidays one or several of the kids sometimes accompanied her and helped with the work. Travelling to the *chacra* involved an eight hour journey by *colectivo* mini-bus; this and the fares meant it was only feasible to go there for extended periods.

On the *chacra* they were growing corn, *yucca* and *pituca* (root crops), various types of beans, bananas and coffee. Coffee had previously earned the family a reasonable income, but the price of coffee had dropped dramatically and now it hardly paid for itself. By the time the bus fares were paid, Carmen usually did not have much money left over, although she brought home food for the family.

We learnt that the family was of Quechuan descent, the direct descendants of the ancient Incas, and that Quechua was their mother tongue, with Spanish their second language. Karina told us how, in the colonial days, the indigenous inhabitants routinely suffered mistreatment, even by the priests, as it was believed that
~~~~

because they worshipped the sun and the earth, they didn't have a soul and so it was permissible to abuse them.

In addition, we were learning more about Peruvian culture, special events and general day-to-day happenings in the lives of our family.

Karina gave us an account of the *Fiesta de Maynay*, a festival held each year in September, in the nearby village of Maynay. She had been a contestant in the competition to be the *Riena de Maynay* – the Queen of Maynay. She'd hired a traditional Quechuan costume and prepared a speech which she delivered to a large audience. Karina told us she was proud to have been honoured as the *Segunda Dama* (Second Lady) and was planning to enter again the following year in an attempt to be crowned as the '*Reina*'. She wrote how sad she was that Michael and I were not there to see her, and that the only family member who had been able to come was one of her little sisters. Her father was, as always, too sick to leave the house and her mother and Mariluz were working on the *chacra* in the *selva.*

~~~~

In an email later in the year, Mariluz wrote: '*You are the only hope my family have, and that hope gives us the courage to live, work, study and struggle with the challenges that present themselves in our lives.*'

She wrote that Marleni was better than before and had returned to school. Margot's health had only improved slightly but she had also returned to school. They had stopped her treatment because it didn't seem to be making any difference.

In September 2003, Karina graduated with high marks from her university preparation course. She told us she wanted to study law. Michael and I were initially not so enthusiastic about her choice of course. In many parts of South America we had seen rows of shopfronts all advertising that they were '*abogados*'. We did not think that there could possibly be enough work and enough money in the country for so many lawyers, and we didn't want to spend years paying for Karina's education only to find that she was unable to get a job. Additionally, we were well aware that, coming from an uneducated family without connections, her job prospects would be much more limited than many of her classmates. We
~~~~

knew that in Peru, as in many countries, family connections played a huge role in finding employment.

We emailed Karina asking her why she wanted to study law. Her answer impressed us greatly.

'I have chosen this career because in Huanta there is a lot of injustice against the poor and needy indigenous people and they have nobody to support them. This has happened in my own family. The authorities, who have the power and the duty, and those who have a profession, all commit abuses against the poor. I have chosen this career so that I can defend these people so they won't be downtrodden.'

After that answer, we gave Karina our blessing and promised to help her financially throughout her studies. At the time, we were not aware that she would still be studying nine years later...

Soon after, we received an email from Karina telling us that on 28 October 2003 she'd heard on the radio that she had been accepted into the *Universidad de San Christobal de Huamanga.*

'When I heard my name read out I began to scream with happiness and the tears rolled down my cheeks and those of my parents. I cannot thank you enough. It is only through your support that I will be able to go to university.'

Karina told us that it should take six years for her to receive the title of *abogada*. For the intervening months she had secured a job at the academy where she had been doing her preparatory course. Her wage would be a meagre 25 soles per week (A$10) and she was planning to save this money to pay for her matriculation from the Academy and her university entrance fees. She found a small room to rent in Ayacucho for 70 soles per month, and started her university course in May 2004.

~~~~

Around this time we began to entertain thoughts of returning to Peru – we were keen to be reunited with our adopted family, and to ascertain that our money was being used wisely. We decided to plan our trip for some time after early August, when Michael would receive his first allotment of paid leave. We wrote to the girls to let them know that we were thinking about coming over later in the year, and we could almost hear the screams of joy through the internet. Wanting to be there when Karina had her university holidays, she told us they would be at the end of August / early
~~~~

September. This worked out perfectly as it also meant we would be in Huanta for the *Fiesta de Maynay* when she would be having her second attempt at becoming the *Reina*.

I wrote to the girls and told them that we had a month's holiday and that we would spend two to three weeks with them, after which we planned to go to Huaraz to do some more hiking in the Cordillera Blanca.

Our flights were booked and we were to fly out from Sydney airport on 24August 2004. Mariluz booked our bus tickets to travel from Lima to Ayacucho.

Peru, here we come...

CHAPTER 9 Reunited with Family

August 2004

The weeks preceding our departure were hectic and stressful. Having found out during this time that the house we were renting was going on the market, we made a rush decision and bought a house up the road. The move, combined with packing for the trip and buying presents to take with us, left us with scant time to think about the long journey we were about to undertake.

It was a relief to be finally underway.

The sense of relief didn't last long. To get to Peru we had to fly first to Chile, a 16 hour flight. Then followed an eight hour wait in Santiago airport, and a four hour flight to Lima. We arrived at 11pm, and within an hour and a half, we were falling into a hostel bed for a few hours sleep. We had hardly closed our eyes before we were jolted awake by the alarm. Sleepily we stumbled outside and found the taxi our hostel owner had kindly booked for us. We were headed for the bus station for the early morning bus to Ayacucho, another ten hours away. The taxi driver warned us to be careful in the crowded terminal.

'There are many *rateros* here,' he told us. Our large backpacks suddenly seemed like neon lit targets, and as we booked them in we just hoped they would arrive in Ayacucho with us.

The bus rapidly began to fill up and Michael and I were glad of our reserved seats. As we travelled, the daytime temperature increased and more and more sweaty bodies piled onto the bus until the air was pungent with the odour of unwashed bodies and became insufferably hot. With a constant stream of people getting on and off, we needed to keep our wits about us to ensure the security of our belongings. As well as carrying passengers, the bus hosted a never ending supply of vendors selling all manner of goods. Some pushed their way through the passengers, handing everyone a few lollies or some other gift, before beginning their spiel about their amazing product. 'You simply must buy these health powders – straight from the mountains – they will ensure eternal youth,' or 'no more headaches with these amazing tablets ...'

Sales pitch over, the vendor squeezed his or her way back through the crowd, taking money from those passengers who had been taken in, and collecting the 'gift' back from those that didn't purchase. Other vendors were selling snack foods or scissors, batteries or magnifying glasses, and a myriad of other things. All the products were 'essential for our happiness and well being'.

The vendors didn't just look after our material comfort. Some clearly saw themselves as God's messengers, getting on the bus purely to lecture their captive audience about the Lord Jesus. Often they competed with the salespeople, each person trying to talk over the other. Blended into this commotion were the deep rumble of the engine and the screeching din of a tinny radio blaring out the latest Peruvian pop songs. The cacophony was at times unbearable, but at least it ensured we didn't fall asleep. It had only been three years since we had last been in Peru, but during that time we had already forgotten about the dubious joys of Peruvian bus travel. Entertaining as it was, we were too weary to enjoy it.

The bus travelled south, heading along the dusty desert coast for about four hours before turning eastwards and beginning the ascent into the mountains. The ascent marked an end to the stream of salespeople and the bus became a little less crowded. We seemed to be climbing for an eternity and as we reached higher elevations the temperature finally began to drop. For the first hour or so of ascent, the landscape was bare with the mountains appearing to be made from sand. Gradually vegetation started to appear, transforming the countryside.

Not long after we'd noticed the appearance of vegetation and coolness of the air, we succumbed to the effects of the altitude. We both felt nauseous and began dropping in and out of consciousness. We'd awake with a start as we gulped down the air in a futile attempt to obtain enough oxygen and then drift off again into a strange altitude-induced slumber, full of weird dreams.

This continued for several hours. I felt like I'd been doped with a sleeping pill that made it difficult to breathe and made me feel queasy. Michael said he felt the same. We were lucky not to throw up; others did though and the smell of vomit added to the aroma on the bus.

We only found out later that the road reached an altitude of 4746m and the bus had remained at over 4000m for a couple of hours. No wonder we felt so ill, having come straight from sea level and being thoroughly exhausted from three days of virtually continuous travelling through changing time zones.

It was a relief when the bus finally began its descent towards Ayacucho, situated at an elevation of 2,800m. We arrived at 6.00 pm and there, eagerly waiting, were Karina and Mariluz.

The four of us all burst into tears as we hugged each other closely. The first thing that struck Michael and me was how small the girls were. We had forgotten how short Peruvians, particularly indigenous Peruvians, are. In our memories, Mariluz had been quite a large girl, a bit on the plump side, but she was not at all as we had remembered. She was now slim. We began to wonder if all the clothes we'd bought for the family would be far too big.

Michael and I were still rather dazed and it was hard to concentrate and take in everything the girls were saying as they excitedly chattered. Our Spanish was rusty and by this stage of our journey we were not very coherent. We did, however, gather that before we headed for Huanta, Karina wanted to show us the room she rented in Ayacucho.

We donned our backpacks, heavy with presents, and followed Karina, who had taken off at a fast clip up the hill leaving us panting and trailing behind. We struggled not just with the weight of the packs and our tiredness but with a lack of oxygen due to the altitude.

Fifteen minutes later we arrived at Karina's spartan, dimly lit room. The furnishings consisted of a small desk, an old bed and books piled up on the floor. The only splash of colour on the grimy walls was a calendar with Australian animals which we had sent in one of our Christmas parcels. 'I use this to plan studies,' she proudly told us, indicating the calendar.

The girls allowed us a few minutes rest before shepherding us back down the hill to the bus stop to catch a *colectivo combi* to Huanta, where the rest of the family would be impatiently awaiting our arrival. We crammed into the crowded van and tried to stay sufficiently awake to chat to Karina and Mariluz. An hour later we arrived at the house of the Carbajal Moreira family.

It was by now quite late and Michael and I had been travelling for 72 hours since closing the door of our home behind us. We were almost asleep on our feet, but as we alighted we were buoyed by greetings from the whole family and a few cousins. Lots of big hugs, tears, cries of welcome and disbelief that we really had come back to see our Peruvian family. Of course we had to stay up and talk and try to remember who was who, who belonged to our direct family and who didn't. And at last we met Carmen and Wilbur for the first time. Carmen, with her long straight black hair and dark skin and the high cheekbones typical of Quechuan women, flashed us a beautiful wide smile and shyly welcomed us into her home. We noticed she was dressed in a plain skirt and blouse.

The family's five dogs, which were all barking and growling at us as we came through the gates, were also introduced to us. They were not quite as friendly towards us as the rest of the family was!

Michael and I were not functioning very well at this stage, struggling to string two words together and wondering where we were going to be sleeping. Eventually Celestino noticed the state we were in and asked the kids to show us, by fading torchlight, to our room which had been especially prepared. It even had a bed, of sorts, that they had somehow procured.

Asking about the *baño*, we were shown the toilet, an open-topped cubicle arrangement with walls on three sides and the opening looking straight out onto the yard. The business end was a concrete slab with a hole in the middle that took the 'goods' down a pipe after a bucket of water was thrown in. Hmmmm, I'm not an overly private person, but going to the toilet in full view... I could worry about that in the morning. At least now it was dark.

We performed our ablutions, wobbled up the rickety ladder and crashed into bed. The narrow single bed was made from bamboo and was deeply bowed in the middle. On top of the bamboo slats was a lumpy cotton mattress. One would have thought that in our exhausted state sleep would have come easily, but it didn't. We lay awake listening to the trucks roar by on the street (their house fronted onto the main road into town) and the dogs barking all night while we tried to get comfortable. Sometime in the early hours of the next morning we both drifted off to sleep.

Michael and I were awoken early by even more loud trucks braking on their way down the hill towards town, by roosters crowing and dogs barking yet again (or still). We also heard the sound of sweeping. A sleepy look at the watch revealed it to be 5.30. We lay in for a short while and then got up to find Mariluz sweeping the earthen backyard with a tree branch. Although the yard was all dirt, the family still had obvious pride in it and wanted it to look spick and span for their special guests. Mariluz or Carmen did this every morning.

By the time we were dressed, the family was all up and waiting excitedly, even though it was not yet 6.30 am. They explained that being Sunday it was market day and hence the trucks that had kept us awake through the night. 'Normally the road is fairly quiet at night,' they told us. That was a relief. They asked us if we wanted to accompany them to the markets later on and we agreed.

Before too long, more cousins had arrived to check out the *gringos*. We wanted some time alone with the family and sensing this, the girls shooed the cousins away and told them that they could come back later. We had a lot of catching up to do and presents to dispense. And they had a few surprises for us.

Michael and I were shown around the house and Celestino apologetically explained why we hadn't been invited inside the house the first time we had been there three years prior. My hints to look inside the house had not gone unnoticed, but at the time they didn't want us to view their basic living arrangements, of which they were quite embarrassed.

'Back then we thought that if you saw how we lived, without even beds or mattresses to sleep on, you would look down upon us, as other Peruvians do,' Celestino said. 'Now, of course, we realise that this would not have been the case.' I mentioned that I had thought that it may have been a Quechuan custom, not inviting strangers into the house, and Celestino explained that in some Quechuan families this is the case, but for them it was purely out of embarrassment for their living conditions.

The living part of the house was the upper level of a two storey structure, with the rooms in an 'L' shape and a covered veranda fronting all of the rooms. It was roughly constructed from bricks, with a rusty corrugated tin roof. Access was via a steep rickety ladder without a handrail. The ladder led to the veranda which was also without a railing. At one end it was dangerously high – about three metres.

On the long side of the 'L' were two large rooms, both about 3 metres wide by 6 metres long, and each only accessible via the veranda. One of these rooms had no floor and was not able to be used. The other room, with rough wooden floor boards, was the sleeping quarters for the entire family. At the end of the veranda was our small bedroom, about 3 metres by 2 metres in size. The room had the lovely aroma of fresh new timber and had obviously only just been completed in time for our arrival. Each room had a window, although ours was the only one with glass. The family's bedroom window was open to the air.

The family bedroom was dark, with nothing to decorate the bare brick walls. It was infused with a sickly-sweet pungent smell, like three day old dirty socks. It was devoid of furniture apart from two single beds, one at each end of the room. Celestino explained that he and Wilbur each had a bed and the others all slept together on the floor, on and under blankets. Michael and I were shocked that Wilbur had a bed, yet Carmen slept on the floor. It was, however, later explained to us that Wilbur had a bed because he too suffered from an illness, caused by a childhood accident. Carmen also told us that she liked to sleep with her children.

The veranda was about three metres by eight and also had rough wooden floorboards. This area had the only mirror of the house and was used for getting ready to go out. It was also used for doing homework, drying clothes and sometimes for relaxing.

On the bottom level the floor was concrete, but this area was little used, except for storage. They explained to us that Celestino had wanted to run a small general store from here and did give it a go but, with his illness, it proved too difficult. This area could not be used for sleeping as it was cold and damp and water poured in during the wet season.

Celestino explained that he had planned the building of the house but, due to his illness and lack of finances, he had never been able to finish it. This was why the second large bedroom did not yet have floorboards and the ceilings in all the rooms were made using plastic sheeting.

Down the ladder from the house, attached to but lower than the living quarters, was another small room with a dirt floor which was used for storing harvested crops. This room was accessed via the yard. Attached to this room, and directly opposite the main house, were two small adobe (mud brick) rooms with uneven dirt floors. One was the kitchen and the other the dining room. Both these rooms were also accessed from the yard.

At one end of the kitchen was a small wooden table on which were a few old pieces of equipment and utensils, and at the other end was an open fire that was used for cooking. Carmen was embarrassed that they cooked on an open fire and asked if we wanted to buy gas and cook on a gas cooker. We assured her that it was no problem for us, and that when we go camping we also cooked on an open fire. She looked relieved.

The dining room had two small tables, one of which was borrowed from their *abuelos* (grandparents) who lived across the road. Also borrowed was an old church pew for seating at the tables. We found out that this family of eight only owned three chairs, all straight-backed wooden chairs. The younger kids had always had to stand up at the table when eating.

Across the other side of the backyard was the *baño*. On mentioning that I was a bit embarrassed about going to the toilet in full view of everyone, Celestino apologised and said that they had bought some plastic sheeting and had planned to string it up for us. He promised it would be done promptly. Next to the *baño* was a large concrete tub with a tap. This tap, which was connected to a water supply, was the only running water the family had access to. Before it had been connected five years previously, they'd had to walk a long way up the hill to cart water.

As for power, the family pirated electricity from the power lines running past the house and had a single bare light bulb in the dining room and one in the main bedroom. They'd only had this access to electricity for about five years.

After the house tour, Michael and I were asked to come into the dining room for breakfast. We were served a hot home-made soy milk drink, a couple of eggs (fresh from the hens this morning), avocado and fresh bread purchased from the passing street vendor. We were a bit embarrassed to be given an egg each, as there were only two, but they insisted that we eat them. Breakfast was served on lovely new crockery plates, which, Margot excitedly explained, had been bought specially for our visit. Margot told us that she was the one to suggest buying the crockery, and that it had been her life-long dream to have the whole family sitting together for a meal, using nice dishes.

We had a long drawn-out breakfast with lots of chatting – we had so much to catch up on.

Mariluz, her thick long dark hair hanging about her face, was now 21 years old and still smiled with her mouth firmly closed, due to her missing two front teeth. She told us she was unemployed and wanted to talk to us later about studying.

Wilbur, who at 19 was the second oldest, looked much like a younger version of his father. He too was missing his front teeth and so he too smiled without opening his mouth. His straight hair was parted in the middle. It was quite long at the front and buffed up to curl over his eyebrows. He told us he had finished school and didn't elaborate more than that.

17 year old Karina had started her law degree and was enjoying university life. She seemed as vivacious and outgoing as ever, and even more attractive than when we'd met her three years earlier. Her dark hair, parted in the middle and loosely pulled back into a pony tail, framed her smooth-skinned dark face with her beautiful big almond-shaped brown eyes. Karina was blessed with lovely straight white teeth and when she smiled her whole face lit up.

15 year old Marleni looked strong and healthy; her lovely round face sported a fringe and she had a winning smile and, as we were to discover, a wicked sense of humour. Marleni told us that her health had improved greatly thanks to our support and although she was not one hundred percent, she was attending the high school in town and getting good grades. In one of the parcels we had sent to the family I had written an individual card to each family member. To Marleni I had sent a card with a photo of a wombat, and in it I had written that I had chosen this animal because wombats are strong and tough like her and I knew that she would fight to recover.

'The card you sent me with the wombat,' Marleni told us, 'gave me the strength to fight against my illness. I knew I could become strong like a wombat.'

It was great to see what the power of thought can do for someone, and Michael's nickname for Marleni became 'Wombat'.

Skinny little Margot had just turned 13. She, like her mother, had the high cheekbones of the Quechuan people and a lovely smile but still looked quite sickly.

'I am a bit better than before,' she told us, 'but I still suffer a lot from my illness. I go to the primary school just down the road, when I am well enough to attend.'

Finally the baby of the family – the cute round-faced 10 year old Nélida, with her high pitched voice and cheeky eyes, told us she was also at the primary school with Margot and that they walked to school in the morning and home when school finished at lunch time.

'I have been getting very good grades at school and I am often the top student in my class,' she told us proudly.

After breakfast, Michael and I gathered everyone together on the veranda and handed out the presents that we had brought with us from Australia. We had Australian T-shirts for everyone, furry toy animals, caps, some tea towels with a map of Australia and Australian birds and animals, hot pot holders and numerous other small gifts.

I had to explain the use of tea towels and pot holders, but they told us they wouldn't use them for that purpose, as they were too nice! Several cousins showed up during the present distribution and luckily I had bought plenty of little koalas, pencils and other small items to hand out. The Carbajal Moreiras all put on their Aussie T-shirts and posed for photos.

Next, they had a surprise for us. Wilbur disappeared outside and then drove in through their front gates in a shiny, brand new-looking bright yellow *moto-taxi*. In big letters emblazoned across the front were our names, 'Imhof Smith'. Also stuck on the front were several Aussie stickers we had sent in an earlier parcel and the Australian flag he had asked us to send.

'How did you get that?' I asked incredulously.

Wilbur looked to Celestino to explain. 'With the money you have been sending,' Celestino began, 'we put a little aside each month until we had enough for a deposit. Then we got a loan, bought the *moto-taxi* and we are paying it off each month. Wilbur goes out to work every day and this gives the family a small income.'

Celestino went on to explain that the *moto-taxi* is in Carmen's name and is an investment for the whole family.

Michael and I found this to be a wonderful surprise, and we could not have thought of a better way of investing our money. It was obvious that Celestino called the shots in the family and, being the clever man he is, was always thinking of the family's future.

Before we'd arrived in Peru, Michael and I had wondered how we would respond if we found out that the family had been using our money for luxuries. We had no cause for concern. Not only did they lack basics such as beds, mattresses and chairs, all of their shoes and clothing were worn out. There were no luxuries whatsoever in their lives.

They didn't have a television, but did have an old radio which kept them up-to-date with the news and the world's happenings. Celestino, an avid listener, had a wealth of world knowledge, despite never having travelled nor been in contact with people from other nations. Celestino explained to us that Wilbur had been pestering him to buy a television with the money we had been sending, but he had made it clear to Wilbur that the money was for essential items only, not for luxuries. Moreover Celestino didn't want his children to be wasting their time watching *telenovelas* (soapies) to which Peruvians with televisions seem to be addicted. We really liked the values Celestino was imparting on his children.

We had greater difficulty conversing with Carmen. She had received only a basic education, having been expected to work as soon as she was able. Spanish was her second language and although she was fluent (which Michael and I weren't), we had trouble understanding each other. She was also quite shy and let Celestino and the children do all the talking. None of the children lacked any confidence and they all talked enough, often all at once, to make up for Carmen's quietness.

Once the house tour and present distribution was over, it was time to head into town to visit the markets to buy the rice and vegetables for lunch. Before leaving, I thought I had better remind the family that I was vegetarian and that I preferred not to eat dairy products. I had explained all this in an email before we left home and offered to do our own cooking if it made things easier. Mariluz had emailed back saying that there would be no problems. On reminding them of my diet, they laughed and said not to worry.

'We also eat vegetarian most of the time as meat is too expensive,' Mariluz told us, 'and we don't drink cow's milk because it's too costly and Dad doesn't think it's healthy.'

I immediately felt more at ease.

Huanta had a population of about 25,000, about the same size as Nowra (our home town) at that time. The town centre is three kilometres from their house, continuing along down the main road. We were invited into the 'Imhof Smith' *moto-taxi* which had a bench seat behind the driver big enough to take three small

Peruvians at a squeeze. Michael and I took our seats and then the kids all began to pile in until we had five people squeezed in at the back, Wilbur in the driver's seat with Marleni standing crouched over next to him and half hanging out. Wilbur thus drove us into town – the first of many trips in the Aussie-fied yellow *moto-taxi*.

The markets were as vivid as we had remembered. There was lots of gentle pushing and shoving as people weaved their way around the different stalls, as often as not a sleeping baby or produce wrapped in a *manta* on a woman's back, swaying as she moved. There was a vendor for every type of fruit, vegetable and grain we could imagine, and many we'd never seen before. One might have her produce displayed on a table, set out to invite buyers. Another had a competing arrangement on a cart. Many more had their wares stacked in bright, perfect pyramids on a sack on the ground. Greens, yellows, reds, oranges – the food on offer and the clothing of the traders were the colours of a carnival. And weaving in, out and around, were the ceaseless voices of buyers and sellers.

The family all clung on to us tightly to ensure we were not separated from them. We seemed to be attracting a great deal of attention as the local people stared at the tall *gringos* with the little Peruvians holding on to them. We had to start getting used to this as Huanta sees few *gringos*. We were quite a novelty and stuck out like sore thumbs. We were not only white, but were also a good foot taller than the average Peruvian.

Carmen did all the bargaining and after we had bought everything, including five new moulded plastic chairs (a present to the family from Michael and me), we headed back to the house in the *moto*, with the chairs tied to the roof. On our return, Carmen and Mariluz began cooking lunch.

When we all sat down together to eat, using the new chairs, Margot began to cry, closely followed by the others. Michael and I looked at each other wondering why the tears, before Margot explained. 'This is the first time our whole family has ever been able to sit down to eat a meal together.'

It didn't take much to bring such happiness to our family and Michael and I also shed a few tears of joy.

CHAPTER 10

Living with a Quechuan Peruvian Family

We had planned to spend a few weeks with the family and the days just passed by, living and being with them. Meal times were usually riotous with lots of jokes and laughter, lively conversation and plenty of loud family arguments, which we never understood, as arguments were always in Quechuan. The kids told us there was an abundance of rude words to call each other in Quechuan. To our ears the language sounded quite harsh and was usually spoken in a raised voice, so we were not always sure when they were fighting or just 'discussing'. Whatever the case, family meal times were much as they would be for any family, with the full gamut of emotions on display.

The silliest of topics could have us all in tears of laughter, such as when the kids recounted the sad tales of a string of Nélida's pet kittens and cats. It shouldn't have been funny, as Nélida had loved each of her cats, but with the help of a wonderfully descriptive new word that we learnt that day, it turned into an hilarity. '*Aplastado*' means squashed in Spanish, and Michael and I, rather naughtily, made light of the serious issue. One kitten had been *aplastadoed* by the kids as they were playing, another had been *aplastadoed* on the road, and yet another had been *aplastadoed* by Nélida as she rolled onto it while sleeping. Even Nélida couldn't help but see the funny side as Michael and I emphasised the word.

Meals also provided an insight into our family's culture from a culinary perspective. Carmen and Mariluz were keen for us to sample all the local specialties and cooked wonderful food for us every day. The Carbajal Moreira family eats three cooked meals a day, as do most people in the region.

For *desayuno*, breakfast, there was always a hot drink made fresh from either soy beans or grains such as *kiwicha* (amaranth), quinoa, corn or oats. Soy milk was the most common, and the process by which it is made is quite laborious. First the dried beans are ground, using a mechanical grinder such as would now be found in antique stores in Australia. When I had a turn at grinding, I was surprised by just how much muscle power was needed. They all laughed when I gave up after a few minutes, complaining it was too hard for my weak *gringo* arms. Water is then added to the ground beans before the mixture is cooked on the open fire for about 20 minutes. A generous amount of sugar is added before it is served.

Carmen sometimes made the soy milk using an alternative method. The whole beans were soaked overnight, then placed in water on the fire and allowed to boil for an hour. Once removed from the fire, it was all put through an electric blender. After seeing the old-fashioned hand-grinder we were surprised that the family owned a modern electric blender and a juice extractor. Mariluz explained that both were left over from a previous job where she'd sold freshly made fruit and vegetable juices in the local markets.

I tried this method at home one day after our return. However, I took my eyes off the stove and the beans boiled over, making a huge mess on the stove top and the floor. In my haste to get to the stove, I slipped over on the wet floor, falling down hard. To add insult to injury, the resulting soy milk was not very good, or in Michael's words, 'disgusting'. I'm ashamed to say I never made another attempt.

To go with the hot drink for *desayuno*, there was always fresh *pan* with avocado, and sometimes *papas sancochidos* (boiled potatoes). *Pan,* which literally translates as bread, generally refers to bread rolls in Peru. While in the big cities you may find loaves of bread, they are unknown in Huanta. The rolls come in various forms and have a different taste and texture than ours. Generally they are lighter and airier, with less substance and little taste. Having said that, we still enjoyed the *pan peruano*. Being special guests we were also regularly treated to freshly laid eggs for breakfast which we insisted on sharing.

Lunch, *almuerzo*, was typically the largest meal of the day. It always contained a colourful combination of vegetables, bought fresh from the market each day, and either a legume such as lentils or beans, or grains such as wheat or *kiwicha*, cooked in a variety of ways. It was served with rice or quinoa, and was always delicious. The rice was first fried with garlic before being boiled. Yum!

Interestingly, although rice is not native to the Americas, it has become a staple food all over South and Central America. Prior to the Spanish conquest, quinoa was one of the staples, originating in the high Andes of Peru and Bolivia. Although actually a seed, it is used as a grain and is highly nutritious, full of essential vitamins and minerals and rich in calcium, iron and protein. The Incas described it as 'the mother of all grains'. Although quinoa is now widely available, and in very recent years has even been grown in Tasmania, most quinoa is still grown in the high Andes in Peru and Bolivia.

Dinner was a small meal which they called '*lonche*'. It generally consisted of another hot drink and then perhaps some bread and avocado or other leftovers.

The problem with having *lonche* just before going to bed was that it increased the likelihood of having to get up at night, usually at least twice, to pee. The altitude also exacerbated this need. It would have been much simpler to refuse the hot drink at dinner time, but this was hard to do as it was always so delicious and virtually forced upon us. '*Te aumento?*' Can I give you more? or '*Más? Más?*' (more? more?) was always the call from one or other family member, after we had finished eating or drinking anything. They thought they had to feed the *gringos* until they almost exploded! Michael and I, finding the food so delicious, had trouble saying 'no', and when we did say '*no gracias*', it had to be said with conviction or we would get another helping anyway.

Going to the toilet in Huanta was not overly pleasant. While I don't have a problem with squat toilets, or digging a hole in the ground to do my business in the bush, poohing into a small hole in a concrete slab is a totally different experience. An extra difficulty for a female, it was impossible to both poo and pee simultaneously into the tiny hole. You had to work out your priorities and get the timing right! The blue plastic sheet, specially hung up for our privacy, was also problematic. As you squatted, it was only inches away from your face and you couldn't help but notice all the urine splatters from previous users. Then with the slightest of breezes, it blew onto your face. Yuuuk! Maybe we would have been better off without the plastic sheet after all!

A bucket of water was kept in the *baño* to wash down the solids. After toileting you simply poured the bucket of water down the hole, taking everything away to who knows where. (We surmised that it ended up, untreated, in the river far below

Huanta). Once finished, you filled up the bucket from the tap next to the *baño* and placed it back inside for the next person. We were instructed not to throw our toilet paper down the hole, but to place it in a different bucket. The family had kindly bought toilet paper for us soft *gringos* – they normally just used old newspaper.

Going to the toilet at night was even worse. We had first to negotiate the rickety ladder, in a semi-conscious state. Once down the ladder, the 'attack dogs' rallied. Having heard one of us getting up, all five dogs came to perform their duty, surrounding us, barking and growling. Despite the dogs not being particularly big, this was initially quite frightening. We yelled at them, and the family, who were by then also awoken, also yelled. The dogs then only backed off slightly, and fortunately didn't follow us into the cubicle.

After a few days, the dogs became accustomed to us and we were accepted into their pack. Night time excursions were no longer a fearful experience, but still not so pleasant. When they heard us coming down the ladder, the dogs all still barked, but instead of growling menacingly at us they came and jumped all over us with their muddy paws, licked us all over, and wanted some attention in return. Yes, we really were becoming a part of the family.

~~~~

For the first few days with the Carbajal Moreira family, Michael and I just participated in general family life. We insisted on helping with the chores such as washing up, but it was an effort to be permitted to help. The family members were all treating us like a king and queen, something to which we were certainly not accustomed and did not enjoy. We wanted to make ourselves useful but they wanted to wait on us hand and foot.

Carmen and Mariluz did most of the cooking and it was all done in one or two big pots on the open fire. The pot was removed using only their bare hands. When I asked if this was not painful, they just laughed and said they'd always done it this way and their hands were used to it. They also boiled all the necessary water for Michael and me to drink during the day, to ensure we would not succumb to any gastric illness.
~~~~

The food they provided us with was amazing. We were quite sure the family did not usually eat so well, and kept on slipping more money to Carmen to help with the food shopping. When we were in town together, we always paid for everything.

Unfortunately the five dogs didn't eat as well as the humans. They were fed a vegetarian diet of a cooked gruel, made from wheat, and occasional leftovers. Although skinny and always appearing ravenous when food was around, they seemed happy enough. And, although starved of meat, they took no notice whatsoever of the chickens that were running around the yard. They would eat the eggs though, if they got to them first.

Highland Peruvians don't seem to pamper their pets, but Celestino, in particular, loved the dogs and caressed them in his own rough way. Two of the dogs were always by his side. Although underfed, yelled at a lot and not given much attention, I imagine these dogs were happier than most pampered Australian dogs that are often left alone all day in a backyard. The Carbajal Moreira dogs spent their days running up the back and barking at any person or other dog that came near the property, and playing and fighting together. Although not confined to their property, the dogs always seemed to stay within its bounds, defending their territory.

Daily activities involved going to town to buy fresh produce, as there was no refrigeration. There was always a long preparation process prior to departure. Peruvians take great pride in their appearance in public, and the Carbajal Moreira family were no different. Any time we were planning to leave the house, the kids' dressing and grooming procedure began.

First, one at a time, they would stick their head under the wash basin's tap and wash their hair, either just with water, or with soap. Then they needed to comb their hair in front of the one small mirror, pushing and shoving each other to get a look in. Once they were all dressed, someone would decide that the pants or the top they had selected was not suitable, so would go and change it. Then someone else would follow suit, often involving several changes of clothes until everyone was happy. The family didn't have a large selection of clothes, instead borrowing from each other and arguing about it at the same time. It wasn't just a girl thing – Wilbur was equally bad if not worse. He spent hours combing his hair and preening in front of the mirror.

Although Michael and I found this procedure quite amusing, it was also frustrating having to hang around waiting for over an hour each time. For us getting ready was easy – put on whichever of our two pairs of pants and our three T-shirts were the cleanest. Michael promised never to castigate me again for taking too long to get ready!

We teased the kids endlessly about their slowness and Celestino kept apologising for his tardy children, but we knew we needed to display some sensitivity to their culture. Although the Carbajal Moreiras were poor, they didn't want this to be displayed in public; poor people are looked down upon in their society, seemingly even more so than in Australia. In contrast, Michael and I – who are comparatively wealthy – prefer to dress down, and more often than not look quite scruffy.

The family all wore Western clothing. Celestino was always dressed in jeans and a flannel shirt and usually a tattered woollen jumper or two. Carmen generally wore a skirt or slacks and usually a blouse or sometimes a T-shirt. The kids all wore shorts or cotton pants or track suit pants and T-shirts.

Interestingly, the kids constantly commented on our clothes. They loved my zip off travel pants, loved our cheap T-shirts and our shoes, and even our supermarket bought, $6 daggy sandals. We could have been wearing rags and they would have loved them as well.

We usually went on foot to town, walking on the edge of the road for the first part, there being no footpath. We always knew when a vehicle was approaching as the local trucks, cars, *combis* and *moto-taxis* were noisy and generated clouds of black smelly fumes. The drivers all tooted their horns regularly, in case we hadn't heard them. There was a lot of rubbish strewn along the roadside and in the town itself, and the smells were often overpowering. Added to the stench of putrefying rubbish was often the acrid smell of urine. Peruvians seemed to be immune to the foul smells and rubbish around them.

We were reminded of an incident on our first trip in 2001. We were travelling in a *combi* through the beautiful *Cordillera Blanca* when a woman, seated in the back of the bus, leaned forward, passed some plastic rubbish to Michael, and asked him to throw it out the window. Michael asked her why she wanted to pollute her beautiful country. She replied 'I know, you're right, we shouldn't do it, but can you throw it out for me anyway?' Michael refused, so another Peruvian did it for her. Many buses even had signs which read: *'Be thoughtful, throw your rubbish out the window.'*

Another passenger explained: 'In years gone by, all packaging was natural and biodegradable. When food was sold, it was wrapped in leaves or corn husks, so it was fine to throw all the packaging back to nature.'

Unfortunately many people hadn't moved with the times and never considered what would happen to all the discarded plastic and bottles.

~~~~

After about three days with the family Michael and I were starting to feel a bit sticky, dirty and smelly. I thought it was time to raise the issue of washing, being unsure of how and where they washed themselves.

'No problem,' said Mariluz, 'tomorrow we will go to the river for a bath.'

So the next day we, along with Carmen and all the girls, grabbed some clean clothes and our towels, and headed for the *Rio* Tablachacra, about a ten minute walk away. They said they normally bathed about twice a week, but before going had to ascertain what day it was. On alternating days the water was diverted from the *Rio* Tablachacra to another river by a series of sluice gates higher upstream, leaving their river fairly dry.

Following the *rio* up beyond the houses, we had to be careful not to brush past the cactus plants with their sharp spines. The cacti are multitudinous and widespread in this semi-arid environment. The dry hard-packed ground is also vegetated with a variety of other spiky leaved plants. Although there was a rough track to follow, the scrub was sparse enough that you didn't really need to stick to it.

Continuing upstream, we passed several women with their children, washing their clothes and bedding in the river. The items to be washed were heavily soaped, using a huge bar of soap, then scrubbed vigorously by hand, beaten into submission on the river rocks then draped over bushes and boulders to dry, creating what appeared to be a bizarre and colourful work of art. This is common
~~~~

practise throughout South America and leads to many rivers being infused with a pungent soapy aroma.

The Carbajal Moreiras now did most of their washing in their outdoor tub, but prior to having the tub installed, they told us they always did their washing in the river. When the family asked me where I did our washing at home, they were amazed when I told them we had a washing machine, and explained the process. 'Wow,' they all exclaimed, 'you must be really rich.' They were incredulous when we told them that most families, even poorer families in Australia, owned a washing machine.

'Even the *campesinos*?' they wanted to know.

'Yes, even the farmers out in the country,' we answered.

Once we arrived at their chosen water-hole, the Peruvians all stripped down to their underwear and we followed their lead. There was no apparent embarrassment on the part of the older girls or Carmen at doing this, even with Michael present. They clearly felt comfortable with us as we did with them. The water was quite cold, but that didn't deter the younger kids from jumping into the shallow pool and imploring the rest of us to follow. Then there followed much splashing and laughter as we played around and washed.

The kids all enjoyed having Michael and me bathing with them and following our first wash, they asked us most days if we were going to the river for a bath, always hoping that we were. On subsequent trips to the river, we were usually accompanied by a few young cousins as well, and the younger kids had a ball as they splashed and cavorted and wrestled each other, much as kids do everywhere. Most of the Carbajal Moreiras bathed more often during our time with them than they normally did.

After our bath Michael and I towel-dried ourselves, and we were surprised to find that our family, who didn't own a towel (nor had they ever seen one), would just don their clean clothes over their wet bodies. We offered them the use of our towels, but most of the time they didn't bother using them and just did as they had always done. It was the dry season and the daytime temperatures were generally in the low twenties, so enjoyable for bathing.

~~~~
~~~~

On our daily trips to town, Michael and I encouraged the kids to walk with us rather than relying on Wilbur and the *moto-taxi*. They had become lazy since the *moto-taxi* was bought, and expected Wilbur to be at their beck and call. We tried to impress on them that using the *moto* actually costs the family money in petrol and in lost earnings, and that the three kilometres was really not too far to walk. It was not the most beautiful of walks and care had to be taken as there was no footpath for the first half of the walk. Although it was the main road into town, it was generally not too busy.

Michael and I couldn't go anywhere without the kids hanging on to us and fighting with each other to have one of our hands to hold. They were so proud to have *gringos* as a part of their family and it was quite special, if at times a bit tiresome, for us to be loved so much by our adopted family.

On many of the shopping trips Michael and I would buy something for the family. Having noticed that the kids each had only one pair of holey socks and one pair of underpants, we bought them all new sets. The joy on their faces at receiving such small gifts was priceless.

As their shoes were all worn out, one day we offered to accompany them to buy each a new pair. What a mistake that was; we should have given them the money to buy the shoes themselves, because we experienced every parent's nightmare – shopping for shoes with teenagers!

I still remember my mother's exasperation at shopping for shoes with me. I would try on a hundred pairs of shoes before I found a pair that I liked and that were comfortable. However, for some reason we thought that the Peruvians would be different. We thought that because they had so little, any pair of shoes would be accepted gladly. How wrong we were! We spent hours traipsing from one shoe shop to another and to many stalls in the crowded market place. The youngest two, Margot and Nélida, were the worst. They wanted to buy nice black shoes for school. They looked at dozens of shoes and said they didn't like any of them. After many hours, when our patience was wearing thin, they found a pair of shoes each with which they were happy. Marleni was not quite as fussy and soon found some shoes to her liking. We decided to call it a day after the three youngest girls were satisfied.

Mariluz and Karina wanted hiking boots so the following day we once again plodded from shop to shop, this time looking at boots. The quality was surprisingly poor and the prices high. Although prices in the shops are marked, Mariluz and Karina always tried to bargain them down. In the umpteenth shop they both found a pair of boots to their liking. Then the hilarious bargaining process began, starting with some light-hearted haggling. Michael and I kept quiet, but the shop keeper had obviously worked out what was going on and was trying to charge the girls *gringo* prices.

'Your friends will be paying for the boots,' the young shopkeeper said to Mariluz, a glint in his eye.

'No, we are paying,' replied Mariluz earnestly.

'Oh sure,' the shopkeeper said sarcastically, although with a grin.

'We are. Really,' emphasised Mariluz.

The good natured repartee continued until a price was agreed upon and Mariluz and Karina walked out happily wearing their new boots.

We also bought new shoes for Wilbur and Carmen, but they were much easier customers.

Celestino liked my el-cheapo $6 sandals. As he had roughly the same size foot as me, I promised to give them to him when I left. He was very happy.

~~~~

Celestino's mother, who the kid's called *abuelita,* regularly waddled over from across the road. She dressed as most of the older indigenous women of the region did, in layers of voluminous skirts and jumpers and with a felt hat perched on her head. Her greying hair cascaded in two long plaits. She was a large woman and she was strong. Calling me *gringita* (little *gringa*), she would grab me and give me a big bear hug, squeezing the air out of me. The kids tried to avoid her rough embraces, something that was harder for us to do.

Abuelita was always chewing on something, often coca leaves, used to ward off the effects of altitude. She didn't speak much Spanish, but that didn't stop her talking to us in rapid Quechuan, and the blank faces we gave her in response just made her laugh, pinch our cheeks and talk louder. The children all thought she was a bit crazy.
~~~~

~~~~

The younger girls frequently asked us to teach them some English, although they rarely ventured far past "good morning", "good night" and the numbers up to ten. We were worse when they tried to teach us some Quechuan. I was unable to remember one single word while Michael, by accident, mastered one. He had mispronounced the Spanish word for trout (*trucha*) and Mariluz and Karina had started giggling, telling him that he had said a *mala palabra* (rude word). The meaning, which had to be prised out of them, was a crude word for a female body part.

Karina was working through a Basic English workbook and wanted to know what a lounge chair and a sofa were. I looked up the words in my English/Spanish dictionary and the Spanish words gave her no further clues. In their environment in Huanta, comfortable padded chairs simply didn't exist. They weren't available in the local shops and probably wouldn't have been found in many other peoples' houses. The family members had all thought that the moulded plastic chairs we had bought them from the local shops were the ultimate in comfort. They had only ever known hard straight-backed wooden chairs.

Karina then asked what a lounge room was. There being no point in looking the word up in the dictionary, I tried to explain the concept of a separate room in the house in which to relax. Karina looked amazed that such luxuries existed. Most people in the Peruvian Highlands don't have the spare time to lounge around anyway, there always being some chores or work to do.

~~~~

All the family were mesmerised by Michael's eyes, and one or other would often comment on their beautiful blue colour. In an area where everyone is dark-skinned, dark-haired and brown-eyed, Michael's blue eyes were something extraordinary and to be admired. Michael enjoyed the extra attention. It was actually surprising that the family didn't refer to Michael as *ojos azules* (blue eyes) because in Peru, as in other Latin American countries, people are often nicknamed for their attribute. Fat people are called *Gordo* and skinny people *Flaco*. Nélida was often called *Chino* for her Chinese looks. But Michael was called 'Mitch a el', as his name would be pronounced phonetically in Spanish, and they pronounced my name, Laní, with the emphasis on the 'í'.

~~~~

Michael regularly walked behind the house and into the home *chacra*, binoculars glued to his face, looking for birds. This caused some amusement amongst the kids – they wanted to know what he was looking through and why. Michael explained their use and told them he liked to look at different birds. He tried to teach them to use the binoculars, but none of them really managed, and the younger ones in particular couldn't see much point in looking at birds. They would try, then giggling, pass them back, not having seen anything. However, after a few days if they saw Michael without the binoculars around his neck they always asked him where they were.

Celestino was particularly impressed with the binoculars and asked Michael to explain how they worked, which he attempted to do. Whether or not Celestino could understand Michael's explanation, he nodded knowingly and said they were a wonderful invention.

~~~~

A couple of times during our stay, Michael and I braved the crowded *combis* and rough winding dirt road to travel the 45 km back to Ayacucho to be given tours of the city by Karina and Mariluz. It was usually a one-hour trip, although on a couple of occasions it took over two hours. One time the *combi* got a flat tyre; the driver replaced it with his spare, a very bald and patched tyre, which only lasted another few kilometres before it too punctured. We then had to wait for another vehicle to pass, so we could borrow its spare tyre. This was a common occurrence, as the tyres used on the vans were invariably old, full of patches and with little tread.

With 33 churches and cathedrals, the oldest being the San Cristóbal Temple of 1540, Ayacucho is known as the 'City of Churches'. The city was founded in 1540 and named Huamanga, then in 1825 it was renamed Ayacucho as a tribute to the Battle of Ayacucho in which Peru gained its independence from Spain. It now has a population of about 140,000.

Karina and Mariluz usually referred to their city as Huamanga, as did most other locals, although maps show the city as Ayacucho. Karina told us that her university, the *Universidad Nacional San Cristóbal de Huamanga,* is the city's main university and also the oldest, having been founded in 1677.

Mariluz told us that Ayacucho is well known for its colourful and devout *Semana Santa* (Easter) celebrations. 'Peruvians come here from all over the country. There are huge parades that take over entire streets and lots of music and festivities.'

Ayacucho is also well known for its beautiful *artesanía* which include all manner of colourful hand-woven goods, pottery, jewellery and clothing made from alpaca wool. The city has another not so auspicious claim to fame. The Maoist terrorist organisation - *Sendero Luminoso*, or Shining Path – launched its bloody campaign against the Peruvian Government from the *Universidad Nacional San Cristóbal de Huamanga* in 1980. The organisation, under the leadership of Abimael Guzmán, terrorised the nation for twelve years until 1992 when Guzmán was captured and imprisoned. Another leader took over the control and the carnage continued, albeit in a smaller way, until 1999, when he too was captured.

In 2001, a 'Truth and Reconciliation Commission' was established to investigate the conflict. It was found that over 69,000 people had died or 'disappeared' between 1980 and 2000 as a direct result of the armed conflict. It was estimated that the Shining Path was responsible for about 50 percent of the deaths and disappearances, about 33 percent died at the hands of the government security forces and the remainder by other smaller guerrilla groups. About 45 percent of the deaths were from the Ayacucho region.

We spoke with Mariluz and Karina about this horrific period of time, and Mariluz told us some chilling stories about abuses, deaths and torture that happened not far from their home and told us how they'd all lived for many years with constant fear and mental anguish.

While walking on the outskirts of Huanta one day, Mariluz indicated a small shelter on a ridge overlooking the village.

'This was used during the time of the *Sendero Luminoso*, as a lookout post for the villagers to spot guerrillas approaching. When guerrillas were detected, the look-outs signalled for the inhabitants to hide.'

She went on to explain that when the guerrillas came to the village they demanded food and goods. If the villagers resisted or didn't comply, they were beaten up or even killed. However, when they did comply with the demands, they were seen as Shining Path sympathisers by the military, and then often brutalised or murdered for having aided the guerrillas. 'It was a frightening period of time, which thankfully is now over.'

It was only on our later visit in 2010 that we found out how closely the Carbajal Moreira family had been affected by the atrocities. Celestino explained the events to us.

'On the 6 September 1983, one of my sisters was killed during a confrontation between the armed forces and the *Sendero luminoso*, in the *selva* where she was living at the time. This was the day that marked the beginning of the political violence in this department, and it was the day that changed my life, leaving me in deep sorrow over the death of my beloved sister. It got worse the following year, when the armed forces arbitrarily detained passers-by, grouping them together until they had 20 people, then taking them to their barracks and killing them. They were buried in mass graves.'

Celestino and Carmen, along with two year old Mariluz and seven-month old Wilbur had fled to another area to save their lives. In 1985, they moved to the Sivia locality, in the *selva,* and built themselves a house. They had lived in constant fear for their lives as the political violence continued and worsened for many years.

Meanwhile, Carmen's family had also been deeply affected by the violence.

'In 1985 my father died as a consequence of physical abuse he received at the hands of the armed forces. At the same time my mother was tortured by the *Sendero Luminoso,* and my sister lost her left hand when a bomb, placed in her house by the members of the armed forces, exploded. I was sent into a deep depression and wondered how we could continue to live in a country so full of violence, which doesn't respect social class or origins.'

Fortunately Huanta and Ayacucho were now experiencing more peaceful and tranquil times, although we did hear that deep in the jungle areas there were still some active *Sendero Luminoso* guerrillas.

CHAPTER 11 The *Chacra* in the Jungle

'Would you like to come to the *selva* to see our *chacra*?' Mariluz asked, her eyes shining in anticipation.

'Yes, of course, we'd love to,' Michael and I replied in unison. 'But is it safe?' Their previous stories about the *Sendero Luminoso* and the possibility that they were still active in the jungle areas concerned us.

Yes, it's now safe,' Mariluz assured us, 'but it is a long journey.'

Undaunted, Michael and I said we were keen to see their *chacra*, about which they had told us so much and where Carmen spends so much of her time.

'Many families from the town of Huanta have *chacras* in the wider Huanta Province, in an attempt to make ends meet,' Mariluz said, 'Like us, they grow coffee and other edible foodstuffs for market and for their own use.'

Mariluz explained that the Huanta Province comprised about 4,000 square kilometres and extended from the highlands to the lowland jungle or *selva*. 'The nearest town to our *chacra* is Sivia, on the Apurimac River. It takes about eight to ten hours to travel there from Huanta, even though it's not so far in distance as the crow flies.'

Carmen, Mariluz and Karina were coming with us to the *chacra*, leaving Marleni in charge of cooking for the others in Huanta for the week and caring for Celestino. Marleni laughingly told us she was really good at cooking – rice. The rest of the family was obviously not going to be eating so well for the week we were to be away!

First we caught a *colectivo* back to Ayacucho and then changed to a jungle-bound *combi*. As with most local transport, the vans heading to the *selva* wait until they fill up and then squeeze a few more bodies in before departing, rather than running to any timetable.

The dirt road is narrow and rough and winds up and down through the mountains, going over several high passes and through many small villages and communities. Each village is different. In one, the roof tops are covered with colourful beans, laid out to dry in the sun. In another village the roof tops are red with bright chillies. In a third, potatoes adorn the roofs and surrounding land. There are scores of varieties of potatoes, each with a distinctive shape and colour that, from a young age, the Peruvian children can identify. Even this many is only a handful of the 200 or more types that are indigenous to Peru. With the harvest in, many fields too are covered with fruit and vegetables being dried for storage or sale.

For much of its length the road is built right into the mountain-side with terrifyingly steep drop-offs. Michael, Karina and I spent much of the time, our stomachs tied in knots of fear, awaiting disaster especially when meeting oncoming traffic. Another car on the road necessitated one vehicle having to back up to find a space to let the other pass, its wheels teetering on the edge. Added to this, much of the journey was in thick fog and rain, on slippery muddy roads.

Carmen, who is accustomed to this long scary bus journey, was wearing her 'Quechuan travelling face' – passive and expressionless – and even managed some sleep. She said she is terrified every time she does the trip, and she does it several times each year, but is resigned to it and endures. Mariluz is a little scared, whereas Karina told us she rarely goes to the *selva* with her mother as the trip frightens her so much.

The driver, who travels the same route several times each week, seemed unfazed by the risks he was taking as we headed deeper into the jungle, with the road becoming steeper and wetter. He took in his stride the many landslides and other obstacles while we were quaking in the back. Carmen told us that it is much worse in January and February, the wet season, when the roads are just slippery muddy tracks.

Despite the fear it was, nevertheless, a beautiful trip, with the verdant green rainforest dripping and shrouded in mist. The villages changed remarkably in character. The houses in these lower altitudes are of wood rather than adobe and concrete and they have thatched roofs. The locals, either wearing gum boots or bare-footed, wander along the wet, muddy verge, straggly dogs in tow, going about their business. Ducks waddle across the road and pigs wallow in the mud.

Once we reached the major jungle town of San Francisco, on the Apurimac River (a tributary of the Amazon), we had to change vehicles and jump into another *combi* for the remaining two hour drive, following the river. To reach Sivia, on the other side of the river, we boarded an outboard-motor-powered long boat.

We stayed the night in Sivia, in the home of one of Celestino's brothers and his family. Rather than the warm welcome we expected, they were quite cold towards us and told us we could sleep outside.

We later found out that of Celestino's five siblings, four of them sought to take advantage of him because he was the oldest and an illegitimate child, having a different father. Ever since he fell ill in 1994, his siblings had been trying to wrest the *chacra* from him as they knew he was too sick to look after it. They didn't give Carmen any credit for the work she did on the property. 'A woman can't look after a *chacra* alone,' they all thought.

During the remainder of the afternoon we walked around Sivia in search of something vegetarian for dinner. We found it to be a strange place and as we wandered around, Michael and I could feel the eyes of the locals boring into us, making us feel quite uncomfortable.

Checking out all the local eateries, we found that the only food available was fried chicken, this information having to be prised out of the unfriendly owners who refused to make eye contact. Michael and I had never experienced so much rudeness and unfriendliness in a Peruvian town before. Unable to find a vegetarian meal, we went to the local markets and bought some fruit, vegetables and bread for dinner.

Later on, Mariluz and Karina explained the situation to us. 'Tourists don't visit Sivia. The only white people that come here are either drug dealers or, on the other side, the US narcotics enforcement police. It's a high coca leaf producing area. Once the leaves are harvested, they are made into cocaine and shipped to the USA.'

Coca leaves have been grown in the Andes for centuries and are chewed by the locals to lessen the effects of living at high altitudes and to dampen hunger. However, of the coca leaves grown in this jungle area, about ninety percent is used for the production of cocaine and the US authorities are trying to eradicate or at least slow down its production. This went some way towards explaining the unfriendliness and wariness shown towards us.

This also explained why, when we had entered the wider San Francisco area the day before, the Peruvian anti-drug police had recorded the names of all the bus passengers on-board. This was after we had been forced to pay a 'toll' to local shotgun-toting bandits.

It was quite a scary area to be in.

~~~~

After an uncomfortable night sleeping on the table outside the relatives' house, we ate our fruit breakfast and headed for the *chacra*. This entailed hiring a car to take us as close to the *chacra* as the road goes, and then walking for several kilometres up a muddy trail with a 400 metre ascent, carrying our gear and some basic foodstuffs. It was hot and humid and we were glad we had started early.

Within a couple of hours, we arrived at the home of Celestino's youngest brother, Edmundo, who is married to Carmen's sister, Antonia. Edmundo is the only brother of Celestino who is not out to destroy him. They live in a small and basic pole house they have built in the forest. It has a thatch roof and walls on three sides, the fourth being open to allow the breeze to pass through and to enjoy the expansive views over the rain-forested valley and down to the Apurimac River. The whole family sleeps in the one big open area upstairs, with mosquito nets to keep the insects at bay. Hanging from the rafters, as if for decoration, were hundreds of cobs of last season's corn, being dried for later use.

In Edmundo's house, we were made to feel welcome. We set up our tent inner in the room upstairs with the rest of the family, to keep the insects out, although we were assured that there was no risk of malaria, it being the cooler winter season.

Downstairs, under the house, was where the meals were prepared, cooked on an open fire and eaten. The area was also used for the sorting and drying of crops, such as beans and coffee, in preparation for market or future planting. At the time of our visit, the family residing there consisted of Edmundo, Antonia and their three youngest children, including a baby. Their three older children were in Huanta living with their grandparents, so they could attend school.
~~~~

The Carbajal Moreira's *chacra* was about half an hour's walk from their relatives' house. As they only had a small hut on their own *chacra*, Carmen had decided it would be better to stay with the extended family for the week. After lunch of fried plantain (a type of large banana, especially delicious fried) and yucca (a sweet tasty root crop), we set off up the hill to our family's *chacra*.

Before arriving, Michael and I had preconceived ideas about what the *chacra* would look like. We had envisioned it being akin to a veggie patch, with neat rows of vegetables planted and maintained. Nothing could be further from the truth. The *chacra* was just a steep hillside of jungle with small areas semi-cleared for plantings. The twisting bean tendrils were mixed in with the native forest and the root crops such as yucca and *pituca* were buried amongst the tangle of forest vines and corn. Banana and plantain trees were scattered around at random in small clearings, as were other fruit trees such as native lemon, papaya and vegetable crops indigenous to the region. Coffee beans were planted in separate clearings.

Carmen guided us to the top of the hill to show us the extent of their land. It was quite a long walk along a rough trail which Carmen slashed at with a machete as we went. We stopped en-route for Carmen to chop down a *palmetto* for us to sample. This 'heart of palm' is a delicacy and was delicious, but we thought it a shame to have to kill a whole tree for such a small morsel. Being unused to the heat and humidity, we all (apart from Carmen) found the trek quite tiring. Viewing the large expanse of verdant jungle, much of it still in its natural state, made it all worthwhile and we got a good feel for the area and the extent of their *chacra*.

Work would begin the next day. Michael and I were instructed that we were not there to work but to have a holiday. We, of course, insisted on helping out. Carmen and Mariluz told us that we were *gringos* and would not be able to handle the work. We flexed our muscles and told them how strong we were and capable of physical work.

The five of us, tools in hand, headed out the following morning. Our first job was to harvest beans. Mariluz demonstrated the technique of running your hands through the whole plant, pulling several pods off at once. Michael and I were not quite so adept and it didn't take long for us to tire of standing on the steep slope performing this seemingly easy task. Carmen and Mariluz were right; we *were* weak *gringos* who couldn't handle the physical work – even though Michael had done plenty of hard physical labouring work in his time.

Karina wasn't much better than Michael and me and she also needed to stop for regular breaks. Teasingly, we nicknamed her *Gringa Peruana* (Peruvian White-girl).

Even when we did persevere with the work, either Carmen or Mariluz would instruct us to sit down and take a break. Then they would hand us some new food they'd just picked or dug up, for us to sample. Carmen and Mariluz worked like Trojans. Carmen, although only short in stature, is as strong as an ox and can keep working all day. She is also capable of carrying large loads on her back, for long distances over difficult terrain – all of this in flimsy plastic sandals. She is an inspirational woman.

While Mariluz shares Carmen's amazing strength, sadly none of the other children seem to have inherited it. Celestino later explained to us that he believes the other children lack the strength and stamina of their mother because they suffered from inadequate nutrition during their childhood years and when they were babies, they were fed on artificial milk as Carmen didn't have sufficient breast milk.

Due to the elevation of the *chacra* over the surrounding land, it has a more pleasant climate than the heat and stifling humidity of Sivia. Although still warm and somewhat humid, the *chacra* doesn't experience the climatic extremes of the lower altitudes, and in the evening the temperature becomes very pleasant. We found ourselves annoyed by biting insects, but we were assured that there were even more down in Sivia and the lower lands, particularly in the wet season.

There was plenty of work to keep us occupied for the week. After harvesting came shelling and sorting. Vladimir, the four-year old son of our hosts, taught us how to pod and sort the beans into their various colour groups and grades and showed us how to lay them out for drying. He demonstrated adroitly how to de-hull the dried corn cobs; the kernels were sorted into feed for the chooks, and seed for planting next season's crop. We knuckled down to help our young teacher. With three pairs of hands the work was completed sooner, allowing Vladimir more play time with his 'truck', a half cut-out bucket that he dragged along by a string. We were amused by his Russian-sounding name; and the family were surprised when we told them that it was Russian – they had just heard the name on the radio!

We helped collect water in buckets from the nearby stream. It was as sweet tasting as it was clear – and we didn't need to boil it for drinking. Michael and I also helped plant the corn. One person, using a bamboo pole, pounded a small hole while the other person sprinkled a few corn kernels into the hole and covered it up. We thus made our way across the hillside. There were also plantains, bananas and other fruits to harvest and root crops to be dug up.

Carmen and Mariluz constantly told Michael and me to sit back and relax, which we frequently did, often getting out the binoculars to do some bird watching. We were hoping to see macaws, but the closest we came were some small parrots.

Eating was another enjoyable pastime. Although some would call the meals monotonous, we loved every one of them and looked forward to them with relish. We ate a lot of fried yucca and fried plantain, neither of which we'd eaten before, both served with lashings of salt. We also ate a lot of eggs (usually fried) and plenty of rice, beans and potatoes. There were also obscure tropical fruits to be enjoyed. Breakfast and lunch were much the same, and dinner *(lonche)* was normally just a hot drink, as in Huanta, with whatever was left over from lunch. Michael and I tried to help with the cooking but we weren't allowed to do much of this.

~~~~

One day, Michael helped Edmundo load his old and sickly donkey with a huge weight of produce to take down to Sivia to sell. I felt sorry for the poor beast as it was whipped and yelled at in order to get it to walk. When I commented to Carmen later about the donkey's treatment, she said that it was well cared for as it is essential to the family for their income. Life in Peru is tough on both the people and their animals.

Michael and I had a lot of time to chat to Carmen and the girls and many tears were shed as they opened up and talked candidly about their lives. Carmen felt that her life was sad: 'I spend a large part of the year working alone on the *chacra* and I get very lonely. I
~~~~

normally live by myself on the *chacra* in our little hut, and I only sometimes visit my sister and Edmundo. I work really hard to maintain the *chacra*, and I worry that when I'm not here, neighbours come and help themselves to our crops.'

Carmen told us about the amazing dream she'd had back in 2001, around the time we had first met her children.

'I was alone on the *chacra* and I dreamt that my children had met some *gringos* who would help us in some way.'

This was the first time Carmen had mentioned this to us and we were dumbfounded. When she had returned to Huanta after that period in the jungle, the rest of the family told Carmen about meeting Michael and me, and she then told them about her dream. The family had no telephone contact at that time and could only pass messages to each other through other people who were travelling to or from the jungle. Carmen's family believes that she does possess psychic powers, and in later years Carmen has told us about other dreams that have come to fruition.

Carmen told us a bit about her background.

'I was born in Huanta in 1960, and was the fifth child of ten; eight girls and two boys. I grew up in a house not far from our current house in Huanta. I attended the local primary school but my parents didn't have the means to send me to high school. After I finished primary school my parents took me to the jungle to work with them and my elder siblings on the family *chacra*. I was 17 when I met Celestino; he was the love of my life. We made a commitment to spend the rest of our lives together and to work hard to create a better future for our children. We bought the land in the *selva* and worked long hours together to clear patches of rainforest in which to cultivate coffee and grow other crops. We were young, in love and very happy doing the hard work together and enjoying each other's company. We worked for several years before starting a family. I was 22 when I gave birth to Mariluz.'

When Carmen and Celestino's children were very young, they had lived on the *chacra* with their parents, but as each child reached school age they had been sent to Huanta to attend school and to live with their grandparents. Although life was hard for Carmen and Celestino, they were happy knowing they were creating a better future for their children. However, when Celestino fell ill in 1994, their lives and that of the whole family changed forever. From

1995, Celestino was no longer able to work on the *chacra*, leaving Carmen to work there alone. She was trying to do the work of two people and spent many months alone, suffering terribly from loneliness due to the distance from her family in Huanta. She had no option however, as it was the only income the family had. Without this meagre income, the family would have starved.

Initially the *chacra* was able to provide for the family, but as the years went by the price of coffee dropped dramatically and the earnings were not enough to sustain them. Carmen told us that we had met her family just when things were looking particularly grim. She saw Michael and me as the family's saviours.

During the week, Michael and I had a few discussions with Carmen about the worth of maintaining the *chacra,* now that it was virtually non-viable, financially. It wasn't even earning enough to cover the cost of Carmen's transport down and back. Carmen had to work on other *chacras* to earn her fare back to Huanta. When working as a *peon* (labourer) on another *chacra,* she was paid ten soles ($2.50) for an eight-hour day. To put that into perspective, one sol bought two rolls of toilet paper. The bus fare back to Huanta was 35 soles ($14). Carmen told us that Celestino wanted to keep the *chacra* in case any of the children wanted it in the future. At the time we were there, none of the children wanted to work on the *chacra* in the future as they all had aspirations to study and become professionals.

After close to a week on the *chacra*, we began our return to Huanta. Michael and I suggested we break the journey in San Francisco rather than facing another uncomfortable night with the unfriendly relatives in Sivia. Carmen said that was possible, but was concerned that we would have to pay for accommodation in San Francisco whereas it was free in Sivia. We assured Carmen that we would pay for the accommodation.

We loaded all our gear onto our backs and headed down the mountain. We were also carrying a large amount of produce to take back to Huanta - kilos of yucca, plantain, bananas, beans and other fruits and vegetables. Michael and I carried the produce in our backpacks while the Peruvians used their age old method of wrapping it all up in a *manta* – a colourful cloth swung over the back. These *mantas* are used for everything, including the swaddling and carrying of babies. All over Peru and indeed South America, one sees mothers carrying babies in *mantas* on their backs and rarely are the babies heard to cry.

Reaching Sivia, we left all our gear at the relatives' house while we visited the local animal park. This was a sad and depressing state of affairs. Many of the local jungle animals, including a jaguar, various species of monkey, wild boar and other unusual animals we'd never heard of, were locked up, looking bored and unhappy, in tiny cages and enclosures. Of even greater interest to us than viewing the animals, was seeing the park workers 'mowing' the lawns by hand, using machetes... At least it kept many workers employed!

After retrieving our luggage from the house, we headed down to the Apurimac River and loaded it all into a long boat for the crossing. Once safely across the river we found a *colectivo* heading back to San Francisco. It was late in the afternoon by the time we arrived and we were all quite tired. We asked at a couple of cheap hotels for their price for two rooms. Carmen said they were all too expensive and led us to the house of a distant relative. We were shown to a filthy, wet, dirt-floored open courtyard and were told we could sleep out there on the ground, for a minimal amount. Carmen and the girls seemed to think it was okay. Michael and I did not. We argued with poor Carmen and told her that we would not stay there.

Carmen didn't want us to waste our money on accommodation and was also afraid of upsetting her relative, but Michael and I were tired and just wanted a reasonable place to stay. Carmen said that she and the girls would stay in the courtyard while we could stay in a hotel. Michael and I would not agree to that suggestion and I told them firmly and in no uncertain terms that we would prefer to pay for all of us to stay in a hotel.

Carmen looked stunned. This was the first argument we had had with our family and it upset them deeply. Although I felt dreadful for causing such distress, I was tired and had wanted to make my point clear so there would be no further discussion.

We walked back to one of the hotels, in which we'd enquired earlier, and booked into two basic rooms which were luxurious compared to the alternative. After a half hour rest and freshen up, we all met for dinner and walked around from one greasy restaurant to the next, looking for the best of a bad lot. There wasn't much choice in San Francisco!

Things were still a bit tense between us all, but Michael and I reassured Carmen and the girls that we still loved them.

'All families fight from time to time,' I explained, 'and now that we are a part of the family, we are also entitled to an argument and loss of temper.'

'I was worried that you were so badly upset that you would abandon my family,' Carmen said, tears welling in her eyes.

We assured her that this was most certainly not the case; we had just been tired and fed up with dragging our gear all over town looking for somewhere to stay.

We all enjoyed a good night's sleep and were refreshed and ready for the continuation of the return journey the following morning. The tension of the previous day had fully dissipated and we were back to our normal happy family relations.

The five of us walked to the bus departure area and were told that we would have quite a long wait. In the last few days there had been a few *combis* attacked by armed bandits and many drivers were fearful of making the trip. The drivers who were prepared to take the risk were travelling in convoy and we would therefore have to wait for enough passengers to fill up three *combis* before they would depart.

Once the journey started, it wasn't long before our convoy halted. A message had been passed along from vehicles coming from the opposite direction that there were bandits on the road ahead. Michael quickly passed the majority of our cash to Carmen who hid it under her clothing. They would be less likely to suspect a local woman of having much cash than two *gringos*. We sat there for quite some time until the drivers felt safe enough for the convoy to continue. Fortunately we never came across the bandits.

Later at a checkpoint we had to alight from the vehicle while it and all our gear were carefully checked for drugs. Nothing was found. There were two other stops to repair flat tyres before we arrived in Ayacucho at close to nightfall.

Another flat tyre during the *combi* trip to Huanta meant we arrived home quite late. This, however, didn't deter the rest of the family and the dogs from giving us an excited welcome home reception.

CHAPTER 12 Back in Huanta

We arrived back in Huanta to warm embraces from the rest of the family and the five dogs jumping up and licking us with excitement. They were all so happy to have us back. Not only had they missed us, they told us, but they were sick of eating only rice, because that's all Marleni had cooked for them!

The following day, Michael and I thought it time to broach the subject of our departure. Prior to leaving Australia I had told the family via email that we would be in Peru for four weeks and that two to three of those weeks would be spent with them. I had carefully explained that after visiting them we wanted to go hiking in the mountains of the *Cordillera Blanca.*

As the *Fiesta de Maynay* was taking place just after our third week and Karina was again contesting to be the *Reina*, we decided we would stay to see Karina compete before leaving. We told the family of our decision and they all promptly burst into tears. 'What have we done to upset you?' they wanted to know and, 'Why are you leaving so soon?'

We assured them that they had done nothing to upset us and that our holiday plans had always been to stay for no more than three weeks. We explained our desire to go hiking in the mountains and our need for some time to ourselves, and reiterated that by the end of the week we would have been with them for a little over three weeks. Holidays? Time to ourselves? These were foreign concepts. Accustomed as they are to living in close quarters with little personal space, holidays were something they really couldn't comprehend, never having had the opportunity themselves. None of the family members could understand our desire to leave a loving family to go on a 'dangerous hike' on our own. It was difficult to convince them that although we did love them very much, we wanted to see Peru's beautiful mountains again and experience the peace and tranquillity that camping there offers, before returning to our busy lives in Australia.

Michael and I were aware that we were upsetting our family deeply and felt badly about it. We knew we were privileged to have already seen so much of their country and had been to places that they had never had the opportunity to visit and probably never would. We pondered whether we should stay for the final week to make them happy, but we both felt that three weeks was long enough and we really felt the need for a few days alone.

During our final week in Huanta we would often find one or other family member in tears. On asking what the matter was, the person concerned would reply: 'you are leaving in so and so many days,' or, 'we only have four (or three or two etc.) more days together.' We felt special but heavy-hearted at the same time. We realised how much joy our simply being with them was bringing to the Carbajal Moreiras. We were about to break that connection.

~~~~

There were many activities still planned for our final week, one of which was a speaking engagement at Margot and Nélida's primary school. I had suggested to the girls that they could ask their respective teachers if they would like us to speak to their classes about Australia. Both teachers responded in the affirmative and arranged a time for us to visit.

We took a few props with us including pictures of Australian animals, a map of Australia and some Aussie money. We had imagined that we would be speaking to two classes of children. Arriving at morning tea time, we chatted to the children in the playground. Then the bell rang and the students were all directed to the hall. Then it dawned on us that we were to speak to the whole school. Oh my God, I thought, what are we going to say to a hall full of several hundred school children? Michael's little Spanish seemed to totally disappear and I was left to do all the talking, while he played the stooge with the props. I talked about life in Australia, our language, the animals and whatever else came to mind. Then I was asked to teach the children some English. I taught some basic words and then the numbers to ten – one, two, three ... *nine*, ten. Well, I thought I was saying 'nine' but we had to laugh on hearing a room full of Peruvian children perfectly mimicking my Aussie accent, saying 'noyne'.

After our talk, any time we passed any of the students in the street, they gave us big waves and greeted us with '*hallo'*. The ice
~~~~

had been broken and the children were no longer afraid of the two big foreigners.

~~~~

Before we had arrived in Peru, Mariluz and Karina had written about the *Lagunas Razuillcas* – beautiful lakes high up in the mountains and after which their voluntary guiding group had been named. Both girls had mentioned having guided groups there previously.

'How long does it take to get to the *Lagunas Razuillcas*?' I asked Mariluz one day.

'Three hours.'

'Can you take us there?'

'Yes, of course I can, but it's a long way.'

Mariluz told us that it would take three hours to the lakes, walking straight up into the mountains, or else three hours by taxi as the road is circuitous and rough. We said we were prepared for a long walk if she and Karina were. They said they were, but only then told us that they had never walked there and didn't actually know the way.

On relating the plan to Celestino, he suggested the girls ask their *abuelo* (his stepfather) to guide us there as he knew the way. *Abuelo* agreed to accompany us the following day. We went to the markets and stocked up on food for the big hike – *Pan*, avocado, fruit and peanuts.

The following morning, Mariluz and Karina sporting their new hiking boots, Carmen wearing her plastic slip on shoes, we in our good hiking boots and *Abuelo* in his worn out old leather boots, all rendezvoused at 7.00. We were concerned about Carmen's shoes and asked if she had any other suitable footwear. No she didn't, but she assured us that she would be fine. Of course she was.

Abuelo set a cracking pace, walking directly behind the house and up into the hills. The rest of us struggled to keep up with this incredibly fit 68 year old. He just kept motoring on up the hill without pausing to draw breath. Several times one or other of us would have to beg him to stop so we could have a break and a drink. We got onto a ridge and could see it stretching way up into the distance – we knew we had a long way to go, but none of us knew just how long.
~~~~

Up, up, and up we followed on the heels of *Abuelo*. Mariluz, Karina and I were getting particularly tired and after about four hours of steady uphill climbing we asked *abuelo* how much further. 'We're nearly there,' was his cheery reply.

Another hour passed. '*Abuelo*, we can't go any further, we are exhausted,' said the girls and I to their grandfather.

'We're nearly there,' he replied with a wicked look in his eyes. The girls explained to me, once he was out of earshot, that their *abuelo* was a horrible man who didn't like them because they were the daughters of Celestino, the illegitimate child. *Abuelo* appeared to be enjoying seeing us all suffer.

After six hours of virtual non-stop walking, we finally reached our destination – the *Lagunas Razuillcas* – and they really were beautiful mountain lakes, coloured steely grey due to the cloud cover, perched amongst the grand mountains. What an achievement! The girls told us that if they had realised what a huge walk it was, they wouldn't have taken us there. It was the first time Karina had walked in the mountains and I think she was wishing she had never met us. Exhausted, we flopped down on the mountain grass to enjoy our well deserved lunch. *Abuelo* then told us about the two times he had walked alone from Huanta to Sivia, over these same mountains, in three days, taking nothing more with him than the clothes he was wearing and a few cooked potatoes as snacks. Although hard to believe, we had seen the stern stuff this man was made of and we could well believe him. Celestino later verified the story.

After a quick lunch and the obligatory photos, we prepared to leave. It would have been nice to linger and soak up the beauty, but it was freezing and we knew we had a long walk to get home. Although the descent was quicker than the ascent, it still took us four and a half hours and we arrived home in the dark. The family waiting for us in Huanta had been concerned, but they knew we were with *abuelo* so trusted we would be alright. And we were, but absolutely and totally exhausted.

Michael and I both claimed it was one of the hardest day-walks we had ever done, and for Mariluz, Karina and Carmen it was equally hard, if not harder. We had climbed from 2,500m of altitude up to around 4,200m and had walked about 25km. We were extremely grateful to Marleni who had prepared a big pot of dinner for us. It was delicious and we ravenously ate huge quantities, proving her siblings wrong when they had claimed that she could only cook rice. Karina virtually fell asleep at the dinner table.

A hot shower would have been wonderful, but a cold bucket wash had to suffice. As cold as it was once the sun had set, I could not have gone to bed without some sort of wash. The others all thought I was crazy, claiming I would come down with the flu, as I poured cold water over myself in the chilly night air. We all slept well that night, washed and unwashed alike!

The following day Michael told Carmen that we would like to cook the *almuerzo* and that we would do all the shopping. He wanted to make vegetarian spaghetti bolognaise. After returning from the markets, our arms weighed down with bags of vegies and spaghetti, we got to work, with a few onlookers. I pulled out our little plastic vegetable peeler I'd brought from home and started to peel the carrots. This caused some amusement. In Huanta they peeled vegetables using their one and only knife, an old, loose-handled implement, which to me seemed rather hazardous. I showed some of the kids how to use the peeler. 'That looks like a great idea,' said Margot, before trying it herself. She couldn't get it to work. Then each of the others had a go but they also couldn't get the hang of how to use it effectively. We left it in the kitchen for future use, but it remained untouched. They preferred their tried and tested old knife.

I described some of our other kitchen gadgets, such as a garlic crusher. 'Why do you need that?' they had asked incredulously, 'we just use a smooth river rock to crush the garlic on the bottom of the pot.' It was equally effective!

The spaghetti was a big success. Pasta was a new experience for them all and there was much laughter around the table as they struggled to eat it, bits of spaghetti hanging from their mouths and slapping them in the face as we explained how to suck it up.

'We love your Australian cooking, Michael,' they all enthused, while we laughed and explained that spaghetti actually originated in Italy.

~~~~
~~~~

'Shall we go on a picnic?' I asked the family one night at dinner.

'What's a picnic?' they wanted to know.

I explained the concept and they told us they'd never done that before. Karina mentioned that there was a waterfall – the *Cascadas de Huanyocc* – within an hour's walk of their house. This sounded like a great place for a picnic. We would go the following day. Unfortunately Celestino wouldn't be able to accompany us, but everyone else was looking forward to the adventure.

Michael and I, along with Carmen and the six kids, walked into town to buy the ingredients for the picnic lunch – fresh *pan*, avocados, tomatoes, carrots, cucumbers and fruit – and loaded them into our backpacks. The route to the waterfall wound up the rough trails behind the adobe houses scattered around the hills. The land was parched after the cold dry winter. We passed through bare fields dotted with cacti before arriving at the village of Huanyocc, near the *Cascadas*. The waterfall was more impressive than we had envisioned, with the main fall about 30 metres high and enough water cascading down to make it quite picturesque.

Carmen spread out her *manta* as a picnic rug. The family was under strict instructions to let Michael and me do all the preparation – they were to relax and enjoy the experience. Once everything was chopped and laid out decoratively, it was a free-for-all as everyone dug in and made up their own sandwiches amid lots of laughter and chatter.

After lunch we climbed down to the base of the falls and the older girls decided it would be fun to get wet. It wasn't long before we were all standing under the cascading water, fully clothed and giggling like little children.

The picnic was branded a huge success and I suggested that they could repeat the experience even when we were not there. They all thought that a lovely idea, but never did have another picnic until we returned six years later.

~~~~

Fortuitously, several events were staged during the time we were in Huanta, one of which was an anniversary celebration of the large high school which Marleni attended. Many of the students, including Marleni, had been practising some traditional folk dances
~~~~

for a concert. Unfortunately, the week before the *fiesta,* Marleni sprained her ankle and was unable to participate. She was terribly disappointed – she was one of the lead dancers and had been looking forward to performing in front of an audience, especially in front of Michael and me.

The celebrations began with an evening *fiesta.* Marleni accompanied us to watch her fellow students dance. Although she tried to put on a brave face, she was visibly sad that she wasn't a part of the performance. It was, however, still a lively evening with lots of noise and excitement, and like all good South American fiestas it concluded with fireworks – South Americans love a good party and the noisier the better.

~~~~

Another day, Michael and I did a day-trip to the picturesque small town of Quinua, an hour away from Ayacucho. Accompanied by Carmen and the two older girls we travelled there in a crowded *combi,* all squeezed in like sardines. I did a quick head-count and counted 24 bodies, all in a small van that in Australia could only legally carry 12. Despite the heat and the crush of humanity, everyone was good natured and laughed and chatted to us as we took photos of our fellow passengers, contorted and crouched over in the van, too low-roofed to fit even the shortest of standing Peruvians.

Quinua is famous for its distinctive ceramic figurines made from the rich red local clay and decorated with mineral earth colours. Virtually every house is of adobe topped with a red-tiled roof and each roof is adorned with small ceramic figurines. Many of the ornaments are religious in nature, such as churches and nativity figures, but there are also comical groups of musicians, llamas and other quirky figures. Even the church has a model church on its roof!

Close to the village of Quinua lies the *Pampa de Quinua* where the Battle of Ayacucho was fought in 1824 between the Spanish Royalist and the Peruvian Independence forces. As Mariluz had previously explained, this was the battle that brought Spanish rule of Peru to an end and sealed its independence. The victory also
~~~~

ensured the independence of the remainder of the South American countries.

~~~~

During our stay, one or other member of the family would often ask Michael and me about our life back home and our belongings, with an especial interest in our household appliances. They were amazed when we told them that as well as a washing machine, we owned a fridge and freezer. 'These are things that virtually every family in Australia owns,' we explained, 'they keep the food from going bad.'

'So you don't have to go to the markets every day?' they asked, and were astonished when I replied that many Australians shop only once a week, and some even less frequently.

Their jaws dropped when we told them that many families also owned clothes driers and dishwashers, although we assured them that we didn't have these machines. They laughed when we told them that we did own a lawn mower and explained its use. They'd never seen lawn.

Michael and I told the family that we weren't rich by Australian standards and reiterated that we could only afford to support them and to travel because we didn't have children of our own. We explained that although our wages were higher than in Peru, we did have to pay significant tax. We tried to give them an idea of the comparatively high cost of living in Australia. We were well aware, however, that if they could see our modest three-bedroom home, their belief about our perceived wealth would be confirmed. Not only do we have an indoor bathroom, we have two; we have carpet on the floor, a television and many toys such as bicycles and canoes. Yes, in comparison to the vast majority of Peruvians, we are indeed rich.

~~~~

One afternoon, some old Carbajal Moreira family photos were brought out to be shown to us. In a few of the photos the family members were dressed up in fine clothing. The young girls were wearing frilly white dresses with colourful waistbands and shiny black shoes. Indicating a photo of herself, aged about seven and looking very girlish, Karina explained that things were different then.

'Before Dad became ill, our parents could afford to buy us nice clothes. We all took great pride in our appearance. We could attend *fiestas* and town functions without feeling self-conscious and could mix freely with our peers. We were never rich and never had savings, but my parents were careful with their money and ensured that we had everything we needed and sometimes something extra as well. Everything changed when Dad got sick and couldn't work anymore. We could no longer afford the niceties of life.'

The family did still have an old radio, although the cassette function on it had long ago died. Celestino enjoyed listening to the news and current affairs programs, while the kids liked to listen to the latest pop music. The girls, in particular Marleni, had a favourite song that was broadcast repeatedly: '*Soy un idiota, te amo*' (I'm an idiot, I love you). I enjoyed it too and once I'd learned the words, Marleni and I sang it together every time we heard it. It became our theme song.

~~~~

During our final week with the family, our discussions became deeper and more intimate as our command of the Spanish language grew and our familiarity with the family increased. Michael and I discovered that we really were in tune with them, despite coming from such vastly different countries and backgrounds. We shared similar core values such as honesty, working hard, being considerate to others and a belief in social justice. Our political views were surprisingly similar, as were our views on other matters such as caring for the environment and healthy living. The Carbajal Moreira family appeared to be quite different from many of the poorly educated Quechuan families, partly perhaps because of Celestino's illness.

Celestino is a very intelligent man and as a result of his illness has had plenty of time to listen to the radio, to read and to think. Realising that traditional medicine had not helped him, he read widely about alternative medicines and naturopathic-type cures and was open to trying new things. He was passionate about eating healthy foods, free from chemical contamination, and adhering to a
~~~~

non-meat and non-dairy diet, which had the added benefit of being more economical. He imparted his wisdom to his family and most of them now hold similar values.

On environmental issues, the Carbajal Moreira family also holds a different view to many of their compatriots. Celestino realises that caring for the environment and the health of the planet is of vital importance to all living beings. He explained that few other people in the local area thought this way. The family was keen to listen to our suggestions on improving their environment. When we noticed that they disposed of their rubbish by throwing it over the fence into the neighbouring vacant lot, Michael asked why.

'That's what everyone does,' replied Celestino.

After discussing the issue with us they realised that there were other ways to deal with it. The family decided that in future they could burn their rubbish, which although not ideal was better than having it blowing around and polluting the village.

The Carbajal Moreiras are now also careful not to throw their rubbish onto the streets in town, as other people do, but seek out rubbish bins and educate others to do the same. Michael and I feel we taught the family some alternative ways of living, but we were only able to do this because they were open to new ideas and keen to learn about improving their country and themselves.

Another area in which Michael and I were influential was in how the family dealt with their fellow Peruvians in the streets and in the marketplace. We noticed that most Peruvians in Huanta were markedly unfriendly and abrupt with each other. We found that when we went to the markets with our family, the shopkeepers stared at us and did not attempt to talk to us. However, when we went shopping on our own, the vendors were generally friendly and interested to find out where we were from, where we were staying, and why were in Huanta. They wanted to know what we thought of Huanta, how we liked Peru, and what life was like in Australia.

The reason for this became apparent as we watched how the family dealt with the shopkeepers. There were no pleasantries such as 'hello' or 'please' and 'thank you', just hard bargaining. Watching other Peruvians go about their business, our family was quite typical, but we felt it did not have to be this way.

Mariluz and Karina told us they had seen the way we smiled and greeted people and used normal Western-style pleasantries and had noticed the different and friendlier responses we received from the vendors. They thought about their approach and decided that even though they were operating within their cultural norms, change must start somewhere and why not with them. They liked the way we interacted with their countrymen and showed respect for all people regardless of their station in life. They said they would make an effort to be friendlier in their dealings with others on the street and take note of the different responses they might receive.

Years later Mariluz and Karina told us how they always kept this in mind and found their interactions on the streets more enjoyable. They said they hoped their new manner of dealing with people would rub off on other Peruvians.

~~~~

Celestino was only able to sit all day as it was too painful for him to stand up for more than a few minutes at a time. He wasn't even able to sit on a normal chair as the pressure caused him too much discomfort. He used a milk crate with an old small tyre on top of the open side, and on this he sat all day, bent over at the waist. He moved around the yard during the day trying to find the most comfortable position within the narrow temperature range that he could tolerate. He was intrigued by the little thermometer I had dangling on my backpack, so I gave it to him and he enjoyed checking at which temperatures he was happiest. He explained to us that his illness had something to do with a lack of kidney function.

He would read at times and listen to the radio, but Celestino especially loved it when Michael or I sat with him to talk. When Michael was talking to him alone, I was often called over to help with translation, although I also had to concentrate hard to understand Celestino as his speech was not as clear as his children's. Michael was particularly frustrated with his faltering Spanish when talking with Celestino as he greatly enjoyed their conversations, finding him to be a fascinating man with many thoughtful insights.
~~~~

Celestino wanted us to tell him all about life in Australia and about other countries in which we had been. He was hungry for knowledge. He wanted us to explain how society functioned at home and to learn from us how things could be improved in Peru.

Celestino told us about his childhood.

'I was born in 1958 in Uyuvirca, a province of Huanta, the first born to my parents. As is the custom, I took my family name from the first surname of my father followed by the first surname of my mother and thus I was christened Celestino Minaya Gonzales. However, my parents split up when I was two years old and my mother married another man – Casimiro Carbajal Quispe. My stepfather Casimiro put in a judicial request for my surname to be changed to his name and so my name was officially changed to Celestino Carbajal Gonzales. At this time I was sent to my maternal grandmother (a widow) who cared for me until I was twelve. I attended the local primary school and when not at school I worked on my grandmother's *chacra* – cultivating corn, wheat, alfalfa and other crops and attending to the livestock.

As I grew up, I found living with my grandmother to be increasingly difficult. She used to get drunk whenever there was a *fiesta* or other celebration and I took on the duty of looking after her and ensuring she got home safely. When I finished primary school my parents (mother and stepfather) decided to bring me home so that I could look after my five younger siblings, while they went to work in the *selva*. During the next seven years, I looked after my younger siblings while completing high school. At the end of my final year of high school, in 1977, I fell in love with Carmen and we started our life's journey together. Realising that I didn't have the economic means to continue my education, I dedicated myself to working hard to create a better future for my family.

My natural father remarried and had another five children, so I have five half siblings, although I have less to do with this side of his family.'

~~~~

Before leaving Huanta, Michael and I wanted to buy a nice present for Carmen, who worked so hard for her family but had little for herself. We thought we would buy her a comfortable sprung
~~~~

mattress. All she had ever known was to sleep on blankets on the floor with her children snuggled up close. However, on questioning Mariluz and Karina, they thought she would prefer the traditional, more natural type of mattress which was basically a cotton filled cover – a bit like a futon.

Mariluz and Karina helped us to choose and bargain for the double size mattress – big enough for the younger girls to share with Carmen – and arranged for Wilbur to meet us with the *moto-taxi*. It proved to be quite a challenge to carry the heavy mattress back home, travelling in the *moto* with the mattress held above our heads. When we presented it to Carmen that afternoon, she promptly broke into tears. She was overjoyed, as were the younger girls who would be sharing the mattress with her.

~~~~

I had another task to do before leaving Huanta. The girls asked me if I could cut their hair as it was expensive to go to the hairdresser. I warned them that my previous hair dressing experience consisted solely of cutting my own hair. This didn't deter them so, after buying a pair of scissors, a makeshift hairdressing salon was set up in the courtyard and I got to work. They were all happy with their new haircuts and I decided I had a new career awaiting me. Mariluz was the only one who declined the offer of a free haircut.

~~~~

The day was fast approaching for the *Fiesta de Maynay* – and our last day in Huanta – where Karina was having her second attempt to become the *Reina*. There was considerable prestige to be gained and also good prize money on offer. Karina had written her speech and had spent the week practising it in front of the family; to us it sounded wonderful. Her speech was about human rights and equality for indigenous Peruvians, something about which she was passionate.

For the event, Karina hired a traditional outfit of the Huanta region – a full maroon-coloured skirt with a green sash, a white blouse with colourful embroidery, and traditional headwear. She looked lovely. Wilbur drove us, along with Carmen and all the kids, the few kilometres to Maynay (in a couple of trips). We spent the morning perusing the different stalls, listening to local musicians, trying various foods, buying presents for the kids and buying lots of *artesanía* to take home.

In the afternoon was the most important event of the day – the competition for the *Reina de Maynay.* We nervously watched the contestants give their speeches and, as lovely as all the girls looked and as well as they spoke, we were convinced (possibly we were biased) that Karina delivered the best speech, spoken with great confidence and self-assuredness. We were sure she would win and she herself was quite confident of a win.

The wait for a result was agonising. And then the placegetters were announced: 'Third place to ... Martina Quispe, second place to ... Beate Golfo,' we waited expectantly, it had to be Karina. 'And first place to ...' It wasn't Karina. She broke down in tears. Our shoulders all slumped forward with disappointment.

She had so wanted to win, especially this year with Michael and me watching and cheering her on. It transpired that the head judge was the town Mayor, a man who didn't like the Carbajal Moreira family as they had supported an alternative candidate for the Mayoral elections. Not surprisingly, all the winners were relatives of the Mayor.

Karina told us, between sobs, that this was how things in Peru always operated. Jobs and competitions were awarded to relatives and to people who gave bribes. She was inconsolable – not only had she failed in her bid to become the *Reina*, in front of Michael and me, but we were leaving Huanta that evening. It was a sad end to an otherwise exciting last day.

We travelled back to Huanta to have a quick dinner before our bus to Ayacucho. It was a sombre dinner with lots of tears and the repeated question: 'When are you coming back?' to which we could provide no firm answer. It had been a wonderful but tough three weeks and the trials of the long journey to Peru and Huanta, and the many scary bus trips were still fresh in our minds. We didn't think we would be back any time soon. The only answer we could give them was: 'Within ten years, *ojalá*.' Hopefully, all going well.

We were all crying uncontrollably as Michael and I hugged each and every one of our Peruvian family. They all begged us to come back soon. Wilbur drove us to the bus stop in town, along with Mariluz and Karina who were to accompany us as far as Ayacucho. We allowed plenty of time for this trip in case of break downs or flat tyres. We only had one.

As it turned out, when we arrived in Ayacucho there was only a small margin of time remaining before our *Cruz del Sur* bus was to depart. Since the overnight trip to Lima was going to take ten hours, and then we were getting straight onto another bus for the eight-hour trip to Huaraz, we had decided to travel with the most comfortable and expensive bus company, something we had never previously done.

After giving Mariluz and Karina one last emotional hug, we tearfully boarded. As we stepped up onto the coach and looked around, we were astounded by the luxury – something we had not realised existed in Peru. The bus had comfortable airline-type seats, air-conditioning, soft ambient music playing in place of the usual loud Peruvian cacophony, and a motor that literally purred. This made our whole departure seem even worse. It was as if we had stepped out of Peru and into another world altogether; but when we looked out the window we saw the sad, teary-eyed faces of Karina and Mariluz waving forlornly. It made the injustices of our world seem even more real. We could afford to travel in comfort. They could not.

The bus quietly departed and our tears flowed freely. It was hard to shake the sadness and despair we felt when we didn't know when we would see our family again. Michael and I began to process our feelings of the previous three weeks. It had been difficult but incredibly rewarding.

In one of our conversations with the family, when they had said how much better life must be for us, living in a wealthy and developed country like Australia, we had tried to make them feel happier about their situation by telling them some of the positives of their life as compared with ours: 'For your family and others such as yours, you are in some ways more fortunate than us. Although you are living in poverty, the family unit seems to be so strong in Peru that it binds people together. In our world, this has largely been lost. Families are often disconnected and spread far and wide.'

How wrong we were! Mariluz explained to us that the three weeks we had just spent together were the first time the whole family had been together for many years. Normally Carmen spends months working in the jungle alone, leaving her family to fend for themselves. She had been doing this for many years, even when the children were very young. The older children have had to care for the younger children and look after their sick father. Prior to Celestino's illness, both parents had worked in the jungle, leaving the school-aged children in Huanta to be looked after by their grandparents, something that is common to the many families in Huanta who own *chacras* in the *selva*.

Our three weeks with the Carbajal Moreira family had been full of jokes, laughter and chatter. We had thought this was life as usual for the Carbajal Moreira family, but the kids were quick to dispel that myth, telling us that life for them is not usually so happy; it involves a lot of pain, worry and hard work. They all commented on the fact that while we were with the family, Carmen smiled the whole time. 'We have never seen *mamá* so happy. This has been the happiest time of our lives,' Mariluz had said, hugging us.

Michael and I discussed how the kids seemed to be caught between two worlds: the agrarian existence of their forebears and the modern world they could see around them, with television and pop music. The kids all strived to be a part of the modern world: they dressed in western clothing and wanted to get an education. They were frustrated at not being able to afford many of the modern-world trappings that their school-mates could. They wanted a television, a CD player and nice things to decorate their house. Yet they still enjoyed harvesting the crops and talking in Quechuan to their *abuela*. Had they lived further from town, way up in the mountains, they might have remained blissfully unaware of how others live in a modern world. They might have been happy to continue with subsistence farming, as their ancestors had for centuries. As it was, times were changing and they were at the crossroads of change.

~~~~

We knew we were going to miss our Peruvian family terribly, and they us.
~~~~

CHAPTER 13

Huaraz and the Cordillera Blanca

September 2004

We had a very comfortable overnight journey on the luxury coach back to Lima, and managed to sleep quite well. Arriving in Lima in the early morning, we had three hours to spare before our next bus to Huaraz. We decided to take a taxi to Miraflores to see where the wealthy *Limeños* live. Here we found the houses and apartments all protected by high brick walls, the tops of which are covered in razor wire and jagged pieces of broken glass. It was quite a contrast to what we had seen in Central Lima where we had spent our first night. We also noticed how different the people in Miraflores looked. Most of them had a much fairer complexion than their counterparts in Central Lima and they were a good deal taller. There seemed to be few obviously indigenous-looking people.

After a quick dash around Miraflores and breakfast, we boarded the bus for Huaraz.

In 2001, when previously in Huaraz, we had befriended a family, in whose *hospedaje* we had stayed, and we were hoping they were still in town. After some searching, we found their house and were overjoyed to find them home and still running a *hospedaje*. They welcomed us warmly, giving us the same room we'd had three years before. Surprisingly, they remembered not only that we had used that room the last time we had stayed, but they also recalled all sorts of little details about us and our family back home. We were amazed by this, given that they have so many travellers passing through their home. They invited us to dine with them that night and kindly cooked a vegetarian meal. Michael once again refused their offer of *cuy* (guinea pig)!

Our Spanish had improved since the last time we were with them so we were able to have a more in-depth conversation. After spending three weeks with a poor indigenous family it was interesting getting a middle-class perspective on the state of the country. We found that our hosts, Fidel and Mimila, held views about their country and Government that were remarkably similar to those of our less well-off family.

'Peru is in a bad way for all but the very rich,' commented Fidel. 'There are many professionals unable to find employment and the pay for those that do have jobs is very low. Most Peruvians are struggling to get by. I work for the Government as an engineer, but it doesn't pay enough to support my family so we augment my salary by running the *hospedaje*.'

On a more positive note, while travelling in a crowded *combi* on the way to the start of our hike, we talked to an agronomist whose job it was to go into the countryside to talk to the farmers and advise them on ways to improve their agricultural practices with a minimal use of chemicals.

'The Government is changing and moving away from the overuse of chemicals,' he said, 'but it is hard to convince the *campesinos* not to use pesticides and chemicals when they get so much advertising from the corporations proclaiming how wonderful their products are.'

On our last visit to Huaraz, we had heard about an amazing lake nestled in the mountains, so this time *Laguna 69* was the destination for our three-day hike. Being late September it was the end of the usual trekking season and the weather was starting to look a bit dubious, but we hoped it would hold for us. We hiked up into the mountains hoping to get a view of Huascarán – at 6768m, Peru's highest mountain. Unfortunately, the weather started to deteriorate and with all the mist and cloud we only managed to get small glimpses of the mountain. *Laguna 69,* however, did not disappoint; the stunning azure-coloured lake was perched beneath towering steely grey snow-capped mountains and ringed by a jumble of rocks and boulders. We stayed there for a long lunch to soak up the splendour.

Camping at 4,200m we felt the effects of the altitude, and after over three weeks of good health, Michael succumbed to the dreaded diarrhoea, requiring several emergency exits from the tent. We now didn't have Carmen and Mariluz looking after us.

Lovely as it was to be on our own, ensconced in the peace and quiet of the mountains, we were already missing our Peruvian family and wondering when we would see them again. We were wishing that Mariluz, Karina and Carmen could have been there with us to share the experience and see the incredible *Laguna 69*, so different from the *Lagunas Razuillcas* to which they had taken us the week before.

It was time to head home.

CHAPTER 14 The intervening years

Home felt surreal. The time spent living with our Peruvian family had left an indelible imprint on us and we returned with a different outlook on life and family, and with new priorities. We found it hard to listen to people whingeing about their pay or their working conditions, or problems with their cars or houses, or the myriad other little things people in a first world country like ours tend to complain about. We talked endlessly to anyone who would listen about our Peruvian family and our experiences with them, hoping others would realise how lucky we are in Australia.

The regular email contact with our family continued and it wasn't long before we were being asked, 'When are you coming back to Peru?' The only answer we were able to give was that we would come back one day. We didn't know when.

Although we returned to regular work-day routines and had the usual run of work and life problems to occupy our time, the Carbajal Moreiras were never far from our minds. There was always something to worry about. There were constant illnesses and many emails to read and to respond to. We found it hard to buy anything for ourselves that was not strictly necessary or to treat ourselves to something as extravagant as a meal out without first thinking and talking about our Peruvian family and discussing how they could better use this money for the necessities of life.

I deposited their regular monthly stipend into the bank account and often extra amounts as needed. We also mailed regular parcels, which always created a great deal of excitement. In one parcel we sent a magnifying glass for Celestino as he had mentioned he had trouble reading small print. Very pleased, he wrote back that he could now read even tiny print. We were delighted that the smallest of things could make a big difference in their lives.

Mariluz's dream of becoming a professional was about to begin. She enrolled in a college in Ayacucho to study to become a nurse, a three year course, beginning in May 2005. She would share Karina's room in the city.

'I am so excited to be able to study and begin along the path to my chosen career. I am looking forward to the day when I will be a professional and be able to help my family,' she wrote.

Celestino and Carmen often wrote letters to us in long-hand, which Mariluz or Karina then typed into the computer and sent via email. In August 2005, Celestino wrote: *'We are happy because the anniversary of your arrival – 28 August – is approaching and we are all awaiting this day. Carmen won't go down to the jungle because we want to spend this important day with our whole family together. We will never forget this marvellous day and we are looking forward to the day when you will return to Peru.'*

Mariluz wrote: *'I'm writing to tell you that I love you a lot and although you won't believe it, I think of you both every day, and now the anniversary date of your arrival last year is getting closer ... and it's a great happiness to us that we'll always be united and nothing and nobody can separate us. Thank you for the love that you have for our family.'*

They were in our thoughts too and we arranged a time to talk by phone. This was quite difficult to organise. First we had to negotiate a mutually agreeable time, taking into account the 15 hours time difference. Then they had to go into Huanta's centre and to the telephone *cabinas*. As most people in regional Peru did not have personal telephones, they relied on these booths. Although a private business, this operates like a public telephone exchange where there are many phone booths within one room and people pay to make a call. They are not supposed to be used to receive calls as no profit will be made, but Mariluz and Karina ingratiated themselves with the operators and organised it so that we could call them. They then emailed the phone number to us so that we could phone them in the *cabina* at the appointed time.

Our first phone conversation with the whole family took place that August in 2005, close to the anniversary date of our arrival. The owner of the *cabinas* probably did not know what hit him as Carmen, with her six excited children and two young cousins crammed into and around a booth designed to take one person, and waited for our call. I phoned the number that had been emailed. It was engaged. We waited. I tried again. Still engaged. We waited. Then our phone rang. It was Mariluz and she gave me a different number to write down. In the excitement I wrote down the numbers incorrectly and still couldn't get through. Mariluz phoned again and I asked her to read the numbers out slower and individually, rather than the Spanish custom of giving the phone number in pairs such as twenty-one, thirty-six, fifty-three. It was early in the morning for us and thinking in Spanish just after waking up was not so easy. I didn't want them to waste any more of their money having to call us.

Finally I got the numbers down correctly and we got through. At their end, the phone was passed from one to another as they spoke with us in rapid Spanish and told us how much they missed us. Each of them asked us when we were returning and said they couldn't wait for the day when we could once again be all together and go on outings, bathe in the river and laugh and joke. Wilbur told us that the *moto-taxi* was now fully paid off and explained that he could now take care of all the necessities alone. Previously Mariluz had to assist him with such things as motor checks, licences and insurance issues as he had not been confident in dealing with anyone outside the family. The younger children told us how well they were doing at school and that they had come first in their class in many of their courses.

Celestino was the only one not present as he was still unable to leave the house. After doing a round of speaking to everyone we started on round two. I told them that we thought we would be able to return to Peru in five or six years and this brought on a babble of excitement. They now had something to look forward to.

After an hour I told them that, as it was getting expensive, we would have to finish the call. Mariluz had begun to tell us of the problems being faced by Celestino with his family, but it was too difficult for us to understand over the phone, so I asked her to explain in a letter. We weren't allowed to hang up until we had farewelled each individual separately, not once but two times. They were all crying, especially Carmen who was sobbing and telling us how much she missed us. We hung up. Michael and I felt emotionally drained.

The following month we received a parcel of letters from the entire family, many of the letters decorated with beautiful coloured drawings by the younger girls.

Carmen wrote: *'I always dream of you and you're always in my mind. Thanks to you my children can study and we have food to eat. I can't but think what would have happened to us if we hadn't met you.'*

Celestino's letter was worrying.

'I am now living in the midst of hate, envy and such injustice within my family – that is my parents and most of my siblings ...,'

He explained that the main reason for this was that he was not the legitimate son of his father, and now his step-father wanted to remove his surname from him. He told us that his step-father, his sister and most of his brothers were telling lies about him and his mother wouldn't defend him in front of the others. They had taken some of his property in the *selva* and wanted to throw the family out of their house in Huanta.

'It makes me so sad to think about all the sacrifices I have made and the hard work for my property. I cry for the bad luck I experience, in my health, for not having a legitimate father, and in other aspects of life.'

Reading all this saddened us as we knew what a good man Celestino was and that everything he did was for his children. He wanted to be able to give them a good education to enable them to get ahead in life.

The letter from Marleni made us both laugh.

'I have to tell you, the shoes I bought with Michael now have a hole and look old, but they'll have to do until you return. I can cook everything now and when you return I will prepare delicious food for you. I miss you and I hope the years pass rapidly until we see each other again in Huanta. When we spoke on the telephone I cried – it was as if we were chatting right beside each other.'

~~~~

2005 was coming to an end. Instead of sending another parcel, Michael and I sent money, with instructions for it to be divided between each family member so they could buy their own Christmas present. It was the first time the children were able to buy themselves something special for Christmas and they were overjoyed.

A letter from Karina reminded us again how different our lives were. I'd recently shared with them my experience of seeing dolphins in the ocean and jumping in to swim after them. I was admonished by return mail.

'Dear madrina, we are happy that you are so strong in the water and that you swam close to the dolphins, but we became sad afterwards thinking about what could have happened to you. You can go crazy in the salt water. Please don't do it again, we don't want anything bad to happen to you....'
~~~~

None of our Peruvian family can swim and none of them had been anywhere near the ocean.

~~~~

One of the big events of 2006 was the arrival of mobile telephone coverage in Huanta. Now those who could afford it were buying their own mobile phones, which made it much easier for people to stay in contact. In the middle of the year, Wilbur found a phone that a passenger had left in his *moto.* He tried, unsuccessfully, to find the owner, so this was how the family acquired their first telephone. We didn't think much of their excited news at the time, as we considered the costs associated with running the phone and paying for calls. However, they were able to buy an inexpensive battery charger and it transpired that pre-paid mobile calls in Peru (as in other developing countries) are very cheap.

In the ensuing years, mobiles made a big difference in their lives. Before phones, when the girls were studying in Ayacucho, they had no communication with the family in Huanta; and when Carmen was away in the jungle, they had to rely on news being relayed from other relatives or neighbours who were travelling between Huanta and the *selva.*

~~~~

Otherwise, 2006 was a difficult year for the Carbajal Moreiras. Early in the year, four of the five family dogs were poisoned and died slowly and painfully. This was hard for the whole family, and especially for Celestino. Two of the dogs had been his constant companions as he moved around the yard trying to find the most comfortable place to sit. The family believed that the dogs were poisoned by potential thieves who didn't want them barking as they entered the property. They now felt uneasy in their home.

Mariluz became depressed about Celestino's poor health, and Marleni and Margot continued to be plagued by one illness after another, mostly relating to urinary tract infections. Mariluz felt she carried the weight of all the family's problems and guilt that, with college, she didn't have time to help or be with them. She had classes and practical experience six days a week. Her days started with classes at 6.20 am, and continued, with a 45 minute break to get across town, until 7.15 pm, when her prac ended for the day. Then there were assignments and homework to be completed.

In June the National elections were held. In Peru, as in Australia, it is compulsory to vote and Peruvians seem to be politically aware: throughout the country one sees political slogans and politicians' names painted all over buildings and walls, often new ones painted over the old. Not an attractive look. The Carbajal Moreiras too were interested and involved in politics and they had their favoured candidates' names painted in large letters across their front wall. Much to their disappointment the new President, Alán García, was a right-wing politician who, they believed, had little interest in improving conditions for the poor. They surmised that under his leadership the rich would continue to get richer and the poor would get poorer.

Carmen continued to spend long months alone in the *selva.* When we had been with them in 2004, we had begged Carmen not to go so often – we were worried about her making the perilous journey so regularly and the amount of time spent alone and away from her family. We had increased their monthly stipend so that she wouldn't need to go there so much, but we learned that it wasn't only about income. After a lull, her trips to the *chacra* in the *selva* again became more frequent and for longer.

'It is necessary,' she explained to us, 'because we are still struggling financially and we are worried that when no-one is there to keep an eye on the place, the neighbours and relatives come and help themselves to our produce. They will gradually try to take it over if I don't keep going there. Celestino and I want to keep the *chacra* in the family in case any of the children want to continue with it. In addition, its value wouldn't make it worthwhile to sell.'

Carmen wrote to us: '*I dreamt of you while in the selva, that we were together once again, and it made me very happy.*'

In August 2006, the second anniversary of our visit came around again and Mariluz wrote:

'My dear Lani and my dear Michael. I am writing to you now from the whole family to remember that another year has gone by since your visit to your Peruvian family. We all remember this date when we were making all the preparations for your arrival. Now it's the same – as if you were once again going to arrive in Peru. Although this year it won't be like that because you are

far away, but very close in our hearts and within our souls we carry you. In our minds we imagine that you are with us my dear Lani and Michael.'

We arranged another phone call and once again they all made sure they were together for this important anniversary date and in the *cabina* waiting for our call. Like last year, we spoke to everyone twice before being allowed to hang up. They told us about what had been going on in their lives and some funny things that had happened. They were all so happy to hear our voices, they told us.

Wilbur told us that he keeps the Australian flag, that we had sent him, on his *moto* all the time and that he was looking forward to our return to Huanta so he can take us on trips. 'When I go out in the sun, I put on the sunglasses you gave me and everyone looks at me,' he said, causing us to chuckle.

When we were in Huanta, Wilbur had so admired Michael's sunglasses that he gave them to him. Although very scratched, Wilbur wore them with pride and loved admiring himself in the mirror. We are quite sure he even wore them on dark cloudy days because he thought they looked cool.

~~~~

That year, as happens frequently in Peru, there were many long strikes. As a result, Karina spent several months having no classes while the university professors were on strike. She found this highly frustrating but still continued to meet with other students so they could work on some of their subjects together. With all the strikes that happened over the years, Karina did not know when she would graduate.

Meanwhile, Celestino's health seemed to be deteriorating. At the end of 2006, he explained the nature of his problems: he had (among other things) chronic prostatitis, an ulcer in the bladder and severe back pain that prevented him from standing or being in an erect position for more than five minutes. He told us he needed an operation. I asked him to find out how much it would cost and he came back with the amount of US$500 for the operation and a further $200 for medicines afterwards. We forwarded money to cover these costs.

Celestino wrote back: *'Many thanks Lani and Michael for understanding what I am suffering day by day. This life is so difficult to lead.*
~~~~

With your offer of economic assistance for the operation, my life expectancy will be extended. Although a complete recovery would be difficult, it's not impossible. I still have hope for a cure.'

Celestino wrote again in May: '*Thank you a thousand times for the money for the operation. The operation will be at the end of June. There is a delay because I have other complications and illnesses that need to be sorted out before doctors will operate. I'm very worried for the bad luck we have and that sickness is always bothering our family. However, with the economic assistance you send us, we are fighting to overcome all, good or evil. I am wounded but not conquered.'*

Celestino needed his fortitude. Because of his pain he often spent whole nights awake, and on other nights considered himself lucky to get three hours sleep. Although he tried to keep his depression from the children, Mariluz was sensitive to his suffering. She found him crying one day and he confided in her that it was not only from the physical pain but also the pain of not being the family provider that he wanted to be.

~~~~

On 15th August 2007, an earthquake that measured 8.0 on the Richter scale shook the coastal regions of Peru, killing hundreds of people and devastating a large area in the Ica-Pisco area south of Lima. Earthquakes are fairly common occurrences on the west coast of South America, positioned as it is at the edge of two tectonic plates that form the Andes Mountains. Karina wrote that they could feel the earthquake in Ayacucho, about 300 km from the coast. She described the fear she'd felt and explained that it was the first earthquake she had experienced.

~~~~

At the start of the next semester, Karina began a course on human rights law at university, and then in October she, along with a few other students, was selected to attend a conference on human rights in Lima.

It was her first trip to the capital and she was wide-eyed at the luxury she encountered, which included a stay in a three-star hotel with sumptuous buffet breakfasts. On her return, she emailed enthusiastically that she had found her vocation: '*I want to specialise in human rights law and continue on to do my Masters on this topic, once I've finished my degree.*'

Michael and I were delighted that Karina was taking such an interest in human rights, as this is something that is also very important to us. We were proud of her for making this decision and wondered if she realised that there would be less money in this area of law. We were not so pleased, however, by her inference that she could keep studying beyond her degree and the associated expectation that we would continue to support her. I conveyed to Karina our pride in her but told her she would need to think first about getting a job and earning her own money, before beginning her Masters. She replied that she understood and that she would do as we suggested.

~~~~

By the end of 2007, Celestino had still not been able to have his operation as his health was still too delicate. Carmen, who had been so excited about the thought of a cure for Celestino, continued to spend a lot of time alone in the jungle on the *chacra*. The long wait for the operation was lowering her spirits too. On her return from a stint on the *chacra* she wrote: '*I was alone in the selva, very sad and lonely, so I went to look for the tree under which we had rested, when we were together three years ago and remembered how happy we'd all been. I was crying and quite sad when, just at this moment, four monkeys appeared and my sadness disappeared. I think of you both a lot when I'm in the jungle and I dream of us all together. I'm very grateful to you both. Perhaps without your help we wouldn't be alive, but with your continued support we are learning to struggle along with what we have.*'

Worry piled on worry. Mariluz wrote to us: '*Marleni has become very ill again – this time mentally as well as physically. She sometimes speaks in a rage and sometimes she's incoherent. She has constant fear of being hurt by someone and of dying. Margot still has problems with her urinary tract and has to urinate every hour. She cries about this as she is becoming a teenager and is different to her peers. She also suffers from constant backaches.*'

Wilbur was angry that his sisters were studying and he had to drive the *moto* to help support his family when he also wanted to study. He complained: '*There are more and more moto-taxis in Huanta so*
~~~~

it's getting harder and harder to make money. I spend all day driving around and only earn enough to buy bread and sugar for the family.'

Carmen was fretting about the *chacra* and the 'bad people' who wanted to take it over. The money she was able to make on the *chacra* was a pittance. The price of coffee had dropped and was hardly worth growing. She confided to us in a letter: *'I am all alone in the selva. I can't do it anymore. My back aches. I was sick for two weeks with a fever, lonely, sad and all in silence. I work for my children so I can buy them one more bread roll.'*

~~~~

The following May, Mariluz finished her studies. She was now the first person in her family with a tertiary education and was looking forward to being able to find work and support her family. *'It's only thanks to you,'* she wrote, *'that I've now finished my studies and achieved my dream. I never believed that I would ever be able to study, and still didn't believe it right up until the day I started my course. I don't know how I can ever repay you.'*

Although she had finished, Mariluz was sad that she wasn't able to attend her graduation ceremony. The additional funds we'd sent her covered the costs associated with gaining her qualification, but not the hire of the gown and the cost of the ceremony. And now we learned that Mariluz hadn't qualified as a registered nurse – the course she had done qualified her as an *enfermera técnica*, a technical nurse. To become a registered nurse is a five-year course, Mariluz explained, like all degree courses in Peru.

By the end of 2008, 18 months after having sent Celestino the money for his operation, we still hadn't been told anything about it. Karina was writing us only short emails and not answering my questions, and Mariluz was writing even less frequently. We began to doubt that Celestino intended to have the operation and we wondered what had happened to the money we had sent. Neither of us liked to distrust the family, but we began to suspect that the money had been spent on other things, even though we remained confident that they would spend the money only on necessities. We wanted answers, but it was several months before we were given them, and only after I had written a terse email demanding answers.
~~~~

Celestino replied, apologising. Yet again, faced with costly problems, they'd been forced to spend some of the money on urgent matters and had postponed the operation. And they'd been beset by more misfortune. Wilbur had had an accident in the *moto*, necessitating repairs, the younger girls were sick again and Celestino's health continued to deteriorate, making him increasingly debilitated and unable to carry out even the most mundane of daily domestic chores. On top of this, the family had planted several avocado trees in their home *chacra* in Huanta and a neighbour's sheep had eaten almost all of them.

In the *chacra* in the *selva* there were more problems: the neighbouring landowner had entered their property and cleared forest, along with many of the family's mature fruit trees, and planted his own coffee crop. They were having trouble resolving the issue. Another neighbour had pulled up about 20 of their taro plants. This was a large proportion of their plants with the consequence that they'd have to buy more food. Celestino had spent money to plant corn and coffee and they'd needed some money to fight the neighbour who'd cleared his land. Prices for staple foodstuffs had all risen steeply. A litre of cooking oil, which had previously cost six soles now cost 14 and the price of other necessities such as sugar, rice and bread had also increased.

Celestino gave a detailed explanation of his numerous additional health problems, all of which had made it impossible for him to have the operation, and for which he'd spent $200 for medications. He was not sure he would ever be well enough to have it, and worried that, if he did, it would fail and he would be left even more unwell. Although we understood the reasons they had spent the money we'd sent, we couldn't help but feel disappointed that, without the operation, Celestino had little chance of a better life.

There was little to ease pressures on the family elsewhere, either. Mariluz was unable to find work, so she spent some time in the *selva* helping Carmen on the *chacra*. They enjoyed this precious time together. When she did find a job, working out of the small town of Sivia, it was in social development rather than in a hospital or health post. She would be providing health and educational support to small isolated communities scattered around the *selva*.

It was several months before we received any news from her about her new position, and when we did, she sounded very unhappy and heartbreakingly lonely. She apologised for not having been in contact and explained it was because she was out in the small communities, none of which had any means of communication with the wider world. The work was stressful and heavy and she worked long days that stretched late into the night, seven days a week. For this she was paid a pittance. Even in those moments she could grab for herself, the internet in Sivia often didn't function. She had been unable to spend Christmas or New Year with her family as she couldn't get back to Huanta, and she was still in the *selva* at Easter, *Semana Santa*, one of the most important festivals for Peruvian families.

Meanwhile Karina was doing a practical work placement at the Public Ministry office. She too was exhausted by her routine. She had classes from 6 am – 8 am, then the practical experience from 8.30 am – 4 pm, followed by more classes until 10 pm. She was often up until 1.30 in the morning studying. Michael and I thought how tough it is for students in Peru; Australian students would never put up with such a rigorous timetable.

Having asked Karina about her unusual class times, she replied: *'because our university professors get paid so little they normally work at another job during the day and then teach us in the mornings and evenings.'*

Karina was expecting to finish her degree in April 2010, and we began making secret plans to visit the family and, with a bit of luck, attend her graduation. She explained that, although she would graduate in 2010, she wouldn't actually be a qualified *abogada* until she had completed her thesis, which she had recently begun work on.

~~~~

In the middle of 2009, Mariluz gave up her job in the *selva* and soon found another job in the neighbouring province of Andahuaylas, in the mountains. Although it was 10 hours from home, even further away than her first job, she found here 'tranquility, peace and friendship with colleagues'. She was employed by the town mayor who, she said, was 'a good man who
~~~~

fights for his people'. This was the first happy email we had received from her for a very long time.

Unfortunately, her new-found joy was short-lived. In September the mayor was replaced and she lost her job. She was glad to return home to Huanta. With a little experience under her belt she soon found another job, back down in the jungle near Sivia. She was employed as an educator on a six-month contract by the National Assistance Program for Food and Nutrition (PRONAA), whose aim was to raise the food and nutrition standards of the people who live in extreme poverty, particularly for pregnant women, lactating mothers and those with children under three years of age.

Mariluz's job involved visiting the communities around Sivia. Getting to these outlying communities meant walking for five hours as the road had been cut by flooding and rock falls, which had also destroyed a bridge. It was a beautiful place and she enjoyed the work, but it was difficult to communicate with her family and difficult to get back to Sivia. She was also called upon to assist in a flood emergency, which she found harrowing, but was proud to have helped people whose homes had been washed away.

In December 2009 Nélida, the baby of the family, graduated from high school. She was 16 but we could barely believe it, as we still thought of her as a little girl. Although she was a year younger than Margot, she was a school year ahead of her as Margot had been held back by her illnesses.

Meanwhile Michael and I announced to the family that we would arrive on 1 April 2010, in time to spend *Semana Santa* with them. Even email couldn't dissipate the air of excitement from both sides of the Pacific Ocean. Unfortunately we wouldn't be there for Karina's graduation, as we'd initially hoped, as it had been delayed by yet more strikes during the year prior to our visit.

But first, before arriving in Huanta, we were going to fulfil one of our dreams – to do a long-distance self-supported bicycle tour in Patagonian Chile and Argentina. We would have seven weeks of cycling before flying to Peru to visit our family.

The family began to count down the days until our arrival, and so did we.

CHAPTER 15 Cycling in Patagonia

February 2010

We flew out of Australia with 100kg of luggage between us, including the boxed bicycles, camping gear, some home-dehydrated food, a bag full of presents for the family, and a jar of Tasmanian honey – a special request from our Chilean friend, Antonio. Fortunately, the luggage allowance was generous.

The fourteen hour flight to Santiago was uneventful, but the fun started on arrival. I told the gruff-looking customs officer exactly what foodstuffs we were carrying, assuming all would be fine as it had been last time. He asked me to pull out our food bags. After looking through them all carefully, he removed the bags with the spinach and the herbs.

'*No son permitidos.*'

'Why aren't they permitted?' I asked.

'Dried leaves, you can't bring in dried leaves,' he replied tersely.

I had been advised that as long as the food was fully dried it would be fine. At least he hadn't noticed that many of the complete meals I had packed also contained dried spinach and herbs. Fortunately I had packed them in pre-used snap-lock bags, so they looked like commercially packed meals – and luckily he couldn't understand the labels.

The next thing to come under fire was the honey. Antonio, an agronomist, had assured me that as long as I declared it as 'trekking food' it would be fine. He wanted to compare Tasmanian Leatherwood honey with the honey from a similar Chilean tree. Trusting his judgement, I'd bought a large, expensive jar. I pulled the honey from the outside pocket of my backpack and noted with dismay that the outside of the jar was sticky.

'Honey is not permitted,' said the gruff customs officer.

'But it's for trekking and my friend who is an agronomist at the University in Santiago told me I can bring it in for trekking food.'

He gave me a menacing look and took the honey away. What neither of us realised at the time was that I did bring some honey into the country – sitting in the bottom of my backpack!

Once we had cleared customs, it was straight into the maelstrom of Santiago airport. Although we weren't spending a night in Santiago, I had booked a hostel room so we could sort our gear and leave some of it there while on the bike trip. The hostel had booked us a special shuttle bus that could take us and our bikes straight there. They'd told me to look out for someone holding a sign saying TRANSVIP.

A man approached and asked if we needed a taxi. I explained that we were fine and had transport organised.

'Who are you booked with?' he asked.

I told him we had booked the TRANSVIP shuttle bus.

'No problem,' he said, 'I am from TRANSVIP.'

After twenty hours of virtually no sleep, and trying to negotiate the airport and dealings in Spanish, I foolishly asked, 'Really?'

'*Sí, sí, sí,*' he replied, showing me a small TRANSVIP card in his wallet, 'follow me.'

'We need to get money first,' I told him.

'No problem,' he said, 'follow me.'

Leaving Michael with the luggage, I followed the *señor* to an ATM out in the parking lot, feeling increasingly uneasy. I withdrew some Chilean Pesos and followed him back to Michael and then we all headed outside the terminal.

'This is your TRANSVIP shuttle,' he said indicating a non-descript van, while instructing the driver to take us to the hostel. Once we had loaded our gear into the van, the *señor* stuck his hand through the window and asked for a '*propina*' for his help. By this stage I realised we had been conned. *Señor* asked me for 5,000 pesos ($12) telling me that 'this is nothing', trying to take advantage of newly-arrived travellers, tired, and not yet used to the money. I told him this was too much and that I'd give him 2,000 pesos. I handed him a 5,000 peso note, the smallest I had, and he handed me back 2,000 pesos, saying '3,000 pesos is nothing'. I was too flustered to argue further. At least I hadn't been mugged while withdrawing the cash. The taxi driver then asked us how much we had been quoted by TRANSVIP and this is what he charged when he dropped us at the hostel, no doubt having made more than his usual fare for the trip.

Welcome back to South America!

We had all day to complete our necessary tasks which included, after a much-needed shower, cleaning the honey out of the backpack, sorting out our gear and heading into town to pick up our ticket for the '*Turbus*' coach that night.

As only Chilean credit cards were accepted by the bus company, I had asked Antonio to make the reservation for us, which he had done. However, he was now away on holidays but had sent us an email with instructions on where to collect the tickets from the *Turbus* office.

We caught the underground train to the central *Turbus* office and were greeted with barely a glance by a bored-looking woman who said she knew nothing about the tickets – we would have to go to the other office 'just out the back.' We wandered 'out the back' and found no more offices. We went back to our 'friend' inside and she looked up, grunted and ignored us. She refused to offer any further help. Eventually we found someone who explained that we had to walk several blocks to find the right office.

On entering the new office, we again encountered unfriendly staff who said they didn't have any tickets there and that the company doesn't do this sort of thing. We were getting quite desperate because we knew we wouldn't be permitted to board the bus without our tickets, even though our names would be on the paperwork. Chileans are very officious and 'by the book'. We were unable to contact Antonio.

I then spied another *Turbus* office. The first man we spoke to gave us a blank look, but fortunately another man overheard the conversation, opened a book and found our tickets stapled in. What a relief! We headed back to the hostel, tickets in hand, for a much needed nap before dinner.

We had a taxi booked to take us to the bus station for our 9 pm departure. We'd made sure to tell them we had bikes, still in their boxes. The taxi turned up on time, but we were dismayed to see that it was a small sedan car.

'*No hay problema*,' said the driver, while pulling out a large octopus strap and fastening the bikes to the roof racks and then loading our numerous bags into the car. We told the driver the name of the bus station from where we were to get the bus, and he assured us he knew it well.

On being dropped at the bus station, we unloaded our gear, paid the driver and the taxi sped off. We were just wondering how on earth we could move our mountain of gear without leaving any piece unattended, when a *señor* appeared with a *carrito*. We told him we were travelling with *Turbus*. He indicated the stand from which it would depart and began loading our gear onto the trolley. We did think it strange that all the different bus companies had their names emblazoned across the front of the building, but there was no sign of '*Turbus*'. The *señor* pushed the trolley the hundred metres to the bus stand, unloaded it and we paid him and waited.

I began to feel uneasy. Leaving Michael with our gear, I went into the nearby offices to check whether we were in the right location. There was no *Turbus* office inside. I asked in a few of the other offices if the *Turbus* does actually come to this bus station and no-one was sure, but they didn't think so. Did they know where the *Turbus* station was? No! Eventually I found someone who thought it was a few blocks away.

We then tried to hail another taxi, but there were no taxis that could take our bikes. We only had thirty minutes until departure time. A man, hearing the distress in our voices, came to our aid and actually did know exactly where the *Turbus* departed from – six blocks away. He then grabbed our little '*carrito* man' and explained where he had to take us. We loaded the gear back on to the trolley and took off at running pace behind '*carrito* man'. We followed him for several blocks and then he stopped with a confused look on his face. We thought he was lost and queried him. '*No, no, está bien,'* all is well, he replied as we turned off into a dark side street. We were quite worried by this stage, but then another couple of turns later we saw the office of *Turbus* and the bus loading passengers outside. Phew! We paid '*carrito* man' generously, breathed a huge sigh of relief and boarded the bus, bathed in sweat, our afternoon shower just a memory.

We were headed for Puerto Varas, 1000 kilometres and twelve hours south of Santiago, at the southern end of the Chilean Lakes District. This was to be our departure point for the bicycle tour.

We arrived feeling reasonably refreshed after the most comfortable bus trip we'd ever taken. Knowing we'd be exhausted from our flight, we had booked *cama* seats. *Cama* means bed, and incredibly the seats did fold down to be totally flat. We'd even had our own attendant who had made up our beds and tucked us in for the night.

After assembling our bikes, we visited the local tourist office where the friendly girl sold us a map and assured us that we didn't need to book the ferry we required in a few days time. 'You just walk on with your bikes,' she confidently told us.

We were set to depart on our seven-week cycling adventure, much of it on the *Carretera Austral.* The Southern Highway.

Fortunately, the first day's riding on our heavily laden bikes was predominantly on tarred roads and, 67km later, we made it to the bustling tourist locality of Petrohué, at the base of the perfectly cone-shaped *Volcán Osorno.* The National Park campsite boasted hot showers, and I needed one. I went first, leaving Michael to finish setting up the tent, and had a refreshing *cold* shower. Michael located a ranger who apologised and said he'd forgotten to light the gas burner. Michael then waited a while and enjoyed the hot shower I had been denied.

My need for a wash as soon as possible upon arriving at our day's destination meant I usually showered first and I lost count of the number of cold showers I had, while Michael scored a hot one. I became quite annoyed at one campsite when he had gone first and luxuriated under a long hot shower, only to find that when it was my turn the gas ran out after about twenty seconds and I was left to *enjoy* yet another cold shower!

From Petrohué we left the usual tourist route and headed into more remote areas. Here we found innumerable hills and unpaved roads (*ripio*). At times the gravel and large rocks on the *ripio* made it difficult to stay upright. With many fast cars and buses blasting dust in our faces and the hot sun beating down upon us, I was wondering if we had bitten off more than we could chew. I knew that the majority of our planned ride was to be on *ripio.*

After our first five kilometres on *ripio* (which took close to an hour), we overtook a road grader (*nivelador*) heading the same way we were. The ungraded road surface was a dramatic improvement. It was here that we learned to fear the dreaded *nivelador* (literally leveller). Rather than the road being smoothed and levelled by the grader, its job seemed to be to scrape all the loose rocks from the edges and dump them all over the road while at the same time creating an impossible camber.

Several days later, on meeting a *nivelador* driver in a shop, I told him what I thought of his levelling job and how difficult it made the road for cyclists. Not understanding the humour in my statement, he gave me a withering look.

~~~~

We generally stayed in small towns or camping areas along our route. Getting nourishing vegetarian meals sometimes proved challenging, but the locals were generally eager to help. In one small settlement we stayed at Nora's *hospedaje*. The price included dinner and breakfast. When I told Nora I was vegetarian, she gave me a blank look and told me that she had never cooked a vegetarian meal. She said she would find something. I later heard her on the phone to a friend, getting some tips. On being summoned for dinner, we took our places and devoured the large basketful of fresh-baked *pan*, lathering it in *dulce de leche* (a sweet caramelised milk spread), before the main course arrived. Out came a beautifully presented layered omelette filled with silverbeet and other vegetables and with rice on the side. It was delicious.

After dinner we chatted with Nora's husband, Carlos, who had arrived home from work. He was a diver in the salmon industry. Salmon farming was a huge industry in southern Chile, and dotted up and down the coast are salmon farms – large cages housing thousands of fish, all tightly packed together. Due to the high density farming, many fish die as illnesses spread quickly. In 2007, a virus spread through the salmon population which nearly wiped out the industry. Carlos's job was to dive down and remove all the sick and dying fish. Not an enviable job in any part of the world, but in southern Chile the water is freezing, even in summer. Carlos showed us the extra thick wetsuit he wears, while explaining to us that since the disaster in 2007 there are fewer salmon farms and they are further spread out.

~~~~

After a week of cycling, we reached Hornopirén. To continue our journey further south from there, we had to take a six-hour ferry trip to Chaitén, where the highway re-starts. We went straight down to the wharf area to procure our tickets for the following day's departure.

'It's full,' the bored looking woman in the office informed us, while stifling a yawn.

'What do you mean it's full?' I asked, as I had been told by several people that there was no need for cyclists or pedestrians to book their passage.

'Sorry, but it is fully booked and I can't do anything for you,' the girl replied, 'and there are ten people on a waiting list before you. The next ferry with vacancies is on Saturday.' Six days away.

Disheartened, we realised our only realistic option was to travel by bus back to Puerto Montt, near our trip start point, and get an alternate ferry from there. I would not cycle back over all the hills and rough roads.

We secured bus tickets for the following morning, found a cheap *hospedaje* and dejectedly ate our dinner. When I awoke early the following morning, I shook Michael awake and said, 'I've got an idea. Let's just pack everything up, go to the jetty and you never know, they may let us on.' I was afraid of Michael's response, knowing his dislike of sudden changes of plan, so I was surprised when he agreed, even though he thought it a waste of time.

We got to the jetty an hour before departure time. They had begun to load the cars and there were many people milling around, including four other cyclists. We entered the office and the same girl, in an irritated voice said, 'I told you last night, it's full, there's no point in waiting.' However, we planned to wait. We chatted to the other 'waiters' and found out that there were four cars, four other cyclists, and six backpackers all without tickets. We didn't hold out much hope, but continued to wait.

All those with tickets boarded. Then the extra cars were, one at a time, permitted to board, with them all just fitting on. The backpackers were then told they could board. The other cyclists were motioned aboard. Then it was just us. Just minutes before departure we were also motioned aboard, being told we could pay on the ferry. We were grinning like two Cheshire cats, as were all the others who'd been allowed to board at the last minute.

A fellow passenger explained the current situation to us: In the past, the ferry would be filled to capacity with cars, and any pedestrians or cyclists would be taken without requiring a booking.

However, about two weeks prior to our trip, a ferry had sunk and four people had died. The operators were now forced to strictly adhere to the stated passenger carrying capacity of the vessel. There had been an officious looking naval officer around at the start of boarding and we think that once he left, the ferry crew were happy to take whomever they could fit on board. It was a huge boat and was not overcrowded even with the extra passengers and bicycles on board. (It was nothing compared to our 'cruise' back in 2001).

It was a glorious day. The views of the surrounding hills and mountains were spectacular and, as we drew closer to Chaitén, we sighted *Volcán* Chaitén with its plume of volcanic fumes. In May 2008, the volcano had erupted and destroyed the town. Fortunately, the residents had been evacuated prior to it being buried in ash. Officially Chaitén was still uninhabitable, but about eighty families had moved back in, despite the lack of Government support. There was no power or water, so generators were used to secure water supplies for the townsfolk. As we pedalled around town, it was heart-wrenching to see the homes still buried in ash, some of them up to their roof tops.

We were now on the *Carretera Austral* proper, where we were to spend the next three weeks of our tour. The further south we ventured the more spectacular the scenery became, with lakes, rivers, glaciers and mountains to marvel at every step of the way.

On a day off the bikes, Michael went kayaking on the *Rio* Futalefú while I went for a walk. The hike ended up being a lot longer than I had anticipated. As I reached the outskirts of the Futalefú township, three young schoolgirls approached me and asked if I had my passport.

'Yes, I do,' I replied.

They then told me that I must give them the passport and come with them.

'Where do you want to take me?' I asked, and told them how exhausted I already was from my 25km walk, and that my husband would be worried about me because I was already so late.

'It's not far,' they said, 'and it's important.'

I agreed to accompany them, despite my misgivings. When we got to the school, ten minutes later, it was overflowing with people and I was relieved when one of the first people I spotted was Michael. He told me he had also been abducted – by a six year old.

The little girl had requested his passport and then asked him to get in the car her mother was driving. It transpired that there was a fun competition on each day that week, to keep the children entertained during their school holidays. Today's challenge was to see which team (north or south of the town) could collect the most foreigners with their passports. There was a celebration as the passports were counted and we were all offered to share a *maté* (strong herbal tea) and sweet treats. Michael had been kidnapped by the winning team, with over 30 passports, while my team had 16.

So our first time being abducted was a fun experience after all.

~~~~

As we headed further into our trip, we noticed that things had improved in Chile in the nine years since we had last visited. This time we met many Chilean families on holidays, most of them in modern cars, something that was only available for the rich Chileans previously. Now there seemed to be a larger middle class who could afford luxuries such as holidays, even if only at home rather than abroad. We also met many students, most of them hitchhiking, and found that many of them could speak English, unlike those we met nine years ago.

At one campsite we were invited to share a campfire with some friendly Chilean teachers. They told us about life as a teacher in Chile. The children start school at 8 am and finish at 4 pm, and the teachers need to do their preparation after that. Their pay is only just enough to make ends meet with little extra for holidays or luxuries. They envied us our ability to travel abroad and said that on a teacher's wage they couldn't afford to do this. They were, however, a happy trio who seemed to have a good lifestyle.

~~~~

After three weeks on the bikes, we were excited to be nearing Coihaique, a city we had fond memories of. We were hoping to be able to visit and perhaps stay with *Señor* Robinson, in whose *hospedaje* we had stayed back in 2001. As we cycled into the city, we were struck by the busyness of the streets, the long queues of cars at the petrol stations and the crowds of people at the *supermercardo.* It certainly hadn't been so chaotic nine years ago.

We entered the tourist office, in an effort to locate *Señor* Robinson, as we couldn't remember where his house was. The information officer was eager to assist and painstakingly waded through each *hospedaje* listing. Unable to find his name, but with our description of where we thought the house had been, she came up with a 'hostel' which she thought may be the one. As that was the best lead we had, we thanked her and headed off to find it.

Arriving at the street, which seemed familiar, we had growing feelings of excitement and anticipation for the reunion. When we got to the house, however, it didn't look familiar and was more an upmarket hostel rather than a *hospedaje.* A middle-aged man approached and asked if we were looking for accommodation. I explained our search for *Señor* Robinson, and he confirmed what we had already realised, that this was not the right house. We asked him if he knew a man called *Señor* Robinson, who we thought lived in the same street. He shook his head, but then as we turned to leave, he said, 'Wait a minute, I do remember *Señor* Robinson,' and went on to describe him as we'd remembered him. 'I'm sorry, but he passed away about two years ago.'

Crestfallen and close to tears, we thanked him and pedalled away to look for another *hospedaje* and find somewhere for lunch.

We were surprised that most eateries were closed. We stopped at a café and asked if they were still serving lunch. Yes, we could get lunch as long as we could pay cash as the credit card facilities were down. The young man then went on to tell us that he didn't know for how long the banks would be closed, when phones would be operational or the internet back on. Giving him a confused look, he added that it was because of the *terremoto.*

'What earthquake are you talking about?' I asked.

'Don't you know about the huge earthquake that hit Chile in the early hours of the morning and the tsunami that followed?'

This sent a chill up our spines as we explained that we had just arrived back into civilisation after camping in the Rio Simpson National Park and hadn't felt any earthquake. It was only later, when watching the television in our *hospedaje,* that we were able to comprehend the full extent of the disaster.

We spent much of the remainder of the afternoon and evening glued to the TV Chile 24 hour news channel and were shocked to see the ghastly images of flattened towns and terrified people. We were saddened by the terrible loss of life. The earthquake had devastated an area from north of Santiago to as far south as Puerto Montt, near where we'd started our cycle trip.

The Santiago airport had been badly damaged and was to be closed for an indefinite period and the highway between Santiago and Puerto Montt had been cut in numerous places, with many bridges destroyed. Chile is a long thin country with only one main route from north to south. All other routes involve travelling through Argentina. Many of the ports were also closed due to damage. People were unsure whether food, fuel and other such necessities would be able to be transported down south, hence the panic buying we had witnessed.

We didn't know whether or not to continue our journey further south. We feared we could have issues with food supply and also wondered if there would be sufficient fuel to keep the buses running to enable us to get back up north. In addition, I was feeling quite exhausted and was not overly enthusiastic about continuing south. We had heard that for cyclists the difficulty increases the further south you go. On the other hand though, we also heard that the scenery gets even more beautiful, not that I could imagine anything more stunning than the sights that we'd already seen.

Late that afternoon we found an internet café that was operational. Upon logging in, we found our inbox full of messages from worried family and friends. And there was an email from Karina, on behalf of the whole Peruvian family.

'We are very worried about you. Are you okay? Please leave dangerous Chile straight away and go to Argentina and then fly to Peru where it is much safer.' (They had forgotten about the devastating earthquake in Peru two years prior).

We assured the Carbajal Moreira family that we were fine and, despite my misgivings, we decided to keep on pedalling south, as originally planned.

~~~~
~~~~

On one steep descent, a couple of days out of Coyhaique, Michael stopped suddenly in front of me.

'What are you doing?' I asked.

'Look,' he said pointing to a sign in front of a house with the words: *'se vende ovejas'*, 'We could buy some for dinner.'

'Do you really want to buy a sheep? I asked.

'Isn´t *ovejas* peas?' he asked.

'No,' I laughingly replied, 'that´s *arvejas*!'

Afterwards, I wished I'd let Michael go in and try to buy an *oveja*. It would have been fun to see the farmer's response as he brought the sheep around and tried to tie it on to Michael's bicycle. We would have to do some more Spanish practice before getting to Peru!

A bit further down the road we stopped at another large sign: '*se vende verduras – zanahorias*'. Michael knew this one to be: 'vegetables for sale - carrots'. When we asked the old *campesino* if we could buy some carrots, he gave us a long answer in rapid 'Chilean farmer Spanish' which we couldn´t decipher. Initially he seemed angry, but I finally worked out that he was just complaining that he didn´t have anything left to sell because travellers kept stopping to buy his vegetables. (The hide of them!)

'*Un momento, por favor*,' said the lovely old man as he limped off to his garden bed. He returned with a few small carrots that he'd just pulled up for us. He then didn't want to accept our payment.

After eight spectacular days of cycling from Coyhaique, we made it to Cochrane, our southern-most point and from where we would catch a bus heading back north, before entering Argentina. There had been no issues with food or fuel supplies and in fact there was no indication that most of the rest of Chile was in chaos after the earthquake and tsunami.

On entering Argentina, we immediately noticed the disrepair of the country as compared with Chile. This was a big contrast to nine years prior, when Argentina was the wealthiest country in South America. In 2002 however, the Argentine economy had crashed and the country had fallen into a slump out of which it was still struggling to climb. While in Chile we had noticed all the new cars, with few old cars remaining on the road; in Argentina it was the opposite. The towns were full of black smoke that was belched out of rusty old cars. The streets, shops and businesses all had a rundown look about them.

We spent the next two weeks cycling around the magnificent Argentinean and Chilean Lakes districts, mainly on paved roads, which was a relief. Our bodies had had enough of being shaken to the core on the *ripio*. Our trip finished in Villarica, about 250km north of where we had started. The hostel owners were happy to have us as they'd had few guests since the *terremoto*. They described what two and a half minutes of earthquake is like at three o'clock in the morning. 'It felt like the earth was moving round and around in circles under our feet. It was terrifying and we all rushed outside. We then spent the next two nights, with our guests, sleeping in the kitchen.'

On our final day in Patagonia, we cycled the 28 km to Pucón to visit Lucía, in whose *hospedaje* we had stayed in 2001. Lucía remembered us and was pleased that we had come back to visit. She later whispered in my ear (amidst giggling) that she remembered Michael's forehead, but this time it was bigger! We asked Lucía how life was treating her and her family. She told us her son was studying at university and her daughter was in her final year of school. It was amazing to think that it was these two children who had once greeted us as six and eight year olds and given us the run-down of the *hospedaje*, while their mother was out shopping.

'I can't complain,' said Lucía, 'but life is quite tough in Chile. I have worked hard to provide an education for my children, but I can't afford to travel.'

I asked her if she got tired of having guests in her house all the time.

'Sometimes, yes, if they are difficult I get fed up, but most of the time I enjoy chatting with them. It's my way of travelling and learning about other cultures. I have a much greater understanding of other countries than my friends. It's also heart-warming when I strike up a special relationship with guests, like you, who return years later.'

We were sorry we had been unable to stay with Lucía this time.

On our ride back to Villarica, our cycle computers clicked over 2,000. We had cycled a little over 2,000 kilometres in seven weeks and had had a marvellous adventure in the process. After dinner, we pedalled to the bus station, pulled the bikes apart and caught the night bus to Santiago. The trip was a couple of hours longer than normal, due to the earthquake damage, but it was impressive that new routes had been forged around damaged sections of road and broken-down bridges.

On arrival in Santiago, we managed to fit the two bikes and our entire luggage in a small sedan. The friendly *taxista* drove like a lunatic (welcome back to Santiago) and we were back at our hostel in no time. We thought the hostel would be empty, given the lack of tourists everywhere, so we were surprised to find it quite busy, not with tourists, but full of seismologists, geologists and volcanologists studying the earth's movements.

Antonio met us for dinner and then kindly took our bicycles and excess luggage back to store at his home, for when we returned to Santiago a month later.

Michael and I were sad that our cycling adventure was over, but we were looking forward to being reunited with our Peruvian family.

CHAPTER 16

Return to Huanta for Semana Santa

31 March 2010

On the early morning flight to Lima, Michael and I chatted with Cinthia, the young Peruvian seated beside us. The 25 year-old professional, who was keen to practise her English, told us she worked for a large gold-mining company and was returning home from Antofogasta, Northern Chile, where she'd been on a business trip to the mines. On arrival, we accepted Cinthia's offer of a lift to the city in her company taxi. The driver warned us that, being the day before the Easter break, there was a lot of traffic on the roads as workers were finishing early and leaving the city. He wasn't exaggerating. Once out of the airport, we witnessed the chaos on the roads and realised we weren't going anywhere in a hurry. I had made an error by assuming that the holidays would start on Good Friday as in Australia, however, in Peru the Easter break goes from Thursday to Sunday. We couldn't have picked a worse day to travel and were stuck in Lima's traffic, much of the time at a standstill, for a couple of hours. We were glad we didn't have to foot the bill.

Moving at a snail's pace, we were able to take a good look at Lima and noted that the streets looked cleaner and more ordered (despite the horrendous traffic) than six years ago. We noticed new highways, cleaner suburbs and expansive areas of green parkland. If the capital city was anything to go by, then it looked like Peru was moving forward.

Cinthia's driver finally dropped us at the bus station and we promised to contact her on our way back through Lima, in a month's time. As our bus wasn't departing until 9 pm, we had the afternoon and evening to explore. So we put our luggage into storage and caught a taxi to the nearby suburb of Miraflores, one of Lima's wealthiest areas.

On finding a park overlooking the ocean, we lay down on the grass for a nap. We nodded off but were soon awoken by raised voices. We looked around to see a shabbily-dressed indigenous man also lying on the grass, with a policeman telling him to move on. The man was obviously not happy and was gesticulating at us. Why were we (wealthy tourists) allowed to sleep in the park while he (a descendant of the nation's people) wasn't? The irony was lost on the police officer who enforced his request, leaving us feeling quite uncomfortable. Ashamed, we also decided to leave.

Walking around the crowded shops in the late afternoon we felt overwhelmed after our two months in quiet, clean Patagonia. Seeing bent-over elderly men and women on busy street intersections trying to sell sweets or other small items while inhaling the noxious car fumes, served as a reminder that although Lima seemed to have moved forward in six years, for many people it was still a struggle to survive.

After dinner we returned to the bus station to catch the overnight bus to Ayacucho. We managed to sleep reasonably well in our *cama* seats, although we did feel the effects of altitude while going over the high passes. Fortunately neither of us vomited. Several others did.

The bus pulled into the Ayacucho terminal at 7.30 am and Karina and Mariluz were there to meet us. We all burst into tears as we hugged each other tightly. After a brief stop in Ayacucho's centre to change money and to see Karina's rented room (a different and much nicer one than she'd had six years earlier), we boarded a *colectivo* taxi for the fifty minute trip to Huanta, with non-stop chatting the whole way. The potholed dirt road we remembered between Ayacucho and Huanta was now sealed, making the trip faster and safer – although with the speed the drivers now drove, we didn't always feel very safe.

Karina had some exciting news for us: 'As I was the top-placed student in my final year of law, I have been selected to represent my university, the *Universidad Nacional de Huamanga,* at a large conference in Lima, in early May.'

She went on to tell us that there would be delegates from universities across the Americas, and that all her expenses would be covered by the university. She and a fellow student would have to present a paper on behalf of the university. 'Unfortunately,' Karina continued, 'it will mean that I'll have to spend quite a lot of time meeting with other students from my year group, to research and write the paper, and will have less time to spend with you. But I will spend as much time as possible with you.'

As we drew nearer to Huanta, Mariluz and Karina, with cheeky grins, said they couldn't wait for us to see the rest of the family and see how much they'd changed, making particular reference to Nélida, whom they didn't think we'd recognise.

The anticipation grew until we arrived at their house. The whole family was there, with huge smiles and open arms, all wanting to embrace us at the same time. It was an emotional reunion and tears flowed freely. We wondered who the tall, slim, attractive girl we couldn't recognise was. Of course, it must be the baby of the family, Nélida, now 16 years old, and a good twenty centimetres taller than all of her sisters and her mother. We thought back to the cute, chubby, round-faced ten year old Nélida we remembered from our last visit and could not believe the transformation.

We looked at them all closely. Margot who had been quite tall and skinny as a twelve year old, had not grown much and was now quite short for her 18 years, however she had filled out somewhat and looked healthier.

Marleni, 'Wombat', now 20 years old, was not well and carrying some extra weight. We were surprised because in one of her letters a few years previously, she had complained that she was sick and too skinny and had asked us to send her some pills to make her fatter. Marleni explained to us that she was now suffering from chronic tonsillitis, and her constant illnesses were affecting her mind.

Wilbur had become a good-looking 25 year old, with a more self-assured look. He'd had his rotten and missing teeth fixed and now showed a lovely white smile. 26 year old Mariluz, who had previously only smiled without showing her teeth, now also sported new front teeth, and with her wide white smile she was transformed into an attractive young woman.

Karina, at 23 years of age, was still as attractive and vivacious as ever and didn't appear to have changed much at all. Carmen was looking a bit older, her face more lined, while Celestino actually looked slightly better, with a healthier skin-colour than we'd remembered from before.

There was another surprise. Carmen was holding a baby, who was introduced to us as Jharol. We asked to whom this baby girl belonged, at which they laughed and replied that 'she' was a baby boy and they would explain more later on.

Celestino apologised for the state of the yard, a quagmire of sticky mud, explaining that it was the end of the wet season and there had been a huge downpour the night before. We noticed that the kitchen was missing from the back of the house. Celestino told us that they'd had to demolish that part of the building a few weeks ago as it was decaying and dangerous. They now had a portable gas stove in the dining-room, and mostly cooked on that rather than on an open fire. Having also noticed the shiny new corrugated roof on the main part of the house, Celestino said they'd had to replace the old one as it had rusted through.

Margot asked us if we noticed anything else different around the yard. We took stock – yes, the open air *baño* was still there, with another blue sheet of plastic for a door. Everything else looked much the same as we'd remembered. She asked us to look closely at the *baño*. Then Michael noticed the shower rose, in the same bricked in area.

'We now have a shower,' Margot proudly informed us.

'Do you use it much?' I asked.

Margot sheepishly replied that in the warmer months it sometimes got used, but not during the colder months.

Michael and I ended up making use of the shower at least every other day, but we never once saw any of the Carbajal Moreiras having a shower. 'It's too cold,' they all said, 'and we'll get sick.' They thought we were crazy for having showers as often as we did, and would chuckle as they heard our yelps on first contact with the cold water.

Noting the absence of the *moto-taxi*, Michael asked Wilbur where it was and he told us that they'd had to sell it. Celestino then explained that as the vehicle was getting older, it had needed too much repair work and was starting to cost a lot. 'If we had waited any longer, it would have been worth even less, so we sold it six months ago.'

We were called to the dining room for breakfast. Carmen had cooked us a feast – fried yucca which she'd just brought back from the jungle, eggs, *pan* and avocado, and a hot *kiwicha* drink. How joyous to be back once again with the family we loved so much and sharing a raucous meal full of lively conversation, jokes and laughter. We realised how much we had missed them all.

After breakfast we distributed the presents – An Aussie T-shirt for each of them (creating much negotiation as to who would get which), a jacket for Celestino, sunglasses for everyone (also to be negotiated), and many other small items. They all loved the sunglasses and, interestingly, were more concerned with them as a fashion item than as something to protect their eyes from the harsh Peruvian sun. Whenever we went into town, the girls would wear their sun glasses and more often than not they were perched on top of their heads rather than over their eyes!

The final gift I pulled out was a digital camera. This was greeted with great excitement from everyone. On our previous trip (pre-digital for us) I had thought about bringing them an old film camera, but then discounted the idea because they would have to pay for films and printing. The digital camera, however, was ideal because there needn't be any extra costs, and once we had taught them how to use it, we were constantly assailed by one or other of the kids waving it in our face, and saying '*sonríe*'. Smile.

After a delicious lunch of '*locro peruano*' – a bean and vegetable stew – Michael and I, along with most of the kids, went for an afternoon stroll towards Huanta town centre. That is, after the girls had preened themsleves in front of the mirror trying to ascertain the best placement for their new sunglasses.

We were impressed by the new footpath from their village, now known as Tablachacra, which extended all the way into Huanta. The footpath was, however, built in true Peruvian style with scant thought to health and safety. At one point the path ended abruptly at an abyss at the edge of the creek, forcing pedestrians out onto the road. Also, in an attempt at beautifying the path, shrubs had been planted. However, these shrubs were covered in lethal thorns (probably chosen so they wouldn't be stolen), and as they hung over the path one had to be constantly vigilant when walking. All this aside, it was still an improvement to walking on the road, which had previously been the only option.

It rained during our walk back, something it did every afternoon and evening for the first half of our stay, until the wet season ended. This kept the yard muddy and made the nocturnal trips to the *baño* even more unpleasant.

During dinner, a long drawn out affair with lots of chatter, we became reacquainted with the family's special Peruvian Quechuan Spanish. They had a delightful way of changing many nouns into the diminutive by adding *'ito'* or *'ita'* (meaning 'little') at the end of words. Nélida in particular made us laugh, as every second noun she used was made into a diminutive, and had us having to concentrate hard to decipher what she was saying.

'Would you like some more egg (*huevo*) and potatoes (*papas*) with your hot drink?' became: *'Quieres más huevito y papitas con tu aguita?'*

(A*gua* literally means water, but our family used the term *aguita* for any hot drink).

It was like us Aussies shortening our words and adding a 'y' sound on the end, or even lengthening our words with the 'y' sound; for example, calling pictures pikkies, breakfast brekkie and biscuits bikkies.

Our bedroom was the same small room we'd used last time, only this time it looked shabbier and was infused with the acrid smell of urine, which we were never able to erase, despite our attempts with burning incense. I'd actually noticed the urine smell as soon as we'd arrived at the house and when I mentioned it to Mariluz, she said it was due to baby Jharol, who didn't wear nappies. I also suspected that at night, the family members didn't walk all the way to the *baño*, but just squatted.

There was a new mattress on the single bed so we thought we would be a bit more comfortable this time. We weren't. After a couple of nights with the two of us sleeping on the bed, the mattress developed a deep concave, giving me a backache. We spent the remainder of the nights alternating between the bed and my deflating camping mat on the dirty floor. Having to reinflate the mat in the middle of the night, twice, was still preferable to sleeping on a bed like a big soft banana.

The second larger room, which had had no floorboards on our first visit, was now fully floored and although it still lacked glass in the window and a door, Carmen and the girls slept in there, while Celestino and Wilbur shared the other room. Normally, when we weren't there, Marleni slept alone in the small bedroom.

~~~~

The following morning Michael and I went for an early morning walk with Mariluz and Nélida, up through the fields behind their house. It was much prettier this time, being so green from the wet season. Most properties, including our family's, had their home *chacras* brimming with long corn stalks swaying in the breeze, their juicy cobs ripe and ready for harvesting. It was a great time of year to be in Huanta - the corn was delicious, and we were to consume large quantities of it in various forms. There was almost always a bowl of corn kernels (hand-picked off the cobs) on the table to be snacked on with meals. Beans and peas were also in season and many fruits were ripe and ready to be picked.

Michael ensured the morning walks became a daily event with whichever of the kids could be dragged out of bed. We were also usually accompanied by one or other of the young cousins (Vladimir and Román) who lived next door. They were like mountain goats, running ahead and scrambling up rocks and trees, finding alternative paths for us to explore. The two young male cousins we had got to know last time were now working with their parents (Edmundo and Antonia) in the jungle, and had been replaced by their younger brothers. The boys were being looked after by their 15 year old sister, Mirian, whom we remembered from last time.

After breakfast we all (with the exception of Celestino, who was still unable to leave the house, and Marleni who was too unwell) walked into town. Instead of following the road, the kids guided us through a new park that follows the *Rio* Tablachacra, the same river that starts in the mountains and forms the waterfall where we'd had the picnic on our last visit, and in which we had also bathed. The park was beautifully planted out with bright flowers, many different trees and shrubs and with one section of the pathway passing through a delightful tunnel of trees. Along the way women were washing their clothes in the river and using the age-old method of drying – draping the garments over the rocks and bushes.

Once through the long narrow park, we followed little twisting and rocky dirt laneways between houses all the way to town. It was a lovely way to walk to town, even though a bit further in distance.
~~~~

The only problem was the fierce dog that accosted us menacingly, barking and growling. Under instructions from the kids, we armed ourselves with rocks to hurl at the dog as it approached aggressively. For this reason the girls were not too keen to walk this way, especially on their own. This dog was not bluffing; it would seriously rip someone to pieces if they weren't armed and ready. There doesn't seem to be rules in Peru prohibiting the keeping of dangerous animals, or requiring them to be locked up.

Having run the gauntlet of the dog, and once safely in town, we stopped off at the *plaza de armas* which also looked magnificent, having been planted out with trees, shrubs and colourful flowers. We were asked to stand in front of the large central fountain for numerous photos, as each family member wanted an individual photo taken with the two of us.

We commented to the family on the huge improvements we had noticed around their town, and they said that the current Mayor was keen to beautify the area, but was not so good at looking after his people. Wilbur had once taken a tree-planting job with the council, but after two months without receiving any pay, he had left in disgust.

While walking, Mariluz told us that baby Jharol was the child of one of Celestino's cousins. This cousin, who has a disability, was the victim of a rape and Jharol was the result. When he was born, it was obvious that his mother would be unable to care for him, so the hospital contacted all the relatives, and the only relation willing to adopt the baby was Celestino. He had conferred with his family first, and although some had had initial misgivings, they all now loved Jharol as their own.

Being Good Friday, the *plaza de armas* was crowded with people enjoying a carnival atmosphere. We sat down to enjoy the ambience, and a group of young boys (about 10 year olds), shoe-shine boxes tucked under their arms, approached, jostling each other to get to us first. They asked us if we would like our shoes shined, while still jockeying for position. I negotiated a price with two of the boys and as they got to work on my and Michael's shoes, the rest of them also gathered around, laughing and joking with each other and with us.

When they had finished, our boots were gleaming. I paid the lads and they stayed and chatted. Then one of them reached under the bench we were sitting on and pulled out a one hundred sol note (about $40). The colour drained from my face, and the boy asked me if I had lost it. I reached into my pocket and found that the hundred sol note I'd placed there earlier was no longer there.

'*Sí, sí*, it's mine, it was in my pocket.' I replied, having realised that it must have slipped out when I got the coins out to pay the boy.

Wilbur, immediately jumping to the offensive, said the boy must have stolen it from me. I quickly stopped Wilbur in his tracks, commenting on the boy's honesty. I was also surprised as this lad could so easily have kept that large sum of money for himself. I thanked the boy profusely and gave him a ten sol note as a reward for his honesty. Although my carelessness with money, especially in front of the family, left me feeling queasy, it was heart-warming to know that there were nice honest children in the town. I would have given the boy more if we'd been alone.

With our polished shoes, we walked around the bustling town centre, having to take care when crossing the roads, which were busy and noisy with hundreds of *moto-taxis* buzzing around like bees.

'It's busier because it's a public holiday,' said Wilbur, 'but the streets are always crowded now, and there are many more *moto-taxis* than before. It's now really hard to make any money driving a *moto*. There are just too many out there.'

During the walk back, Mariluz told me that the family had a special job waiting for me. I had thought that little Jharol was a girl due to his long dark wavy locks of hair. However, he was a one year old boy who had never had a haircut. Mariluz explained that in the Quechuan tradition a child's first hair cut was a special occasion and that the first lock of hair had to be cut by someone very special in the child's life, followed by all the other significant people each cutting off a lock. The family wanted me to make the first cut, an honour which I felt I had to refuse, as I thought it should be someone from the immediate family. I volunteered to do the finishing touches.

The following morning Jharol was seated on a plastic chair wearing a bib-type covering. It was decided that Celestino would make the first cut, followed by the other family members in descending order of age. Each time a lock of hair was cut, the person cutting had to place a coin on the chair. The money thus raised was later used to buy a present for the baby. After everyone (including me) had cut off a lock, I took the scissors and finished off the haircut, making him look like a little boy. The gift the girls later bought was a pair of socks. Funnily enough the motif, written in English, was 'baby girl'. When I told them the meaning, they all laughed.

After the formalities were over, we went up the back to harvest *pacay* and peas. The *pacay* tree grows up to twenty metres tall and produces long narrow pods up to 30 centimetres in length. The pods house large black seeds, around which is sweet, juicy, edible pulp. *Pacay* is known in the English-speaking world as the ice-cream bean, so called for its taste.

Carmen and some of the kids climbed into the trees to harvest the pods. First they gave the branches a solid shake, causing many of the pods to fall to the ground, and then, using long bamboo poles, the ends of which were forked, they snared the remaining pods and dragged them down. Those of us on the ground had to collect and bag the pods. We had to take care that the heavy *pacay* pods didn't land on our heads, causing much laughter while ducking and weaving to avoid being hit, and stern warnings of '*Cuidado!*' (Take care!) when there were near misses. We were worried by how high the kids climbed, but they assured us that the branches of the *pacay* tree were very strong and that even the smaller ones wouldn't break.

As we worked we ate many, and developed a taste for these strange legumes. The large shiny black seeds were spat out, while the sweet fairy floss-like white pulp was eaten.

After carrying the many bulging sacks back to the house, we emptied them on to the ground in a huge pile to be sorted. The better pods would be taken to the markets to be sold. We also picked a bag full of peas and took them back to the house for shelling for our main meal, *almuerzo*, in the middle of the day.

Celestino's mother, *abuelita,* shuffled over from across the road, dressed much as we'd remembered, with several layers of skirts and jumpers, topped with an apron, the pocket of which was always filled with food. With her two long plaits, now fully grey, framing her lined and weather-beaten face and with few remaining teeth, she looked much older than her years. She came over to give

Michael and me a huge strong bear hug as she babbled away in Quechuan, spitting as she talked, her mouth full of coca leaves. She grabbed my cheek in a solid pinch, laughing loudly and calling me a *gringita bonita.* She was still remarkably strong and her hugs and back slaps actually hurt. We could see why all the kids tried to avoid her when she appeared in the yard.

Abuelita then picked up some *pacay,* peeled it, crammed the contents into her mouth, and then spat the four centimetre-sized shiny seeds, which shot out of her mouth like missiles, at whoever was closest, breaking into peals of laughter as she took aim.

The kids explained that *abuelita's* mind was going, and that she was quite unpredictable, which we had quickly realised. Any time she subsequently came over to the house she would be chewing on something, and often came with some food to offer us – cooked corn cobs, bread, or fruit. Thrusting it at us, she would demand that we eat: '*Come! Come!*', (pronounced comay). We often tried to avoid eating *abuelita's* food, as her hygiene was dubious and we were usually full from having just eaten, but sometimes we had no choice, as she stood over us asking why we didn't want to eat her food. Admittedly, it was usually tasty.

In the afternoon some of us went out to harvest more *pacay,* while Michael and Wilbur began digging out huge rocks from where the old kitchen had been. The family wanted to flatten the ground to make a small kitchen vegetable garden. This was a big job which was to continue for almost the entire time we were in Huanta. Many of the boulders were so big they required many workers, using wooden planks as levers, to move them. Michael and Wilbur did most of the work, and whoever was around at the time was called in to help when needed. Celestino would even get up for five minutes at a time as he hated watching others work without being able to assist. Although it caused him a lot of pain, he wanted to contribute to the job.

Late that afternoon Karina took out the laptop computer a friend had lent her, and I inserted the USB stick with the images from our cycling trip. It was surreal sitting outside on the rough veranda and looking at a modern computer screen with our photos. They asked us many questions about our bicycles and the gear we had travelled with. They wanted to know what the *Chilenos* were like. Peruvians are generally not too fond of Chileans and they all looked surprised when we told them how friendly we'd found the people to be.

'Ah, that's just because you're *gringos*!' said Marleni, with a scathing look.

Carmen wanted to know how we had cooked our meals. There was one photo which showed our little Trangia methylated spirit-burning cooking stove and Celestino, with his inquiring mind, was particularly interested in how it worked. He asked me to send a clearer photo when we returned home so he could try to make something similar.

We all also enjoyed reviewing the photos the family members had taken with their new camera, and those we'd taken with ours.

Lonche (dinner) was a soy milk drink with a *mazamorra de maíz negra* (pudding made from black corn). The corn really was black and was picked from their home *chacra*. This sweet dessert dish is made by boiling the whole corn cob, removing the cob, and then adding pineapple, apple and sugar to the remaining dark coloured liquid, before thickening with cornflour. It becomes jelly-like in both flavour and texture.

~~~~

On our early morning walk on Easter Sunday, up behind the houses and around the *chacras*, we were only accompanied by Karina, Nélida and Vladimir. As we were walking along the concrete channel that carries the water down the hill to the village, I slipped and fell into the viaduct. Ludicrously, I was wearing good walking boots while the girls were wearing flat-soled slip-on shoes, and I was the one to slip. I would have laughed but I'd winded myself, twisted my ankle and banged my elbow. Karina and Nélida rushed to my assistance and worriedly fussed over me. Once I regained my breath, I assured them I was fine and didn't mention the ankle or elbow, as I knew how much they worried. They were blaming themselves for my fall, saying they hadn't looked after me well enough and were worried what Mariluz and Carmen would say. Then they noticed my wet clothing and worried that I would catch a cold. I assured them that I would be fine. Only then did they notice my bleeding elbow, and this brought on another bout of concern.
~~~~

'Mariluz and *mamá* are going to be really angry with us for letting this happen to you,' Karina said, concern etched into her face.

'They don't need to know about it,' I replied. 'I'm not going to tell them, are you? It can be our little secret.'

The girls gigglingly agreed that we would keep it a secret and I promised them that when we returned I would sneak into our room to get changed without anyone seeing me. Vladimir was also sworn to secrecy, not that he thought it any big deal.

Once back at the house, I was able to get changed without being spotted, came out and winked at the girls. While having breakfast, however, Marleni noticed the graze on my elbow. 'How did that happen?' she wanted to know, 'Does it hurt much?'

I told her that I'd just brushed it against a rock and that it was nothing to worry about. She turned to Karina and Nélida and demanded to know why they hadn't been taking better care of me. Jumping to their defence, I assured Marleni that it had nothing to do with them, was really nothing, and didn't hurt. Marleni was placated and gave me a stern warning, '*Cuidado*!'

The whole family thought of themselves as our protectors. If we dared to cough or blow our nose, they'd ask us in a concerned voice if we were sick. If one of us stumbled in the yard, someone would be at our side immediately, asking, '*Estás bien*?' Are you alright? Such was the huge concern over their precious *gringos.*

After breakfast, all the able-bodied family members set off to walk into town to view the Easter Sunday celebrations. My ankle was quite sore, but I did my best to walk without a limp so as not to arouse concern. Fortunately, everyone was too excited to notice. As we drew closer to the *plaza de armas,* we could see the crowds of people and noticed some of the roads were cordoned off.

'That's for the *Corrida de Toros*,' Carmen informed us.

'What? They really have a running of the bulls?' I enquired, with visions of the famous spectacle in Pamplona, Spain.

'*Sí, sí,*' she replied and continued to say that she didn't like it and thought it dangerous.

I asked if we could have a quick look and we took our places in the crowd, behind the barricades. Suddenly the spectators erupted in a loud cheer and then we saw the scared young steer being prodded and cajoled to run down the street ahead of a mob of young men and boys. The calf didn't want to play, but with a few slaps to its flanks, it trotted on down the street with the yelling and cavorting youngsters in hot pursuit. A little later the scene was repeated with a new calf. The crowd was enjoying the spectacle and although it was quite harmless and non-aggressive, Carmen dragged us away. She was nervous amongst crowds of people and was worried for us and for her children.

Carmen led us to the markets to buy fruit and vegetables for the day. As we followed her from vendor to vendor, Michael and I felt the stares boring into us. No-one tried to talk to us and our attempts at interactions were evaded with downcast eyes, making us feel uneasy. We had forgotten from last time how wary people were of us tall *gringos* being so close to their townsfolk.

Carmen negotiated with the *palta* vendor, a weathered *campesina* sitting cross-legged on the ground, her coloured skirt covering her legs, felt hat tipped to one side, her produce laid out before her. Being an avocado aficionado, I was almost salivating. There was a large basket full of small *palta*, black and green, next to that were neatly stacked pyramids of medium-sized fruit, and then the high rise pyramid of huge avocados, the size of small footballs. The price negotiated: one sol for four *palta*, about ten cents apiece. Heaven! Carmen explained that the small and medium-sized fruits were tastier than the massive ones. Good, at least we didn't have to destroy the tower! They were all flabbergasted when I told them that in Australia we pay, on average, about two dollars for a small avocado and sometimes more. It was good to be able to give the family some perspective about living costs in Australia, so they could understand that although we earn a lot of money in Australia compared to Peru, our expenses are also much higher.

It didn't take Michael and me long to become tired of the hot and smelly markets, having to push our way through the sea of humanity, so we were pleased, although surprised, when Wilbur appeared in a *moto-taxi* and asked if we were ready to go home. 'I sometimes hire a *moto-taxi* to earn a bit of cash, even though by the time I pay the rental fee and for petrol, there isn't usually much money left over. But on a *fiesta* day like today, I should be able to earn quite well,' he explained.

~~~~
~~~~

That afternoon when I entered the larger bedroom to recharge our camera battery, I noticed the television. I remembered Celestino's comments six years ago when he told us they would not spend our money on luxuries such as a television, despite Wilbur's desperate pleas. Celestino had obviously succumbed and bought a television for the family.

My initial reaction was one of mild annoyance that they had spent 'our' money in this way, but, on giving it further thought, I banished this ill-feeling from my mind. How could I begrudge them this simple pleasure when they have so little entertainment in their lives? I chided myself and thought how dare I judge them like this when we have so many luxuries in our lives, and not one but two televisions in our own house. And, as Michael so rightly reminded me, we were supporting the family to give them a better quality of life and should be pleased that they too could now enjoy what most other people take for granted. Additionally, for Celestino, it was a great means of getting some light entertainment in his otherwise difficult and mundane life. He told us that he liked to watch documentaries, as he wanted to continue learning.

Another day I was shown the full set of junior encyclopaedias in the girls' room which Celestino had bought second-hand. He'd thought them to be an important purchase for the education of his children, believing strongly that education is the key to escaping poverty.

I had finally come to the realisation that even though we were giving the family money, it was not up to us to judge or control how they spent that money. We had to trust them to make the right decisions for themselves, and they appeared to be doing a good job of it.

CHAPTER 17 Work and Family Matters

4 April 2010

Late Easter Sunday afternoon, as Michael and I were helping Karina with her English lessons, I looked across the yard and noticed Celestino, Carmen and Mariluz, heads huddled together, all deep in discussion. Mariluz had tears running down her face. I went over to see if I could help. Michael and Karina soon followed.

Mariluz was facing a big dilemma. She had received a job offer down in the jungle, with excellent pay and good future prospects. The only problem was that she would have to leave the very next evening for the *selva*, and wouldn't see us again before we left. We'd spent just four days together.

Michael and I exchanged a few quick words; we could understand Mariluz's dilemma, but to us it was an obvious decision.

'This sounds like a fantastic opportunity,' I told her, 'and we have supported you in your studies so that you could become a professional and obtain a good job. It sounds like this job offer is too good to pass up. Michael and I think it is in your best interests to accept the job, even though it will mean missing out on time together.'

'If you don't take this job,' I asked Mariluz, 'what are the chances of you getting another good post like this one?'

'Opportunities like this are very rare in Peru,' she replied, her voice shaking with emotion, 'but it's more important to me to spend time with you. You have come all this way to see us and I've been waiting for years for you to come back to Peru, and now you're here, I don't want to go away.'

I tried to clarify our position. 'If you don't take this job, we'll be able to spend the next two weeks together with you, but after that we'll be gone and you'll be without a good job. However, if you accept the position, although you will miss the two weeks with us, you will have a good, well-paid job for the rest of the year and beyond, and your future prospects will be enhanced.'

Mariluz then explained to us how she felt about our being there with the family. She emphasised our importance to her, describing us as equally important as her blood family. She stressed that it meant so much to the family to have us with them, and that spending time with us was of far greater importance than any job. She didn't know when, if ever, she would see us again. Carmen, Celestino and Karina were all in agreement with Mariluz, saying it was more important that she stayed with us and with the family for the short time we were in Huanta.

Michael and I felt torn. We wanted to spend more time with Mariluz, but we also felt that it would be crazy to pass up this opportunity. The timing was unfortunate and we asked Mariluz if she could plead with the person who had offered her the job, requesting another week's extension. She explained that they'd already told her if she didn't start the next day, they would hire someone else. She did try again, but they refused to negotiate.

We told Mariluz we still thought she should take the position and even went as far as saying, that if she didn't take it we would have to reconsider our support for the family. We hated to be so harsh, but felt that her future happiness could depend on this job.

Mariluz, in the course of the conversation, seemed to have already made up her mind that she wasn't going to take it. We asked her what her other job prospects were.

'I could take up another contract with PRONAA, my previous employer. The pay is much less, and I have to cover my own transport and photocopying costs, which are substantial. I quite liked the work, but I was lonely. I was stationed out in the communities for long periods, alone and without phone or internet contact.'

Mariluz was even considering refusing the PRONAA contract, as that would mean starting in a week's time and still missing out on a week with us. She told us that if she didn't take one of these jobs, she would be unlikely to find another job for the rest of the year, as this was when all the contracts were being finalised.

Michael and I suggested a compromise. She could take the PRONAA contract, giving us another week together, but still with a job at the end of it. Mariluz tearfully agreed. She would talk to her boss in Ayacucho the following day.

That night Karina had to go back to Ayacucho as she had classes all week. We wouldn't see her again until the following weekend. Mariluz went with her.

That same night I woke up in the middle of the night, doubled over in pain, with severe stomach cramps. And then the diarrhoea started. Having to do the ten second bolt is not much fun at the best of times, but even less fun when the trips to the *baño* necessitated wading through the muddy yard and into the unpleasant loo several times a day. It was even worse at night, when the rickety ladder, still without a railing, had to be negotiated in a hurry and my knees, troublesome at the best of times, would threaten to collapse on my way down. It was usually raining, often heavily, and the *baño* was still without a roof.

After a couple of nights of this I had reached my limit. In addition, I was fed up with the fleas biting and crawling all over me and through my sleeping bag, sick of the little flies whose bites itched like crazy; I'd had enough of listening to the dogs barking all night... Crying, I told Michael I wanted to go home, even though I knew that wasn't a possibility. I could never do that to our family, who loved us so much and who had been waiting years for this reunion.

I was angry with myself for feeling like this. Here I was, in the home of the family I loved, living as they do, and I was daring to feel sorry for myself. Michael had little sympathy for me and told me, in no uncertain terms, to pull myself together. We were here for the family and I was acting like a spoilt child.

It wasn't only the sickness I was struggling with but also the relative inactivity of our stay. After having just spent seven weeks cycling through amazing countryside and having adventures every day, here I was spending my days with little activity (apart from the short walks and the many trips to the *baño*), with not much change of scenery. I needed some action, but was too lazy to help Michael and Wilbur dig in the yard (and I didn't want to get my clothes all muddy). I was definitely behaving like a prima donna!

I was also trying to keep out of the sun. During our cycling trip in the far south of the continent, my skin had been badly affected by the sun. In Huanta, although the family told us it was the 'cold' season, the days were still quite warm and I could feel the sun's ferocious bite. The nights did, however, get quite chilly. The girls told us that in winter (June/July) it gets much colder and they struggled to keep warm. We could well believe them, as they didn't have many blankets and with their bedroom lacking a door and window glass. We could also understand why in the middle of the year they always seem to suffer from colds, coughs and flu. It is the same in January and February when it is theoretically summer. Due to its proximity to the equator, Peru experiences a wet season in summer, when again the girls always seem to suffer from respiratory illnesses.

~~~~

I spent the next couple of days taking it easy and doing very little. It was hard to refuse the delicious food on offer, and Marleni kept telling me that I could eat the food, as long as it wasn't hot. According to Marleni, it was my eating of hot food that had caused me to get sick. She instructed me to eat my food *tibia* (luke-warm). For the rest of our time with Marleni she kept drumming it in to me, *'come tibia'*, and even once she'd left Huanta she would phone me to ensure I was eating *tibia.*

I was given many home remedies to cure my diarrhoea. One of these involved boiling the seed of an avocado and then drinking the water, which took on a slightly nutty flavour. Other times various local herbs were added to boiling water before drinking. The problem was that I would think I was cured, eat normally, and then it began all over again.

~~~~

During our first few days in Huanta, we saw little of Marleni. She didn't leave the house and didn't always join us for meals, saying she felt too ill and complaining of a sore throat. She asked us to buy her some special and very expensive medicinal honey from town to soothe her throat, which of course we did. It must have worked because by the end of our first week in Huanta her health improved and she regained some of the cheekiness and humour that had endeared her to us six years before.

Michael and I wondered why it was that she and Nélida had not looked for work. We instigated another family discussion, this time with Marleni, Nélida, Celestino and Carmen. We suggested to Marleni that now that she seemed a little healthier she could begin looking for work. We thought it would probably do her the world of good, both mentally and physically, to get out of the house and go to work. As for Nélida, who at 16 had finished school and was just hanging around the house, we told her we couldn't understand why she wasn't out looking for a job. Michael and I thought that she was just being lazy, and explained that we had both had part time jobs from when we were in our early teens.

'The problem is,' said Celestino, 'that there are no jobs in Huanta.'

'But there are,' I contradicted, 'when Michael and I were walking through town we noticed that many shops had handwritten signs advertising their need for a worker. Nélida needs to grow up and go in and ask about these jobs.'

Marleni then explained that the problem with these jobs was that they expected you to work long hours, late into the evening, and you got paid so little that by the time you paid for your *moto-taxi* fare there and back and bought lunch each day, you wouldn't have any money left over. It was okay for those that lived in Huanta's centre, who didn't have the extra travelling expenses, but because they lived a few kilometres out of town, it wasn't worth their while. Celestino added that he also needed Nélida to help him in the house and to look after baby Jharol.

Marleni, however, appreciated my explanation that the family couldn't expect our support to continue forever, and that they had to learn to fend for themselves. 'You are right; I will go and see my *padrino* this afternoon. A while ago he mentioned the possibility of a job. I'm not lazy.'

True to her word, later that afternoon, Marleni got changed out of her track suit pants and the many old jumpers she wore. She suffered terribly from the cold, and even when the rest of us were dressed lightly she still complained that she was feeling cold, despite her layers of clothing. Once she'd put on a pair of jeans and a nice jumper, brushed her hair and flashed her gorgeous smile, the transformation was amazing. She no longer looked like an unhappy, grumpy, sick girl, but an attractive confident young lady.

Having visited her *padrino*, Marleni came back that night with a big smile. 'My *padrino* might have a job for me. He asked me to come back tomorrow, and he'll let me know.'

~~~~

On Wednesday, Michael and I travelled by *colectivo* to Ayacucho to meet up with Mariluz, as she hadn't returned to Huanta since she'd left on Sunday night. Having asked us if we wanted to visit the lookout, she guided us through the city and then up a steep hill. We all made it, even though I was feeling quite weak and only eating bananas all day to try to shake the diarrhoea which hadn't abated, and Mariluz was wearing her good high-heeled city shoes. It was worth it. We had almost a 360 degree view over the city.

We took this opportunity to find out more about the family. We were interested to know why her parents had had six children – whether it was through lack of family planning knowledge, or otherwise. Mariluz surprised us by explaining that it was intentional.

'My father had always wanted a boy who could work with him and then look after him in his old age and take over his affairs. Although Wilbur was the second born, he was a sickly child who was not expected to survive. For this reason, *mamá* and *papá* kept on trying for another boy. After Nélida (child number six) was born, *mamá* said she couldn't go through any more pregnancies. So they stopped there, realising they had to give their six children the best education they could. Despite having wished for another son, *papá* loved all his children unconditionally and taught us all good principles and values by which to live.

'We were brought up to believe that family is paramount and that the whole family needs to care for one another and work together. Honesty was of utmost importance to my *papá*, and no matter how poor or desperate we were, he taught us that we must never steal. We grew up knowing the importance of helping our neighbours and being kind to others in the community, even if they didn't reciprocate.'

Mariluz told us that Celestino shunned drinking and smoking and instilled in his children that both are expensive as well as being
~~~~

bad habits, not only for one's own health but for that of the community as well.

We had noticed underneath their house in Huanta, a large piece of butcher's paper on which quotes were written. Mariluz explained that Celestino used to sit them all down regularly and run through his teachings so that his children could use them as a basis to succeed in life.

On one page was written:

To live with philosophy is:

a) to find an answer to the meaning of life
b) to have 'x' reasons to live with optimism
c) to conquer our inner world, not just the outside
d) to know that 'impossible' doesn't exist, only impossibilities
e) to give meaning to our lives and,

There are no geniuses, only perseverance

On another sheet of paper were some words written in Quechuan, and I asked Mariluz for a translation. She said that they are the values that her parents taught them to live by: *ama llulla* (don't lie), *ama yella* (don't be idle or lazy), *ama sua* (don't rob).

At the same time, Mariluz told me, they were taught the following principles to be good people: love, respect, responsibility, punctuality, humanity, humility, courage, honesty, peace, freedom and generosity.

On other sheets of paper, spread around the house, were various proverbs including:

'God delays but doesn't forget',

'Patience is bitter, but its fruits are so sweet',

'If you spit up to the sky, it returns on your face' etc.

~~~~

Mariluz told us more about the continuing problems between Celestino and his siblings. She explained how her father had grown up with nothing and had worked hard for over twenty years to make something of himself. He and his brothers had bought, and divided between them, a block of land in the *selva*, so that each of them could have their own *chacra* to grow food for their respective families as well as produce to sell.
~~~~

Celestino and Carmen had grown coffee as a cash crop on their *chacra,* and Celestino had built a small hut on his parcel of land for his immediate family. He had also built, together with his brothers and sister, a house in Sivia, which any of the siblings or their families was theoretically free to use. (This was the house we had been made to sleep outside of in 2004).

After working hard at their *chacra* for several years, Celestino and Carmen had raised enough capital to buy a car and Celestino started up a business transporting people and goods to and from the *selva.* He'd worked extremely long hours between his different ventures, and described himself as a 'workaholic'. Suddenly his world imploded in 1995 when, in his late thirties, he fell ill and found himself unable to work. He believes that his illness is due to the incredible amount of work he was doing at the time, coupled with inadequate nutrition. Celestino moved his family back to Huanta to be closer to medical care.

Celestino's brothers promised to look after the business for him while Carmen continued to look after the *chacra.* The brothers however, taking advantage of his illness, took over the business and the car without paying him a cent. There was nothing he could do about it. His siblings are still trying to take over the *chacra,* saying that a woman alone cannot look after it, and they have told Celestino that the house in Sivia does not belong to him at all.

Mariluz was attempting to go through legal channels to resolve the issue, but this was becoming quite costly and time consuming.

~~~~

I had another question for Mariluz. I had noticed that she spells her second surname differently to her siblings, with a 'y' instead of an 'i', and I asked her about the origins of their family name. In Peru, as in many other Spanish descendent cultures, a person's surname is derived from their father's first surname, followed by their mother's first surname. So, although all of the kids are Carbajal Moreira (apart from Mariluz), their parents have different surnames. Celestino's surname is Carbajal Gonzales and Carmen's is Moreira Rojas. Mariluz explained that on her birth certificate her mother had spelt Moreira incorrectly with a 'y', and thus Mariluz's official name is Mariluz Carbajal Moreyra.
~~~~

~~~~

We met up with Karina for a late lunch, after which Mariluz, Michael and I returned to Huanta.

As we walked through the front gate, Marleni raced over excitedly. 'You won't believe it, but I've got a job in the *selva* doing translating work in the communities. I'll be translating from Spanish into Quechuan and reverse for the medical teams.'

'That's wonderful Marleni, when will you start?'

'I'm being picked up by a 4 x 4 vehicle at one o'clock in the morning.'

We were flabbergasted.

'Are you serious? Are you really leaving in the middle of the night, *tonight*?'

She affirmed that was the case, and we gave her a big hug and burst into tears. We hadn't meant for her to get a job so quickly; she wasn't yet fully recovered and we worried about her making the long journey in her weakened state. Nor were we ready for her to leave us, and we worried that she was doing this only to prove a point. We would miss her terribly and wished we'd never said anything, but it was too late to change her mind now – it was all set.

Marleni assured us that the work was only for a week, and that she would be back before we left, easing our minds a little. We still found it impossible to fathom that she had only seen her *padrino* the day before, and now she was to be leaving this same night. Mariluz later explained that this is how things work in Peru and that Marleni always makes snap decisions and sticks by them.

We went to bed not believing it would really happen. Then at about 2 am we were awoken by the bleating horn. Marleni really was leaving.

We were left feeling quite shaken – what if something happened to her? We would never forgive ourselves. We began to question our own morality in relation to work. We had been imposing our own work ethic onto an indigenous family who believed that family was of utmost importance. We *gringos,* with little understanding of their culture, were telling them that work was more important than time with family. Maybe it was actually *we* who needed a lesson in what is important in life.
~~~~

~~~~

The next day Nélida and I walked into town to do the grocery shopping, leaving Michael and Wilbur digging in the back yard. We bought a large quantity of fruit and vegetables, loading it all into my backpack. I tried to get Nélida to carry it some of the way, but she complained that it was too heavy – which it was for someone of her slender build and unused to carrying a load. (It probably weighed around twelve kilograms). As we approached the house I gave the pack to Nélida, saying that as a joke, we'd tell everyone she had carried it the whole way back from Huanta. When her parents and Margot felt its weight they were most impressed with her strength.

A couple of days later Michael and Nélida walked into town alone, and when they returned Nélida was again carrying the pack and complaining that her back hurt as the pack was so heavy. I asked if she had carried it the whole way, and she said she had. Later on I asked Michael if she had really carried it all the way, and he confirmed that she had, even though she'd whinged the whole way back saying her back hurt and it was too heavy. I berated Michael for being so cruel.

'But you made her carry it all the way back, and it was even heavier then,' replied Michael, surprised at my reaction. I explained to him that it had been a joke and that she hadn't carried it far at all.

Nélida complained that her back hurt for the next few days, but she didn't seem to hold it against Michael of whom she was particularly fond.

~~~~

Michael and I were looking forward to Karina's return for the weekend, and we told Carmen that we would like to cook Saturday's lunch. Having enjoyed the spaghetti Michael had cooked on our previous visit, she asked him if he would prepare that again.

This time we were able to convince Carmen that we could walk into town by ourselves and manage the shopping on our own. On the previous days when we had walked into town to buy groceries, hoping to be able to spend some time alone, Carmen had always insisted that Nélida join us. Nélida, although not so enthusiastic about walking, enjoyed the outings because she could always talk Michael into buying her an ice-cream or some other treat. Having discovered a fresh juice bar, this also became a regular indulgence on most trips to town. We usually chose a *surtido* – a delicious blend of pineapple, papaya and carrot juice.

Shopping on our own, we once again found the vendors to be friendly and happy to talk to us.

We approached the stall in which a young woman was surrounded by huge sacks filled to the brim with quinoa, rice, wheat, *kiwicha*, ground corn, soy beans, chick peas, lentils or any other type of legume or grain imaginable. I asked to buy quinoa.

'Which one do you want?' The vendor asked, 'do you want the quinoa for 4 sols or 6 sols per kilo?'

'Um, what's the difference?' I asked.

She looked at me as if I was stupid, but patiently explained: 'this one,' indicating a sack to her right, 'is washed and is of a superior quality,' while this one,' indicating another sack, 'is coarser and may contain more husks.'

We opted for the superior quality – still cheap by our standards, although I was surprised at how expensive it was compared to all the other local foods. We found out later that since the Western world discovered and popularised the benefits of this super-food, the international demand for quinoa has become so high that it has driven up the price in Peru and Bolivia, where the poorer people now cannot afford their once staple foodstuff. This adversely affects their health as they are missing out on its nutritional benefits.

When buying the rice we went through a similar procedure, there being several choices. The rice was however, much cheaper. The *garbanzos* were easy – there was only one sack. I now had the chick peas to make a hommus dip for the family. They had never tried it. I was unable to buy tahini, but would improvise with something else.

We bought some olives, thinking they would make a tasty addition to the meal and something the family may not have tried.

Once home, Michael and I began chopping up the vegetables for lunch. We shooed Carmen out of the kitchen, telling her that she should relax while we worked. She was so unused to relaxing that she didn't know what to do with herself. Eventually she took a chair and sat with Celestino. It was lovely to see the two of them together laughing and chatting – a rare occurrence.

Mariluz came to be our *peon* in the kitchen, washing and chopping while Michael directed, jokingly scolding her if it wasn't up to scratch.

Karina arrived just in time for lunch and even Celestino joined us in the dining room. Often he stayed outside and ate his lunch alone, because it was too hot for him in the small crowded dining room.

Everyone had been looking forward to Michael's spaghetti but then we noticed, as they started eating, there were a few funny faces made and we watched Karina and Nélida picking out the olives. They were clearly not impressed by this strange new food. The others all politely said they enjoyed the meal, although no-one was too keen on the olives. The leftovers were polished off by Vladimir and Román, who miraculously seemed to appear at meal times. They always ate whatever was offered to them. They didn't mind the olives!

~~~~

In the afternoon I suggested it was time to relive old times and go to the *río* for a bath. The kids excitedly agreed. Although the water was considerably colder than on our previous visit, I still thought everyone would go in. For years now, the younger girls had been writing how they *'longed for the day when we could once again all go bathing together in the river'*. And every time we talked on the telephone they would mention the fun we'd had together in the river. However, despite my best persuasive efforts, only Carmen, Mariluz, the two young cousins and I braved the water. Karina, Margot, Nélida and Michael all complained it was too cold. I was disappointed, but there would still be plenty of time to go to the river again before we left Huanta.

~~~~

Michael, Mariluz and I wanted to plan a special Sunday outing for everyone. We came up with the idea of a walk to the *Christo Blanco*, a huge white statue of Jesus Christ high up on the hills behind Huanta, followed by a picnic at the same cascades and waterfall where we'd been six years before. Michael and I said we would prepare all the food, including the hommus, as well as cooking the breakfast. Everyone happily agreed.

For breakfast I made a thick hearty porridge, something the family had never tried. They sometimes made a milky drink from oats, but had never made porridge as we know it. Everyone was enthusiastic about the porridge (apart from Michael who never eats it), and Carmen said she would make it at home in the future.

We knew it would be a long and difficult walk so Wilbur would drive the hired *moto-taxi* (which he'd kept for the week) with Carmen and the baby, and Margot who was unable to walk far due to her aching back. The walkers were joined by cousins Mirian, Vladimir and Román, taking our group to eight. It took us one and a half hours to reach the *Christo Blanco*, with some of us (especially the *gringos*) struggling to climb the many stairs to the top. Even though we had been in Huanta for only ten days and should have maintained some of our cycling fitness, Michael and I were still struggling with the altitude. Wilbur timed it well and arrived not long after the walkers.

The *Christo Blanco* was enormous from up close, towering 15 metres over our heads. I was amazed that we hadn't noticed it last time we were in Huanta, but Mariluz told us that it had only been finished a couple of years ago. The view was fabulous. We could see all of Huanta and the orange-coloured ranges across the valley.

I pulled out the special treats we had brought with us from Chile, but first I asked a cheeky question: 'Who likes Chile?' The younger kids all said they liked Chile, while predictably, Mariluz and Karina stated their dislike. 'In that case,' I teased the older girls, 'you wouldn't like to eat Chilean chocolate and biscuits.'

'I'd rather die than eat *Chileno* food!' was Mariluz's grinning response.

On sharing out the sweet treats to all the others, but excluding Karina and Mariluz, the temptation of chocolate (a rare treat) proved too much for Karina who eventually capitulated and said she liked Chile. Mariluz remained steadfast in her convictions and said she wouldn't eat Chilean food. (I did save some for her, and later that night when she ate it, she had to agree it was very nice chocolate)!

After a good break and lots of photos, the walkers headed off cross-country in the direction of the *Cascadas* Huanyocc, with instructions for Wilbur to meet us in the village of Huanyocc. We took a few wrong turns and ended up in private properties, which stressed the girls. 'What if we are seen?' I told them not to worry – I'd just tell the property owner we were lost *gringos*. We only met one landowner on whose property we were trespassing, and he smilingly gave us directions.

Wilbur and his passengers were waiting for us in the village, wondering why it had taken us so long. We then all headed up to the cascades together on foot. The narrow path became steeper as we neared the *Cascadas* and with steep drop-offs. Carmen said she didn't want to go all the way to the falls carrying Jharol, so we picked a grassy embankment on which to have the picnic lunch.

It was hard to keep the ravenous walkers away from the food while Michael and I laid it out. Before calling out *come,* I explained what to do with the hommus, and then it was a free-for-all as everyone attacked the food. The idea of the hommus spread was quite novel to them as the only spreads they'd ever tried (apart from avocado) was the peanut butter and vegemite we had brought them on our previous visit. The hommus was definitely more popular than the olives had been, with most saying they loved it.

The picnic was once again a huge success. Margot commented how nice it was to have most of the family together, but Celestino and Marleni were sorely missed.

Once our hunger was satisfied, we left Carmen and Jharol behind and continued on up to the *Cascadas* to enjoy the waterfall. We waded across the shallow creek to get closer to the falls, and had a moment of panic when we saw the water level in the creek suddenly rising. They must have opened some sluice gates upstream. We had to take great care on crossing back, with the fast-moving water now up to our knees.

All of us, including Carmen with Jharol and Margot, walked back to Tablachacra following the river, while Wilbur departed with the *moto* to earn some money. On the way back we stopped for a bath, this time with most taking the plunge, but we still couldn't get Nélida in the water. She couldn't remember the last time she'd had a full wash – either in the river or under the shower – so Michael nicknamed her 'stinky'. (She did periodically wash her face and hair under the basin tap in the yard).

The weekend was over all too quickly and Karina had to go back to Ayacucho for classes the next day. We missed her terribly during the week when she was away.

After farewelling Karina, we (Carmen, Mariluz and I) set to work picking a large bagful of corn from the backyard *chacra* in order to make *humitas*. Peru is home to numerous varieties of corn with the large-kernelled type we picked that day being the most common, each kernel being up to one and a half centimetres in diameter.

Once back at the house we peeled the husks from the corn, taking special care to keep the leaves intact. They would be needed later. The next job was to painstakingly hand-pick each individual kernel off the cobs. Although a time consuming job, the Peruvians were so adept at it that it didn't take as long as I'd expected. Then the kernels were laboriously ground in the hand-grinder. Carmen and Mariluz happily chatted while grinding away, but when it was my turn I tired quickly, surprised by just how much muscle power was required. Special spices and sugar were then added to the corn. Finally, a small quantity of the corn mixture was placed in a corn husk, along with a couple of sultanas, wrapped into a little parcel and then packed into a large cooking pot. Carmen and Mariluz were incredibly proficient at making the *humitas*, with little fuss. I caused much laughter as I clumsily and messily assembled my parcels, most of which fell apart as soon as I'd finished. Once all the mixture was used up and all the parcels neatly stacked in the pot, it was filled with water and boiled for half an hour.

The result was delicious and we enjoyed the *humitas* for dinner, and then breakfast the following day. They were quite different to the *humitas* we'd enjoyed in Chile, a bit sweeter and less spicy, but just as nice – although Mariluz said that of course the Peruvian *humitas* were *far* superior to the Chilean ones.

~~~~

That evening, Wilbur didn't arrive home. Everyone was very worried as it was unusual for him not to come home, and the
~~~~

family relied on him to bring the *pan* and *palta* for dinner. They had previously told us that they didn't like him driving at night because there had been two *moto-taxi* drivers murdered during the last couple of years.

By nine o'clock when we were all getting ready for bed, Wilbur had still not appeared and Celstino and Carmen were beside themselves with worry. Michael and I drifted off to sleep hoping that everything was okay. In the middle of the night we were awoken by a commotion and were relieved to hear Wilbur's voice. We dropped back off to sleep, knowing we would find out in the morning what had happened.

Wilbur didn't make an appearance until late into the morning and then, with a sheepish look, he gave us an explanation. 'I worked on into the evening as I was getting plenty of fares. Then some of my friends asked me to come out with them. We drove out of town with a case of beer, and my friends got very drunk. I only had a couple of beers because I knew I had to drive my friends back home and I couldn't afford any more. I got home at two o'clock in the morning.'

Celestino was furious with Wilbur for being so irresponsible. He told him he needed to think about his family and provide for them, rather than wasting his money on alcohol. He called him a bad ungrateful son and told him he was ashamed that he had behaved like this while Michael and I were with them. Celestino asked Michael and me to speak firmly to Wilbur telling him how irresponsible he'd been and that he needed to behave more responsibly in the future. Apparently this was the second time something like this had happened.

Although we could understand Celestino's anger, Michael and I actually thought it quite amusing that at 26 years of age, Wilbur was now pushing the boundaries and doing what most young people do as teenagers. We believed him when he said he'd only had a couple of drinks, however we impressed on him how worried we'd all been. Wilbur apologised profusely and promised to be a good son in the future. We reassured him that we still considered him to be a responsible son who does look after and provide for his family.

CHAPTER 18 Final Week in Huanta

12 April 2010

Monday morning and Michael and I managed another solo shopping expedition to town, to buy ingredients for the stir-fried vegetable dish I was planning to cook for *almuerzo*. We were able to locate most of the items we were seeking, but ginger was proving difficult to find. I was sure that it must be available, but with all my attempts to ask for *jengibre* I was met with blank stares. Thinking it must be my pronunciation, I showed the shopkeepers the entry in the dictionary, but they still had no idea what we were after. Just when we'd enquired at the umpteenth stall and were about to give up, I spotted some, hidden amongst the potatoes, and made my purchase. On our return to the house I asked Carmen what they called this root, and she gave me a totally different name. Our guess was that it was called by its Quechuan name in Huanta rather than the Spanish name.

Many fruits and vegetables are known by different names in Latin America from those in Spain, and then many are even different in the various South American countries. Avocado is called *palta* in Chile, Bolivia and Peru, but once we got to Ecuador we found it was known as *aguacate*, as it is in Spain. Likewise, beans had different names. In Chile we had to ask for *porotos*, whereas in most of the other Latin American countries, including Peru they were *frijoles*. It kept us on our toes.

I prepared the stir-fry much the way I would at home, using only a sparing amount of oil. This was quite different to the way the Carbajal Moreiras are accustomed to cooking, using large quantities of oil. They tend to eat a lot of deep-fried food. I explained the health benefits of using less oil and also the savings to be made as oil is quite expensive. They could see my point. Most of the family said they enjoyed my cooking, although I think they may have considered it better with more oil!

That afternoon Mariluz received a call from her boss telling her that she had to report immediately to the office in Ayacucho. She was to prepare all her materials ready to leave for the *selva* the following day. Mariluz was understandably very upset, as they had told her that she wouldn't be leaving until Thursday. With tears streaming down her face, she told us she didn't want to leave and was going to quit her job. We convinced her to go, sad as we were to see her depart.

With Mariluz now gone, only three of the young Carbajal Moreiras remained in Huanta. During the day, Nélida was the only one with whom we could do things, as Wilbur was working and Margot was either at school or studying at home. Carmen, Celestino and baby Jharol were also at home.

The high school operated with two sessions – a morning session and an afternoon session – in order to cater for the large number of students in Huanta and its surrounds. Margot's timeslot was the afternoon, from 1 pm to 6 pm, although she often arrived home earlier because either her maths or her English teacher hadn't shown up. She said they'd been without an English teacher for most of the year, and without a maths teacher for a few weeks. 'I get so frustrated,' she said, 'I really want to learn, but how can I when we don't have a teacher?'

I often sat down with Margot and went through some English work, but the teaching she'd had was very basic and, as often as not, incorrect. It led to a lot of frustration on both sides.

'That sentence is incorrect,' I'd say pointing at the words Margot had written in her exercise book.

'No, it's not,' Margot would counter, 'it must be correct because my previous teacher told me it was. We would argue back and forth and poor Margot wasn't sure who to believe. Due to the dreadful teaching, her English was pretty well non-existent, even though she had supposedly been learning for a few years.

On one of our *colectivo* trips to Ayacucho I chatted to the woman seated next to me, a retired school teacher. She explained that teachers' salaries were so low that she and her husband, a school principal, still needed to supplement their income by running a business on the side. She told me that it was due to the inadequate pay that many schools had difficulty attracting teachers, especially in more remote areas. This explained why Margot was without teachers.

~~~~
~~~~

On Tuesday afternoon Mariluz phoned with the good news that she didn't have to leave for the *selva* until Thursday, although she would have to remain in Ayacucho to participate in training. We arranged to meet her and Karina for lunch on Wednesday.

During lunch, the girls told us more about their younger years and about their brother. Mariluz's explanation of Wilbur as a sickly child helped us to gain a greater understanding of him. We knew that Wilbur didn't like manual work, as Michael had to cajole him into helping with the rock removal in the yard and, later, with digging a trench for a water pipe. Wilbur would make all sorts of excuses to get out of the work – it was too hot, or too wet, or he didn't feel like it now. Wilbur, however, idolised Michael, and couldn't refuse when Michael asked him to work alongside him. Wilbur lacked the stamina to work for long periods, but did as much as he could.

What Wilbur wanted more than anything in life was a *cuatro por cuatro*. He talked incessantly about buying a four-wheel drive and how he would, one day, be able to afford one, even if it meant selling the family home. He explained how he would take loving care of it and drive around looking 'cool'. He said he could also use it as a taxi to earn a living. He was obsessed with cars, and asked us if we could send him one. When we explained the prohibitive cost, he suggested we could just send the motor from our old car!

Michael and I often told Wilbur tall stories about our car. 'It's a huge 4WD, as big as your dining room, and it has wheels as big as a tractor's. It can even drive itself automatically.' The stories got taller and taller until he eventually caught on that we were teasing him, although the jokes continued throughout our stay. We promised to send him a photo of our car when we returned home.

Wilbur was teased mercilessly by his sisters (and by us), which he took in good humour. When we were looking in the *artesanía* markets that afternoon in Ayacucho, Mariluz spotted some little painted clay figurines of cars with passengers hanging out the window. She cheekily suggested we should buy one for Wilbur. Although she was only joking, Michael and I took the bait and picked out a yellow car with 'taxi' inscribed across the front.

This was Mariluz's final day in Ayacucho and she had several things to organise for work. She had to photocopy reams of notes, for which she had to pay, and then pick up all her materials to take down to the jungle. She was returning to Huanta with Michael and me as from there she would be leaving for the *selva* at 2.00 am. We hired a *colectivo* taxi and were astounded by the many heavy boxes of written papers, posters and materials that she was responsible for transporting to the communities in the *selva*, at her own expense. Not only this, but she wouldn't receive her salary until she had worked for a month. Michael and I could not believe how things were organised in Peru, and could now well understand Mariluz's reluctance in accepting this job.

She explained to us that when she arrived at Sivia, she would have a few days for preparation and to organise some way of transporting all the heavy boxes and materials to the communities, which were a five-hour hike away. The road, which had been cut by flooding the previous year, had still not been repaired. She had no idea how she would manage this.

~~~~

When we got back to Huanta it was already dark. We placed the little car on the driveway out the front of the house, found Wilbur and told him we had bought him a *cuatro por cuatro*. His eyes lit up. 'Where is it?'

'Parked out the front,' Michael told him.

A huge smile spread across his face as we said, 'come on, come and see it.' He really believed us, and we felt a bit cruel as he walked out through the front gate, looked around and said he couldn't see it.

'You walked right over the top of it,' we told him. He walked back, looking at the ground, and found the little car. Although obviously disappointed, he appreciated the joke and was thrilled by the model car. 'I will put it in my room until I get a real car. Then, I will put it on the dashboard, so when I drive around with Jharol everyone can see it.'

Like his siblings, Wilbur wanted to study. He wanted a job where he got to sit, all day, at a desk in a nice office. We don't think he realised that people sitting at desks actually had work to do, and are sure that he imagined himself sitting there looking important and doing absolutely nothing. He saw an office job as an easy option which, in a country like Peru, it undoubtedly is.
~~~~

Unskilled workers in Peru do it even tougher than in other countries. For example, here in Australia the 'lollipop' workers hold up road signs, such as 'stop' or 'slow', and can be seen leaning on their sign, in a relaxed pose, their legs crossed over. In Peru the signs only have short handles and the workers have to hold them up in the air for hours at a time.

Wilbur had told us back in 2004 that he'd wanted to study, but we'd told him then that as the family had bought the *moto-taxi* for him to drive, he needed to earn money for the family first and his time to study would come later. Wilbur believed that it was now his turn to study – he had been working for all these years, Mariluz had finished her studies and Karina was soon to finish. He was the second born, after all. We couldn't argue with his rationale, although we remained dubious about his ability to complete tertiary education. He wanted to study accounting at a business college, and his family thought he had the aptitude to complete the course, so we were unable to refuse the family when they requested a small sum to cover his application fee.

~~~~

After an evening full of tears and emotion, we were awakened at two o'clock in the morning, yet again, by the sound of a car horn, this time to take Mariluz away. We got up to bid her farewell and the tears were still streaming down her face as she repeated that she didn't want to leave. Michael and I both felt worried and sad for her.

Later in the morning we were relieved to get a phone call from Mariluz announcing her safe arrival, but we weren't so happy to hear that she'd spent the entire seven hour journey crying, and was still crying into the phone as she told us she missed us and wanted to come home. It was heart-wrenching.

~~~~

Over the next couple of days Michael and Wilbur continued with the rock removal and then they commenced a new project. Celestino wanted to put in a pipe to carry water closer to the kitchen / dining room. He asked the boys to dig a trench, from the basin in the yard to just outside the cooking area, about ten metres in length.

Michael also took on another job of his own accord. He commented to Celestino that the access to their property was a bit difficult. It was now a steep and muddy, slippery ramp.

'It has been like that ever since the council built the new footpath right out the front of our house,' Celestino explained, 'and that was about two years ago.'

So Michael decided he would try to improve the access by building some mud-brick steps. When Celestino and Carmen heard the digging outside, they went out to investigate and saw Michael hard at work. Michael explained to them what he was doing and asked, '*Está bien*?' to which they giggling replied, '*Sí, está bien.*' Then Michael asked them what the neighbours might think of the fact that they had a *gringo peon.* They exchanged a few words in Quechuan and then replied, still giggling, that it would be better if he came inside the back yard to work, as the neighbours might think it a bit strange.

~~~~

On one of our morning walks, Margot and Nélida showed us how they collected *cochinilla* from the cactus plants, which grow wild and prolifically around their area. As they painstakingly scraped the cochineal off the fleshy parts of the plant with a spoon, Nélida explained that great care was needed to avoid getting spiked by the cactus spines. 'It can take many hours to collect a tiny amount of *cochinilla*, but even small amounts can be sold at the markets for a few soles. We don't earn much from our many hours of work, but when it is later sold overseas, it fetches huge sums of money,' she said.

'When we were younger, Margot continued, 'we all used to spend hours after school, collecting the *cochinilla* to make some pocket money.

Cochinilla are actually tiny insects that when crushed release a bright red colour. Back in the time of the conquests it was the third most valuable commodity after gold and silver. Even though synthetic dyes have largely taken over, the *cochinilla* still fetches a good price and continues to be used in lipsticks and for the dying of fabric.
~~~~

~~~~

During our quiet week in Huanta we had a lot of time to talk with Celestino, who told us he was suffering terribly with all his afflictions. He hated having to watch Michael and Wilbur doing all the hard manual work without being able to assist.

'I used to love to work,' he told us, 'and now all I can do is sit around. I can't stand up for more than five minutes at a time as the pain becomes too great. You don't know how much I would love to be able to help with the manual work.' When Celestino did get up to help with some of the work, for a few minutes at a time, the pain on his face was clearly visible. 'My worst affliction now, 'Celestino confided in us, 'is that I am going blind and every day my sight deteriorates further. Soon I won't be able to see at all. He had been an avid reader, but now he was unable to read and was finding this difficult to tolerate. We couldn't do any more than commiserate with him his misfortune. It wasn't until several months after our return that Mariluz wrote that Celestino's blindness was caused by cataracts, which had now grown right across his eyes.

~~~~

During one of our discussions with Celestino, he told us about the many jobs that remained to be done around the house, such as installing ceilings in the bedrooms (the current 'ceilings' were still sheets of plastic pinned to the walls) and installing a door on the bedroom shared by Carmen, Margot and Nélida. He rued the fact that the house was still so basic and had seen so few improvements since our last visit, but explained that he was unable to do the work and Wilbur wasn't strong enough.

I mentioned to Celestino how much I disliked walking up and down the ladder to the bedrooms and how dangerous I thought this was, reminding him of the time a few years earlier when Marleni had fallen from it and sprained her ankle. I suggested a handrail would make it much safer for everyone, and was a job that Michael and Wilbur could manage. He thought that a wonderful idea and said he would see what he could find under the house. He emerged with some planks of wood and later directed Michael and

Wilbur in its construction. Everyone in the family was most impressed with the handrail and they wondered why no-one had thought of that before. I wished I'd mentioned it at the beginning of our stay.

~~~~

On Friday, Michael and I again travelled to Ayacucho to meet Karina for lunch. She told us more about the conference for which she had been busily preparing over the past weeks. It was called MOEA – the 'Model of the Organisation of American States General Assembly'. There would be 500 students from 41 universities from across the Americas, including the USA and Canada. The conference was designed to promote democratic values. This year's theme was 'Peace, Security and Cooperation in the Americas'. The students had to draft, negotiate, debate and approve resolutions based on the position of the country they represented. The resolutions that were approved by the students would, the following month, be presented to representatives of the Governments who would be meeting in the 'General Assembly for the Organisation of American States' (OAS). Karina and her fellow students were working on a paper on indigenous human rights and the environment, something about which she was passionate.

This whole conference sounded like a wonderful opportunity for Karina, and would give her invaluable experience, especially as her ultimate dream was to work for the United Nations in the area of Human Rights. Although this sounded like a hefty goal for a poor indigenous girl, knowing Karina as we do, with her incredible drive, motivation, passion and charisma, we know that she has every chance of fulfilling her dream.

Karina also told us more about the thesis she had begun working on and the reason she had chosen to go down this path. The thesis was not a part of the degree, but was a component in the completion of her studies to become a fully qualified *abogada*. She would be finishing her degree in the next few weeks, but would still not be able to practise as a qualified lawyer until she had undertaken further study of some type. She explained that there were three ways to complete this further study. She could complete several more months of course work, she could do an extra six
~~~~

months of practical work, or finally she could become fully qualified by writing a thesis.

'Although this is by far the most difficult path to follow,' she carefully explained, 'I have opted to write the thesis, as it will give me greater prestige and superior job prospects. The negative side of writing the thesis is the cost involved and the amount of time needed.'

Karina outlined her projected expenses, which included having to pay for a supervisor and for a professor to review and approve the thesis. As her thesis was based around discrimination in *campesino* and native communities, she would have to travel to many distant places to conduct interviews and there would be considerable travelling costs. There would also be costs for photocopying and printing, and she might also have to buy some books.

Michael and I had been thinking that Karina would finish her studies this year but instead here she was outlining close to another year of study. We had hoped that she would soon be earning her own living, not creating further expenses. Although she didn't ask us for money, she did mention that she didn't know how she would cover all her expenses. 'I will try to get some work,' she said, 'but until I finish my thesis I won't earn very much, and it would be hard to finish while working full-time.'

Michael and I had a little private discussion. We were proud of Karina and how well she was doing but wished she had chosen an easier path. On the other hand, we couldn't help but admire her incredible ambition and her dedication to pursue the most difficult (but ultimately superior) path. We decided to offer her more assistance and told her we would give her enough money to cover her costs. She promptly burst into tears of gratitude and assured us that she would not waste this opportunity. She would make us proud and one day she would have enough money to come and visit us in Australia.

We accompanied Karina to the local credit union where, with much excitement and emotion, she opened an account, her first ever bank account. We then withdrew the sum of money from our account and Karina deposited it into her new account. Her eyes were shining with gratitude. We impressed on Karina that this money was to be used only for the costs associated with her thesis.

It wasn't to be given to her father for other household expenses. Karina assured us that the money would all be spent on her thesis.

After lunch, we went with Karina to see her university and she proudly stood for a photo with each of us in front of her faculty building, on which was inscribed in large letters, '*Facultad de Derecho y Ciencias Políticas*'. Faculty of Law and Political Sciences. Tears of pride for our *ahijada* welled up in our eyes.

Michael and I walked back to the city centre and then walked around Ayacucho making enquiries at the bus stations. As we walked from one end of town to the other, the choking fumes of the *moto-taxis* and old cars were getting to us, as were the crowds of people everywhere we walked. We felt for the people who had to live with this every day. We were also fed up with travelling to and fro between Huanta and Ayacucho. Even though it was only a fifty minute trip in a *colectivo* taxi, or a bit over an hour in a *colectivo combi,* the cheaper alternative, it was often a hair-raising trip along the winding roads. The faster drivers, of whom there were many, screeched around the bends and overtook other vehicles on blind corners, causing our stomachs to be tied in knots.

Although we knew we would miss our family, Michael and I were ready to leave Peru; however we had one small holiday still to organise. Before leaving home, we had talked about taking two of the older girls on a holiday to Arequipa and the Colca Canyon, one of the deepest canyons in the world, and located in southern Peru. Michael was a bit dubious about the idea, but agreed that it would be a lovely end to our holiday and would give the girls an opportunity to see some more of their country. However, neither Mariluz (due to work) nor Karina (due to her studies and the conference) would be able to accompany us. Mariluz and Karina begged us to take their mother, saying how much she deserved a holiday and adding that she had never had one in her life. They suggested we could also take Nélida with us as Marleni was still in the *selva* and Margot had to attend school.

Of course we had to agree to their idea although I was a bit nervous about travelling with Carmen as we found communication with her a bit difficult at times. Even though her Spanish was much better than ours, she used it differently and was unable to change the sentence structure around or use different words, if we didn't understand something. We also often had trouble making ourselves understood and then required one of the girls to assist us. Michael, however, was delighted with the idea of travelling with Carmen.

I asked Carmen if she would like to accompany us (half hoping she'd decline), and her face lit up in excitement. We were committed. And seeing her enthusiasm, I couldn't help but be equally thrilled.

The only place, apart from the *selva*, to which Carmen had travelled outside of Huanta was Ayacucho, and that was only to connect with transport. She didn't like the big city with its crowds of people and she had never been to any other towns or cities in Peru. By this stage of our trip, however, Michael and I had both had enough of long scary bus trips and decided we couldn't face the 16-hour bus trip to Arequipa, so we suggested instead, that we take Carmen and Nélida to Pisco, on the coast, for three days. Everyone thought this a wonderful idea and we set Tuesday as our departure day, four days away. Carmen was unbelievably excited, like a young child, but she was worried about how we would get there, where we would stay, how much it would cost, what we would eat and all manner of other details. She wanted to know how we would be able to organise everything when we'd never been there before. We told her she was not to worry about anything as we would take care of the details and assured her that all would be fine. We reminded her of all the travelling we'd done in South America.

Marleni phoned us that evening and said she was feeling a little better and her work was going well. It was so good to hear her voice. Due to the warmer climate, her health was usually better when in the *selva*. We asked her when she was coming home, and she tearfully replied that her *padrino* told her he needed her to work for the second week and wouldn't allow her to come home. This would mean we wouldn't get to see her before we departed. We asked her to talk to him again and explain the situation and beg him to allow her to return on the weekend.

Later on Mariluz also phoned, in tears, saying how much she missed us, and wished she hadn't taken the job. She told us she had organised a donkey to travel with her to carry the boxes of materials to the communities, and she would be leaving on Sunday. After this she would be out of phone contact with us, causing her even more grief.

Marleni called again the next morning with the news that she'd been given permission by her *padrino* to come home on Sunday, but would have to pay for the return transport, as she wasn't staying the second week. I told her we wanted to see her before we left Huanta and assured her that we would pay her fare and also give her the hundred soles she would have earned the second week. She had proved her point that she could work, and we just wanted her back home to spend a bit more time with her and to farewell her properly.

Karina arrived on Saturday morning but could only stay a few hours as she had a meeting back in Ayacucho in the afternoon, but she promised to return on Sunday. Time was now passing rapidly and we weren't going to have much more time together.

On Sunday we waited for Karina to arrive, then walked to Huanta along with Nélida, Margot and Mirian, and then on to Quinrapa, where we had first met on that fateful day nine years before. The memories came flooding back, although the tiny quiet village was nothing like it had been during *fiesta* time. We walked over the same ground where Karina and her friend had sweet-talked the locals into giving us samples of their produce. We remembered and laughed about the bullfight, and how this one chance encounter had changed all of our lives forever.

After walking home and lunch, those of us who were left went to the *rio* for our final bath together. Even though the water was cold, everyone went in, including Nélida who'd finally been persuaded to have her first wash in over a month!

Although, with our western sensibilities, it sounds terrible for someone to go so long without a wash, in the dry climate of Huanta you don't get the same body odours as you do in a more humid environment. Even though we called Nélida 'stinky', as a joke, she actually wasn't smelly, even after going for so long without a wash.

Late that afternoon we were overjoyed with the arrival of Marleni, but that joy was tempered by her being quite unwell again. She complained that the seven hour return trip had been awful with cold air blowing on her the whole time, causing her illness to flare up again. Michael and I felt culpable, having begged her to come home before we left; nevertheless, she was as happy as we were that we would have some more time together before our departure in two days. We asked her if she'd also like to accompany us to Pisco, but she declined, stating she wasn't well enough.

On Monday, Michael and Wilbur finished off the trench and laid the pipes to the kitchen. Under Celestino's instruction, they installed a tap and filled in the trench. However, it wasn't long before we all noticed the yard becoming increasingly wetter. It appeared that one of the sections of pipe attached to the tap was leaking. A crack was found, and Celestino admitted that the piping was very old. There was nothing Michael could do about it as we were leaving the next day. And by the time we left, after it had been leaking all night, the yard was once again a quagmire. We just hoped that Celestino and Wilbur could sort out the problem.

Our final day, Tuesday, was an emotional day of farewells. Using the new digital camera's video function we videoed each person giving a farewell speech and they videoed us giving ours, so we would all have a lasting memory of our visit. Tears were cascading down everyone's faces, including Carmen's, even though she was travelling with us to Pisco. Poor Margot was beside herself with grief, and we were told later that she didn't stop crying for several hours.

We had grown much attached to the sensitive Margot and were also very sad to be leaving her. Margot lacked the natural ability of her sisters, but possessed an incredible driving spirit to succeed, and she put an immense effort into everything she did. Often, during English lessons, I would become frustrated with her doggedness and eagerness to understand concepts, which even after repeated explanations she still couldn't comprehend. I ran out of patience long before she did, and even though at times I felt like screaming at her, I loved her all the more for her determination and perseverance. We often found her lying on the mattress she shared with Nélida, in virtual darkness, with her books out, studying. She had had numerous obstacles to overcome in her eighteen years, but she was determined to succeed and make something of herself, despite ongoing health issues. We were going to miss her.

~~~~
~~~~

We had our final day all planned out. Michael and I, and Carmen and Nélida were going to spend the night in Ayacucho, before getting the bus to the coast on Wednesday morning. But, we wanted to spend some time alone with Marleni and Karina. So, Marleni accompanied Michael and me to Ayacucho to meet Karina for our final lunch together. Then after lunch, while Karina attended a meeting, Marleni and I went on a mission to find a CD with 'our song', *("El idiota: te amo")* from our 2004 visit. She also hadn't heard the song for many years and we were both keen to hear it again. We had asked at all the music shops in Huanta but had not been successful. Now in Ayacucho, we traipsed from one music shop to another until we found a compilation disc with the song on it. The shopkeeper played the song and happy memories came flooding back, to a time when Marleni was in a much happier and healthier state of mind. Delightedly I bought a copy for each of us.

Later in the afternoon, we met Carmen and Nélida in Karina's room, where they would be spending the night. Carmen's smile was as wide as her face and Nélida was equally excited. We sadly farewelled Marleni who had to travel back to Huanta before it became too late, and then took Nélida and her mother to *Mi Casa,* the same hostel we'd stayed at in 2001, and where Michael and I were going to spend the night. Karina joined us at *Mi Casa* after her meeting and we stayed up late into the night talking. Karina assured us she would be at the bus station in the morning to see us off, but it was still hard to let her go. We recorded a long and tearful message on the camera's video and finally it was time to say a heart wrenching good-bye to our gorgeous *ahijada* whom we knew we would miss terribly.

CHAPTER 19 Holiday in Pisco

Carmen, Nélida and Karina were already waiting at the bus station when we arrived at 8 am. Sadly, the time had come for Michael and me to bid our final farewell to Karina. The three of us found this to be incredibly difficult and emotional. With all her university commitments, Michael and I felt we hadn't been able to spend as much time with Karina as we would have liked. She felt the same. Now, with tightness in our chests and tears cascading down our faces, we had to say good-bye, not knowing when, if ever, we would see one another again. We were leaving Karina in Ayacucho to continue her studies while taking her mother and baby sister on the holiday we had wanted to share with her and Mariluz. We consoled each other with the parting words that the next time we met she would be a lawyer, and that *ojalá* we'd see her in Australia one day.

We had chosen Pisco as our holiday destination for a number of reasons. Firstly, it was on the coast and neither Carmen nor Nélida had ever seen the ocean. And, offshore from Pisco are the *Islas Ballestas*, which, with their incredible wildlife, have been likened to the Galapagos Islands. Secondly, it was not too far to travel, taking about six hours on the Lima-bound bus.

As we were travelling during the day, we had booked one of the cheaper buses, and even these were a huge improvement on the buses of six years ago. As we settled down in the comfortable seats, we thought we'd made a good choice of bus company. From Ayacucho the bus snaked its way up the hills and into the high Andes. Michael and I realised that of the five times we had travelled this route, this was the first time we were able to enjoy the views. Three of the previous journeys had been overnight and the other was on our way to Ayacucho in 2004, on the last stage of the gruelling three day journey from Nowra when we were exhausted and not yet acclimatised to the altitude, so hadn't been able to stay awake.

We passed through many picturesque small communities of little adobe houses enclosed by hand-built dry stone walls. The vast green high plains were dotted with sheep, alpacas and llamas. We were offered a snapshot of a traditional way of life as the *campesinos*, dressed in colourful traditional attire, herded their livestock, tended their fields and just went about their daily business.

We also passed through wilder, seemingly uninhabited, areas with gushing waterfalls and crystal clear rivers. We were fortunate to glimpse herds of vicuñas (the wild cousins of the alpacas), wild deer and soaring condors. We also spotted some rare flowering *puya ramondii.* This unique plant is the largest member of the bromeliads (pineapple family). It is found only in a few isolated areas high in the Andes of Peru and Bolivia. It takes a hundred years to grow and then flowers in a huge spike, up to ten metres tall, covered by up to 20,000 tiny flowers.

We continued winding our way up and down the mountains for several hours, delighting the senses. The highest pass on the road was 4,746 metres and the surrounding mountains well over 5,000 metres high, yet strangely there was no snow on the peaks. This is due to their proximity to the equator.

As beautiful as the first few hours in the mountains were, the final two hours of the trip were torturous. As we began the long steep winding descent into the desert coastal hills, the vegetation changed rapidly from the beautiful lush green pastures of the heights to dull brown and barren hills. The rivers, which had previously run so clear, began to look brown and polluted and the small typical communities gave way to dirty towns, cars and contaminated air.

The further we descended the hotter it became, and we realised that there was no air conditioning in the bus (or it wasn't functional), nor were there any windows that could be opened. The heat became oppressive, and many people were feeling the effects. Poor Nélida began throwing up and continued to do so until we reached San Clemente where, with huge relief, we left the bus. We were pleased we didn't have to continue to Lima, another three or four hours away. We promised Nélida and Carmen that we would make sure to book them an air conditioned bus for their return journey, whatever the extra cost.

We were now 20 kilometres from Pisco, so we took a taxi for the fifteen minute drive to the town centre. As we alighted, a tall, dark, good-looking young man approached.

'*Hola*, my name is William. Would you like to book a tour to the *Islas Ballestas?*'

'First we need to find some accommodation,' I told him.

'I can help you with that,' he responded, 'What sort of place are you looking for?'

Although I am normally wary of smooth-talking types like William, there was something about him that made me feel he was trustworthy. He assured us that he could find somewhere suitable to stay and within our budget. We followed William at a fast trot down the road. Not being comfortable walking on the busy road as William was, we walked along the footpath.

'Don't walk on the footpath,' William warned us, 'pieces of concrete are still falling down from the buildings even though the earthquake was over two years ago.'

The aftermath from the disastrous earthquake, which had made world news headlines in 2007, was still very visible in the piles of rubble that lay everywhere, the large cracks in buildings and in the air which was full of dust being blasted by the wind.

'Pisco used to be a beautiful clean town with clear air, but now it's all still such a huge mess and the air is always full of dust,' William said. 'It's so sad to think what it used to be and what it has been reduced to. We don't know when, if ever, we will recover from that disaster, but we are taking one step at a time and trying to encourage tourists to return to Pisco. It's not easy though.'

William took us to a hotel. When the attendant stated the price, Carmen shook her head forcefully. Even though by our Australian standards it was relatively inexpensive, we could tell that Carmen couldn't fathom that anyone could pay so much for a night's accommodation. I explained to William that we would prefer a hostel-type accommodation, and gave him our maximum price. He thought for a minute then told us he had another place in mind that might be more suitable.

While almost jogging to keep up with William's fast pace, he wanted to know how it was that two *gringos* were travelling with two indigenous Peruvians. I explained to him our relationship with the family, and sensed that he thought it a nice story and that he would be willing to go out of his way to assist. He took us to a rather plush looking hostel, and we were dubious that it would suit our budget. William approached the well-dressed and made-up bottle-blonde owner, telling her our maximum price and asked if she could help us out. The *Señora* replied that her rooms were more expensive than our top price. William pleaded with her, and told her we couldn't afford to pay any more than that. She capitulated and agreed to give us the two rooms for our agreed maximum price.

We asked the owner if there was a kitchen we could use to prepare our own meals. She said that although there wasn't a guest kitchen, she would make an exception and allow us to use the staff kitchen. She then pointed out the lounge room with its computer and internet connection, and said we were welcome to use that as well. We thought this all sounded wonderful and asked to see the rooms.

First we were shown Carmen and Nélida's room with its two single beds beautifully made up with frilly white bedspreads. 'We don't need two beds,' piped up Nélida. 'Mum and I will share one bed.' I explained to Nélida that we had to pay for two people and two beds. 'But that's a waste of money when we only need one bed,' Nélida stated.

Feeling my face turn red with embarrassment, I stole a furtive look at the *Señora* to see her reaction and was relieved to see her still smiling and seemingly unconcerned at Nélida's outburst. 'Nélida always shares a bed with her mother or her sister,' I explained and then commented that the rooms were lovely and that we'd like to stay.

The *Señora* told us that each room had an en-suite bathroom with hot water, and each was equipped with cable television. Nélida's eyes were growing wider by the minute and a smile spread across Carmen's face, which up until now had been quite impassive.

Prior to our trip to Pisco we had wondered how we would be received in hostels and tourist locations, travelling with an indigenous woman. Although Carmen didn't dress in traditional clothing, she definitely looked indigenous and her speech and posture reinforced this. We knew that the indigenous people of Peru were marginalised and seen as inferior, as in most other countries and cultures. We thought it might be a bit strange in a hostel with other young backpackers, so we were quite relieved that this hostel was a little more upmarket than most backpackers, and the *Señora* seemed lovely and willing to please us.

We thanked William and told him we'd come back to see him later in his office to organise a tour for the next day. The first thing we wanted was to shower and wash our hot sweaty bodies and smelly clothes, although Nélida seemed more interested in playing with the television and using the remote control to flick through the channels – something at which most children in the developed world are adept but a totally new experience for Nélida.

Michael and I craved some personal space and suggested to Carmen that we all have a shower followed by a short rest, and then meet in our room in an hour. Michael and I each had a cold shower, washed our clothes, draped them over the towel rail, and lay down for a short nap.

All too soon there was a knock on the door. Carmen wanted to know where she could hang out the washing. She didn't have the confidence to ask the *Señora* herself. I found the owner and she told me we could go up to the rooftop to hang the clothes on the lines there. (This is where most town and city-dwelling Peruvians hang their washing).

I asked Carmen if she'd enjoyed her shower.

'Yes,' she said, her eyes gleaming, 'that's the first hot shower I've had in my life; it was wonderful.'

Funnily enough, hot as we were at that time, Michael and I could think of nothing better than a cold shower, but for someone who had never had a hot shower, it was a real treat. Carmen told us that Nélida had also enjoyed her hot shower and was now glued to the television, which came as no surprise to us.

We went up to the roof-top to hang out the washing, although with the thick dust in the air, we thought it would come back dirtier than it had started. From the roof we had a great view of the city and could see the earthquake destruction all around. There were large piles of rubble, half-demolished houses and giant cracks in some of the buildings still standing. It was obviously going to take many more years to repair and rebuild the city.

It was difficult to prise Nélida away from the television, but we managed to do so and walked back into town to find William and organise a tour to the *Islas Ballestas* for the next day. When Carmen found out how much the tour was going to cost, she turned to us and whispered, 'I don't want to go, it's a ridiculous price. We're being ripped off.' Michael told Carmen that this was her holiday and it was her job to just enjoy it. 'You are not to worry about the cost, we are paying for everything and we don't want any arguments.' I mentioned that it would have been silly to come all the way to Pisco without experiencing these amazing islands, and that William had actually given us a good price. Carmen agreed to the tour.

William explained the morning's procedures. It would be an early start as that was when the ocean was at its calmest. We would be picked up at 7 am and driven to the neighbouring village of Paracas from where the boat tours departed. We would be on the boat for three hours, during which time we would cruise around the islands and see a huge array of sea animals and birds. Carmen was nervous about the safety of the boat and William assured her that the boats were all new, stable and safe, and said that all passengers had to wear a life jacket, which allayed Carmen's fears somewhat. After the tour we would be picked up and brought back to Pisco.

After walking back through town and looking at the shops, we went back to the hostel. Nélida went straight to her room and turned the television on, while Carmen seemed at a loss. Not ever having experienced leisure time and being out of her usual routine, she didn't know what to do with herself and was waiting for suggestions from us. We asked her if she wanted to watch TV with Nélida or come into our room and chat or go to the lounge room. She went into her room, and we found her there a little later, sitting upright on the edge of the bed looking at the wall, not knowing what to do and obviously not finding Nélida's channel-surfing very interesting. She was clearly quite uncomfortable in these unfamiliar surroundings, whereas sixteen year old Nélida was adapting quickly.

We found a small restaurant for dinner, where the owner obligingly said he would prepare something vegetarian for Michael and me. Carmen and Nélida enjoyed ordering off the menu, another new experience for them. Carmen was worried about the cost of the meal which, although cheap by our standards, was quite a bit more than a meal in Huanta. We reminded Carmen of our previous conversation about it being her holiday and she smiled and ordered her meal.

After dinner, we went to the supermarket to shop for breakfast food. Nélida's eyes widened in amazement as she saw all the available food choices. She had never been into a supermarket before and she excitedly began taking photos in all the different aisles until a security guard approached her and gruffly told her that she wasn't allowed to take photographs in the store. Apparently this was for security reasons. I explained to the guard that she was from the highlands and had never before seen a supermarket. He told her not to take any more but fortunately didn't ask her to delete those she'd already taken. She was pleased that she'd already taken quite a few!

We found some breakfast cereals and explained to Carmen and Nélida what they were. They had never seen breakfast cereals before, nor had they seen soy milk in a carton. Carmen laughed when I told her that it was soy milk and she asked how it could be soy milk when you have to soak the soy beans then cook them to make the milk. I asked Carmen and Nélida if they had drunk tea before and explained the use of tea bags to make a quick cup of tea. They agreed that it would save time in the morning and were happy to try it, along with the cereal and soy milk. I chose a tea infused with cinnamon and cloves, a tea I'd remembered enjoying on our first trip to Peru.

Both Carmen and Nélida were astonished at the quantity and variety of processed and packaged food on the shelves. They only rarely bought pre-packaged food. Virtually everything they bought in Huanta came from the markets and was bought from bulk quantities. On the rare occasions that anyone in the family bought a sweet treat for themselves, it would be a homemade item bought straight from a street vendor. They didn't buy pre-packaged biscuits or chocolate, as they were too expensive and anyway not so readily available. In Huanta, if they were hungry, they would snack on whatever was growing in their *chacra* at the time – corn, peas, *pacay*, or other fruit or vegetables.

We were up early to have breakfast before our 7 am pickup. Carmen and Nélida both said they enjoyed the breakfast cereal and the tea. Carmen was really relishing all her new experiences. We asked them how they'd slept in their comfortable beds. They had shared the one bed, as we suspected they would, and said they'd had a wonderful night's sleep.

On the way to Paracas, as we drove alongside the perfectly calm ocean, Carmen asked us the name of the 'lake' beside us. She squealed in delight when we told her it was actually the ocean. 'Really?' she asked, 'I always thought the ocean would be a darker colour and really rough.' I told her that the ocean colour can change depending on depth and location and that it was nice and calm now in the early morning but would probably get rougher in the afternoon. She became quiet when I told her that very soon she would be on a boat on that same ocean.

We were pleased to see the boats were quite big and new looking, as William had promised, and were equipped with a large high-powered outboard motor. Apparently there had been a few boat accidents in recent years and the tour companies had been compelled to buy safer boats and adhere to new strict guidelines.

Stepping down into the boat, we were allocated our seats and then given instructions on adjusting the life jackets. Being the last ones to enter the boat the four of us weren't all seated together, although fortunately Nélida was able to sit next to Carmen. I was watching Carmen's face and she was looking very nervous. Taking her hand, Michael assured her that it would be fine. Nélida looked totally relaxed, taking it all in her stride and with a big beaming smile on her face.

The boat took off slowly and travelled adjacent to the shore to the first point of interest, 'The Candelabra', a three pronged motif, over 100 metres high and 50 metres wide, etched into the hillside. It is not known by whom this geoglyph was made or its significance, but one theory is that it is connected in some way to the Nazca lines a little further south.

The boat then headed away from shore. The faster the boat travelled, the more nervous Carmen looked. Once a long way out from shore, the driver put the boat into top speed and I myself was feeling a bit nervy as it jumped from swell to swell, each time coming down with a loud thud. I turned around to smile at Carmen to assure her that it was fine and this was normal, masking my own discomfort. The tour guide, noticing Carmen's look of terror, knelt down beside her to reassure her.

Fortunately it was a quick trip out to the islands and, as we approached, the boat slowed down and we all breathed a sigh of relief. The guide explained the history of the islands. In the mid nineteenth century, this area was highly important to the Peruvian economy due to the large quantities of guano (droppings) produced by the sea birds. It was exported to Europe for use as fertiliser and became the most important source of revenue for Peru at the time. He explained that while the guano is still collected, the modern use of synthetic fertilisers now renders it less important for the economy. Tourism has taken over as being the major source of revenue for the country.

It soon became clear where all the guano came from. As we cruised slowly around the islands, thousands of sea birds flew around us. It was an incredible spectacle. Each species of bird had a separate roosting location. One rock island was home to thousands of Peruvian Boobies, while another was home to Peruvian pelicans. Other rocks were covered in cormorants, while scores of red-beaked terns wheeled in the sky around us. One island was home to hundreds of Magellanic penguins.

As for mammals, there were thousands of sea lions lying on gravelly beaches and swimming in the ocean. They could also be spotted lying on the rocks soaking up the sun, many appearing as if they were posing for the tourists.

We were all enthralled by the experience and, looking over at Carmen, we were pleased to see that her nervousness had disappeared and she was enjoying every minute of being so close to the animals. Nélida had a huge smile on her face as she snapped away with the camera.

The trip back to Paracas was thankfully smoother and Carmen's face was still beaming as she alighted from the boat.

'I loved it,' she enthused, 'all the *pajaritos* (birds) and *animalitos* were so gorgeous and so cute. I'm so happy you took us. Thank you, thank you. I will remember this day for the rest of my life. I can't wait to tell the rest of my family about the wonderful animals and show them the photos.'

We had never before seen Carmen so animated and excited; it was a delightful experience for us all.

~~~~

Carmen had been anxious about procuring her bus tickets to go home, so I made enquiries and found out that we would have to
~~~~

travel back to San Clemente to do this. Our hostel *Señora* told us where to find the *colectivos* heading for San Clemente, but beseeched us to be careful as the bus stop was in the busy markets area of town. Michael gave me the job of accompanying Carmen, who became nervous on hearing the *Señora's* warning, but I assured her we could manage it. And we did, leaving Michael and Nélida to their own devices. In San Clemente, we enquired at the various bus terminals and I made sure that I booked them a bus with air conditioning. Carmen was already feeling apprehensive about having to travel to San Clemente without us, and I assured her that Michael and I would travel with her and Nélida to the bus stop, and then get our onward bus from there.

Carmen and I caught another *colectivo* back to Pisco and found Michael and Nélida, who sheepishly told us that they'd been eating *papas fritas* (hot chips) and *helados* (ice creams), despite the huge Chinese meal we'd earlier had for lunch. We all walked back to the town centre to find William and tell him what a wonderful day we'd had and to book another tour for the following morning. He recommended a private tour of the Paracas National Reserve.

'I can find you a special driver and I am sure it will be an equally enjoyable tour,' he told us. We agreed on a price and then William made some phone calls. 'I've booked Luis for you as your taxi driver and tour guide. I am sure you will like him and he'll give you a great half-day tour. You won't be disappointed. Luis will pick you up from the hostel at 7.30 am.'

On the way back to the hostel we stopped off to buy some bread, eggs and avocados for dinner. Carmen and Nélida were horrified at the price of the avocados, which were at least five times more expensive than in Huanta.

'We can't buy those,' said Carmen, 'these people are *rateros*.' I explained to Carmen that things were cheaper in the highlands because the produce was grown close by and didn't have to travel so far. All food on the coast was a lot more expensive, as was housing and other living expenses. Wages were generally higher on the coast as well. It was good for Carmen to get some perspective on where she lived and to realise that, although they live in a poorer area, it did have its advantages. She couldn't understand how people could afford to survive in Pisco.

Back in the hostel, we fired up the computer and looked at the photos we'd taken that day, and both Carmen and Nélida loved reliving their time with the birds and animals. When the *Señora* asked Carmen how her day was, she even had the courage to answer her, 'it was *bonito* (beautiful),' she said with a beaming smile.

Michael introduced Carmen to the internet and she was astounded at what could be found there. He then had the wonderful idea of looking at Google Earth to give her and Nélida some understanding about the world and where Australia sits in relation to Peru. He went further than that, found our house and zoomed right in. I was also impressed, as I hadn't realised you could get so close, but Carmen's eyes were like saucers, trying to fathom how we could get such a clear picture of our house in Australia here on a computer screen in Peru. She was amazed at the well-kept gardens and lovely green lawns, something unknown in her world.

'Where are all the people?' she wanted to know, because in Peru there are always people everywhere. 'There is so much space and it's so tranquil and there's not one person on the street.'

Carmen, who now seemed so much more relaxed, said she was going to have a rest before dinner, and we were pleased she'd taken the initiative to do this on her own. Nélida went to watch television and Michael and I had a long talk with the *Señora*, telling her the whole history of our connection with Carmen's family. She thought it wonderful how we Australians were helping a Peruvian family and wished more people in her own country would be more philanthropic. We were lucky to have found such a lovely warm and understanding person with whom to stay.

While eating our picnic-style dinner that night in the dining room, we heard a huge bang and looked out the window to see a large commotion outside and crowds of people all looking up at the building. We went outside to see what was happening and discovered that a large piece of the concrete facade had come crashing down off the building next door, narrowly missing passersby. Now we understood what William had warned us about on the day we'd arrived.

~~~~
~~~~

Luis picked us up at the appointed time in the morning and drove us back past Paracas and into the *Reserva Nacional de Paracas*, a large peninsula, the whole of which is devoid of vegetation. It had the appearance of a red lunar landscape and was quite beautiful in its own way. The first place Luis stopped at was an old midden with mounds of large sea shells. Carmen went into raptures and asked Luis if she was allowed to collect some. Luis gave her a plastic bag and she delightedly filled it with shells to take home to Huanta.

Our next stop was a lookout overlooking Cathedral Rock, a large rock island jutting out from the sea and covered in sea birds and their guano. The sea was quite rough and beating onto the rocks below, scaring Carmen who wouldn't come right to the edge of the lookout to look down at the water. Our next adventure was to go down to the beach via a rough path through steep sand dunes. Carmen was terrified and held our hands tightly the whole way down. We could not believe that this was the same woman who could walk up steep, slippery and treacherous muddy tracks through the rainforest in the *selva*, and who could happily climb trees in Huanta to harvest fruit. Here, out of her element, she was like a fearful young child. Nélida, however, seemed totally unfazed by all her new experiences.

We walked along the beach, keeping a wide berth from the small crashing waves, with Carmen tightly clinging to us the whole time. Despite encouragement from us, Carmen refused to go closer to the water saying: 'no no, it's too dangerous.' Instead she collected more shells and rocks from the beach to add to her bulging plastic bag.

The next excursion was a walk across the dunes to another three lookouts. From the first we had a spectacular view along the coastline with its cliffs interspersed with red sand beaches. The next lookout had us looking down upon a seal colony and many more nesting birds. At the third were more seals and a few penguins. This time we were able to convince Carmen to come right to the handrail at the edge of the lookout, although the final twenty metres took her about ten minutes because of her fearfulness. She needed to have a person on either side holding her tightly and found it difficult to look over the edge, but was pleased with herself for being able to come so close.

Our final stop was at a small enclosed calm bay where Luis told us we could swim if we liked. Carmen was keen for me to show her how I could swim as she had never seen a person swim before, but as it was a bit cool I declined, a decision I later regretted. We encouraged her to take off her shoes so she could wade into the water. First she wanted to know: 'Is it safe?' We assured her she would be fine. She eventually worked up the courage to take her first tentative steps into the ocean, holding Michael's hand and looking up with a beaming smile across her face.

'It feels good,' she enthused. 'I never imagined that I would ever do this.' Michael then encouraged her to stick her finger in the ocean and put it on her tongue to taste it. 'Ooh, it's so salty,' was her response.

We couldn't persuade Nélida to take her shoes off and go in the water. She had been unable to fully enjoy the morning as she was affected by car-sickness with all the driving up and down on the sand dunes. I promised to get her some travel sickness pills from a pharmacy before their return trip to Ayacucho the next day.

Luis dropped us back in Pisco and, having found him to be friendly and trustworthy, we booked him to take us to San Clemente the following morning.

Nélida seemed to recover quickly on arriving back in Pisco, and it wasn't long before she was begging Michael to buy her *papas fritas* and *helados*. She knew Michael was easier to influence than me!

That evening, after dinner in a different *Chifa* (Chinese restaurant), we all went for a long walk down to the ocean for a final look. It would, in all probability, be the last time Carmen would ever see the sea. She was still somewhat fearful of walking around Pisco, especially in the dark, but the *Señora* in the hostel had assured us that it was safe to walk around town in the early evening. We sat on the sea wall discussing our few days together in Pisco. Carmen said she was looking forward to going home back to her familiar surroundings and she thanked us profusely for giving her such a wonderful holiday.

'Although I am happy to be going home, I will be sad because it will also mean having to leave you, and I don't know if I will ever see you again.'

Although Carmen had relaxed somewhat after three days in Pisco, she still felt uncomfortable there and unable to converse with the people. Whereas in Huanta, when she went down to the markets to bargain for her food, she was imbued with confidence, here in Pisco, out of her familiar surroundings, she was too shy and insecure to communicate with other Peruvians, and I usually had to do the talking for her. She even found it difficult to talk with the lovely *Señora* in the hostel, and found it hard to look her in the eye. In contrast, Nélida had the confidence to ask for whatever she wanted from the local people although, as a young teenager, she lacked the skills to have a meaningful conversation with them.

Breakfast the next morning was a tearful affair with the knowledge that our time together was coming to an end. We walked to the *plaza de armas* where Nélida wanted to take our last photos before Luis arrived to drive us to San Clemente.

With many tears, we said our farewells as Luis dropped us each off at our respective bus stops. Michael and I had decided it would be better not to wait with them for their bus as it would have just prolonged the emotional farewell.

We would head towards Lima along the coast, and with two days still remaining before our night flights to Iguazu, we decided to spend the time in Lunahuaná, a holiday town two hours from Lima, rather than in the capital.

CHAPTER 20 Leaving Peru

Lunahuaná is an attractive little town surrounded by high barren hills. Running through the town is a fast-flowing milky-coloured river which is used to run commercial rafting trips. It is a tourist town, although frequented by wealthy *Limeños* rather than foreigners. Michael and I were impressed by the town's cleanliness and the lack of urine smell, usually ever-present throughout Peruvian towns. Although possibly helped by the presence of the *Limeño* tourists and their dollars, the local people clearly had pride in their town.

Trying to get a vegetarian meal proved challenging. Being a tourist oriented town there were several restaurants around the *plaza de armas*. Standing out the front of many of these were touts trying to encourage potential diners. Speaking with one young man outside his restaurant, I explained I was vegetarian.

'We have fish,' he told me.

'Sorry, I don't eat fish.'

'We have chicken.'

'No, that's an animal and I don't eat any animals.'

'We have llama.'

'That's another animal.'

'What about *cuy* (guinea pig)'?

By now I was having trouble talking as I was laughing so much, as the young fellow earnestly went through his list of 'vegetarian animals'. He could not fathom what I was talking about.

Every other restaurant around the plaza was the same. We finally found a little family restaurant, away from the town centre. The owner offered me a bean dish. She and her family couldn't have been more helpful, so we ate at her restaurant for the next two days.

It was time to head back to Lima.

I had been in email contact with Cinthia, the young woman we had met on the plane a month earlier, and we arranged to meet in her office. After arriving in Lima, Michael and I took a taxi to the address she had given us in the central business district. We entered the tall modern building and were approached by the smartly dressed concierge. Wearing our dirty travelling clothes, packs on our backs, we felt out of place in this sterile environment.

'We have an appointment with Cinthia,' I told him.

'*Un momento, por favor*,' he replied as he dialled Cinthia's number. 'Come with me,' and he showed us to the elevator, pressing the correct buttons for us. 'Have a nice day.'

We stepped out onto the polished floor, so shiny you could almost see your reflection, and Cinthia breezed up to welcome us. She indicated a place to stow our packs and then showed us around her clean and airy open-plan office and introduced us to some colleagues, all dressed in smart business suits. This was all so otherworldly and in stark contrast to the conditions we had become accustomed to. We hadn't realised that such modernity existed in Peru.

We then followed Cinthia outside to where she had arranged for Ricardo, her boyfriend, to pick us up for lunch. Ricardo drove us a few blocks, found a parking space and led us into an expensive-looking restaurant, replete with white tablecloths. We felt even more out of place. Our seats were pulled out for us by a formally dressed waiter and we were waited upon as in any classy restaurant, something Michael and I are never comfortable with, especially not here in Peru. Looking at the menu, I could feel the heat rising to my face. The prices were exorbitant and I couldn't help but think that one meal here could feed the entire Carbajal Moreira family for a couple of months. I felt ill at ease. Michael, sensing my discomfort, gently kicked me under the table and gave me a look, as if to say don't worry about it.

The dishes were predominantly seafood and there was nothing vegetarian on the menu. Cinthia told me not to worry and spoke to the waiter who told me that the chef would make something special for me. And special it was. The risotto he created was indeed delicious. Michael joined Cinthia and Ricardo in a seafood platter and said it was sensational. Up until now we hadn't realised that Peruvian cuisine is in fact world renowned.

During the meal, Michael and I told Cinthia and Ricardo all about our stay with the Carbajal Moreiras and about the holiday to Pisco with Carmen and Nélida. Ricardo seemed unable to comprehend our accounts of the basic living conditions of the family and then his jaw dropped almost to the floor when we mentioned Carmen's first ever hot shower in Pisco. From the course of the conversation, it was clear that Ricardo had grown up in a rich family in Lima. He had led a sheltered life and had no idea that there were people in his own country living such a simple life. We got the feeling that he felt uncomfortable even talking about it, and didn't want to know about the vast majority of his countrymen and women who were living in poverty. Cinthia didn't seem quite as surprised. She had grown up in Trujillo, a city in northern Peru, and had travelled more.

Once I relaxed, we enjoyed our lunch with this young couple. When the bill arrived Cinthia insisted on paying, despite our attempts to cover our costs.

Before heading home, Michael and I were heading to Iguazú in Argentina to see the famous *Cataratas de Iguazú.* As our flight from Lima wasn't departing until 1.15 in the morning, Cinthia suggested we leave our backpacks in her office so we could look around Lima unencumbered. She told us she had an English lesson that evening in Miraflores, so we arranged to meet her and Ricardo after that.

We spent the afternoon around Lima and explored the Huaca Pucllana pre-Inca ruins that had only recently been unearthed, having been buried beneath the city for 1600 years. They were fascinating and a long way ahead of their time in terms of earthquake preparation. The buildings were built using the book shelf technique whereby the adobe bricks were positioned vertically with gaps between them to be able to withstand the earth's movements. These ruins are surrounded by modern apartment buildings which will no doubt crumble well before the ruins.

We found our way to the English college at the appointed time and Ricardo also met us there and drove us back to the office to collect our luggage. Cinthia then tried to hail a taxi for us. This proved to be a lengthy procedure as most taxis which pulled over didn't have the required authorisation to enter the airport. Finally, an authorised taxi pulled up and Cinthia asked the driver his price to the airport. He quoted 30 soles. Cinthia told him that was too expensive and let him go, although Michael and I would have been happy to pay the 30 soles. It was some time before another taxi pulled up. He also quoted 30 soles but Cinthia bargained him down to 25 and we got in. I felt uncomfortable with her forcefulness as we thought 30 soles was quite reasonable.

During the journey we chatted to the friendly *taxista*, who told us he was actually a police officer who drove taxis in his spare time. His family couldn't survive solely on the policeman's wage of 1200 soles (under $500) monthly. Michael and I could now understand why one hears of so many corrupt police officers who accept bribes in Peru and in other Latin American countries.

Our *taxista-policía* inserted a disc into the car's CD player and loud modern Peruvian pop music blared through the speakers.

'Do you like it?' he asked earnestly.

'Not really,' I replied honestly, 'I prefer the more traditional Andean music.'

He then removed the CD and replaced it with another one. The soothing sounds of pan pipes filled the car.

'I love this music,' I told him enthusiastically.

When we arrived at the airport he ejected the CD and handed it to me as a present. I paid him 30 soles for the trip, being the original price he'd quoted, as I'd intended to do all along.

Our last day in Peru had been wonderful and it was with warm hearts that we were leaving, having been touched by the kindness of a Peruvian couple whom we barely knew and by a taxi driver who was a total stranger. We guessed that Cinthia must have been earning a good wage (by Peruvian standards) with the mining company, but we also surmised that she wasn't rich. Although the meal had seemed to be extraordinarily expensive to us at the time, having just been living in the highlands, if we had put it into Australian dollar terms it was probably the cost of a meal in a reasonable, but not high class, restaurant in Australia. With the value of our dollar the meal would have been much less costly for us than for Cinthia with her Peruvian soles, yet she had insisted on paying. As for the taxi driver policeman, he'd had his normal price bargained down, yet he still chose to give us the CD to take home as a memory of Peru.

~~~~

Our 1.15 am flight was delayed, meaning a few more hours in Lima airport which was surprisingly one of the nicest and most spotlessly
~~~~

clean airports we'd been in. Fortunately we were able to find an isolated dark corner in which to sleep, on padded chairs. We finally flew to Buenos Aires from where we had another flight to Iguazú, arriving at two in the afternoon, to a lovely warm sunny day. Our timing was fortunate because it had been raining torrentially for a week and the river was in flood.

Iguazú Falls, which were made famous by the movie 'The Mission', form a section of border for three countries – Argentina, Brazil and Paraguay.

We spent the next two days at the *cataratas* on the Argentinean side and they were the most spectacular falls we'd ever seen. The huge and powerful Paraná River, with a width of about two kilometres at the falls, drops over a series of ledges creating an incredible spectacle. Due to the flooding rains, the normally white frothy falls were brown-coloured and the huge volume of water was an awesome sight to behold. Even though we were unable to get to some of the vantage points due to the walkways being underwater, we weren't disappointed.

The walkways that we were able to walk on hovered only about a metre above the roaring cascade of water, which was quite unnerving. The large stanchions supporting the walkways were actually in the flooded river and we surmised that in Australia these walkways would undoubtedly have also been closed for safety reasons.

The lush rainforest surrounding the falls is magnificent. While walking along the trails we were mesmerised by a myriad of beautifully coloured butterflies gently fluttering around us. There were strange birds to admire, including the comic-looking toucan with its big colourful bill, and a variety of animals, including monkeys and the cheeky semi-tame coatis, which look a bit like a raccoon with a long tail sticking straight up in the air like an aerial.

Although we tried, we never made it to the Brazilian side of the river as we didn't have a Brazilian visa and they don't issue them at the border.

We had a wonderful few days in Iguazú before returning home to Australia (via Chile to see Antonio and pick up our bikes), but once again we couldn't help thinking about our Peruvian family and how unfair it was that we Australians had the opportunity to enjoy this incredible natural spectacle while the Carbajal Moreiras, who live in the same continent, probably never would.

Karina was often in our minds as we wondered how her preparation for the big MOEA conference in Lima was going. It was being held a week after Michael and I returned home and we were looking forward to hearing all about it.

CHAPTER 21 Karina Graduates

August 2010

'The MOEA conference was an incredible and unforgettable experience,' Karina wrote, 'it was like a United Nations conference. There were hundreds of students from across the Americas and we were all seated around a large oval table with our countries written on a card in front of us. Each university was charged with preparing and proposing a resolution, which the main body of the conference then had to vote to accept or reject. There were nine other students from my university's faculty of law and I was the leader of the 'third commission' where my resolution about the rights of indigenous people to live in a clean environment was proposed and accepted.'

Karina told us she had enjoyed mixing with students of many differing nationalitics and backgrounds. Once again she revelled in the luxury of the hotel, so different to what she was used to. She'd had her first taste of being on the world stage and had loved it.

A few weeks later she was selected to attend another conference in Lima – for the top students from all the universities of Peru. From her university, the first place student from each faculty was selected. The conference themes included leadership, ethics and the inclusion of marginalised communities, this final theme resonating strongly with Karina.

Through sheer hard work and dedication to her studies, Karina was rewarded with these amazing experiences which should serve to improve her chances of success in her chosen career.

On the 28th August 2010, Karina's graduation ceremony was held in Ayacucho. Unfortunately Celestino and Marleni were both too ill to attend, however the rest of the family were present to witness the conferring of her degree. We could only imagine their pride as Karina appeared in her faculty's graduation gown to accept her degree. Michael and I topped off her wonderful day with a surprise phone call in the evening. As she shared the day's excitement with us, we were undeniably proud of her achievements.

'It was so wonderful sharing the day with my family, but I wish you could have been here as well,' she told us, her voice full of emotion, 'you were, however, present in my heart.'

Carmen, Mariluz, Wilbur, Margot and Nélida were with Karina in her room in Ayacucho and they passed the phone from one to the other so we could talk to each of them. Karina's siblings were equally proud of their sister and we could hear the pride in Carmen's voice as she spoke about the ceremony and the excitement of having the first university graduate in her family.

'I was overcome with emotion on seeing Karina receive first her degree and then after that the special award for coming first in her year. I could never, in my wildest dreams, have imagined that this could happen in my family.'

~~~~

After the excitement of the graduation ceremony, reality set back in. Although after over six years of study Karina had gained her degree, she was not yet a qualified lawyer. In order to qualify, she had to complete another four months of practical placement, which she was doing at the Auditor General's Office of the Nation, including the submission of a detailed written report at the end. Then she still had her thesis to write, leaving her a considerable amount of time before finishing.

In October, when Karina was only about two months from completing her prac, a new scheme was put in place whereby students could opt to be paid a basic living wage for their work. She decided to take up the offer, even though it would mean having to forgo the four months of already completed prac and having to complete another six months. Her thinking was that at least she would be able to cover her own living expenses while she continued to work on her thesis. She would be paid 500 soles ($200) a month.

During this time Karina received another award and trip. The National Superintendency of Public Registries (SUNARP) – the national governing body of public records – invited all first and second place legal students to a special award ceremony in Ica, on the coast not far from Pisco. SUNARP would cover the costs for accommodation in a good hotel and transport.
~~~~

Having obtained permission from her prac supervisor to attend, Karina, along with her colleague, caught the night bus to Ica. Arriving at 4.30 am, tired but excited about the trip and ceremony, they hailed a taxi and asked to be taken to their hotel. However, they were given the fright of their lives when the *taxista* turned out to be a *ratero*. He drove them to an isolated place, pulled out a knife and, holding it threateningly in front of them, demanded they hand over all their valuables.

Karina and her friend, in fear for their lives, pleaded with the driver not to harm them, stating they were just two poor students from Ayacucho. The driver took their cameras, mobile phones and all their money. They were left there, by the roadside, to fend for themselves. Fearfully, they walked back to town and found their way to the hotel. Fortuitously, Karina had stashed 50 soles ($20) in her shoe and this was all the money the pair had to spend for the next two days.

Karina told us that although not physically harmed, she and her friend were both incredibly traumatised by the incident and were unable to fully enjoy their award ceremony. This was the second time Karina had been the victim of an armed robbery and it left her feeling insecure and afraid in her own country. In addition, she was disappointed that she didn't have any photos by which to remember the event, apart from an article and photo that was published in Ica's local newspaper.

Karina apologised to Michael and me for having lost the camera and told us that her family was angry with her and very upset that the camera, with all its memories from our visit, was gone. We reassured her that it wasn't her fault and a little later we sent over a replacement camera.

~~~~

Once back in Ayacucho, Karina continued with her prac work and her thesis. Speaking with her in early 2011, we found her in a depressed state.

'I can't see any way of completing the thesis,' she moaned. 'Now that I am being paid for my work, I am expected to put in long hours and by the time I get home, I am exhausted. My thesis
~~~~

is only advancing very slowly as I don't have the time or energy to devote to it.'

Adding to Karina's worries were the continuing illnesses of her father and Marleni. Additionally, a close family friend had just been killed in a car accident. He'd been on his way to the *selva* when his car rolled. Michael and I had briefly met this man in Huanta. He was a Mayoral candidate for the upcoming council elections, and he'd come to the family home to paint his name, in huge letters, on their front wall. Karina and Mariluz had worked closely with him on human rights violation issues. They had been hoping that Huanta would finally get a Mayor with a concern for human rights and who wanted to combat corruption. With his death this hope was dashed.

Michael and I were concerned that Karina wouldn't be able to complete her thesis in a reasonable time frame. We realised that she wasn't going to get anywhere by earning just enough to cover only her basic living expenses. Her thesis was integral to being able to earn a decent living. We decided that we would like to provide Karina with the means to finish it as soon as possible. Only then could she start to earn a real wage.

I wrote to Karina with our offer: She could leave her prac as soon as she had finished the minimum required time and we would then pay her the 500 soles per month for six months, so that she could devote her entire energies to finishing her thesis.

'I feel embarrassed that I am causing you further expense,' Karina replied, thanking us profusely, 'but I would like to take up your generous offer. I will finish my prac and the accompanying report at the end of April, and then I will begin working on my thesis full-time. I promise that I will work hard and finish it as soon as possible so I can get a good job and start earning a real wage to assist my family,' she wrote.

~~~~

In July 2011, there was great excitement within our family and amongst the poorer people of Peru. In the National General Elections, Ollanta Humala, an indigenous Peruvian representing a party from the centre left, narrowly defeated Keiko Fujimori, daughter of the now infamous Alberto Fujimori. Humala promised
~~~~

to improve the living conditions of the huge impoverished population while still maintaining foreign investment and economic growth. The less well-off people of Peru believed they finally had a Government who would take care of their well-being and many Peruvians had high hopes for this Government.

Later that same month, we received en email from Karina telling us that she had been offered a job in Lima. She was seeking our advice. Excitedly, I phoned her straight away. The position was with the Government, she told us, but she was worried that Michael and I might be upset if she took a job before finishing her thesis. On the contrary, we were ecstatic. I told her that she had our blessings to accept the job, and asked her to tell us more about it.

'I will be working for the *congresista* who has just been elected to represent the district of Ayacucho, in the new Government of Peru, in their National Congress. My work will involve human rights issues as well as other projects for the whole country, such as auditing against corruption,' she explained.

I asked what her job title would be.

'I am being employed as an *abogada,*' Karina proudly told me.

'An *abogada...* Really?'

Whooping with excitement, I ran out to Michael and screamed, 'Our goddaughter's an *abogada*. She's got a job as a lawyer. We have a lawyer in the family.'

We hugged each other and cried. We were possibly even more excited than Karina and couldn't believe that after all these long years Karina was finally employed as a lawyer. She would start work on August 8th, as an *ABOGADA*.

Throughout her early years of study, Michael and I had been concerned that Karina would complete a lengthy course and be unable to secure a job at the end of it. We didn't think she would have the all-important contacts – vital in a country like Peru. However, after several years we realised that our intelligent, vivacious *ahijada* was able to make her own contacts through her studies and we were less concerned. Then, when Karina kept achieving the first place in her year, we were reassured that she would be fine. And now, seven years later, she had her first job as a lawyer.

I asked Karina how she had in fact got the job when she hadn't been actively searching. She explained that her new boss, the congressman, was a friend of her sister's. Mariluz had told the *congresista* that Karina had just finished her law degree, gaining first place in her year, and mentioned how hardworking and intelligent she was. The congressman phoned Karina and asked her to come to Lima with her curriculum vitae for an interview. She was offered the job on the spot.

So, for Karina, it was in fact through contacts that she'd been offered the interview, but she'd still won the job on her own merit.

Karina explained to us that until she finished her thesis she would not be receiving a lawyer's pay. Her pay would be a meagre 1500 soles ($600) per month and out of that would be taken 100 soles for health insurance, 100 soles for superannuation and then her rent, which in Lima is substantial. The rest would have to cover all her travel and living expenses. She wanted to be able to help with the family budget, but there wasn't going to be much left over after her expenses. She also mentioned that although she would miss her family terribly and wouldn't enjoy living in a big city like Lima, it was a better place from which to finish her thesis. For this she required many books, most of which were more readily available in Lima than in Ayacucho.

Michael and I were nervous about our little *ahijada* in the big bad city of Lima. I impressed upon her the need to pay a little more for rent to be sure she was in a safe area. She assured me she would do this.

Late at night in Nowra, on the 8th of August 2011, when it was the morning in Peru, Michael and I went to sleep thinking of Karina as she started her new job. We were both so happy for her and unable to wipe the smile from our faces for days. We could only imagine how proud she and her family must be feeling.

We knew the family would have mixed feelings – pleased she had the job, but worried about her in Lima and unhappy that she was so far away. With the 11-12 hour travel time, and the expense, Karina would not be able to travel home very often.

I phoned Karina after her first week at work and she told me it hadn't been too difficult a start, as all the employees were new and learning the routine. Apparently when a new Government is elected in Peru there is a complete staff changeover. She was confident that she would enjoy working there and her new work colleagues seemed friendly, but she was already feeling the distance from her family. The job would be for a minimum of five years, which is the term of office for the elected government.

It took Karina some time to find an affordable room to rent. The small one she eventually moved into cost her 380 soles per month. She said it was a bit smaller than her room in Ayacucho, which was about eight metres by four (and had only cost 100 soles), but it did have an en-suite bathroom, a luxury for Karina. In Peru it is common to rent a room rather than a house or apartment and it often entails having to share a bathroom, as she'd had to do in Ayacucho. All Karina got for her money was a room and a bathroom in a mediocre area. Although initially told there was hot water, she soon found out that it was only rarely hot and she had no access to any cooking facilities. She was about thirty minutes (depending on traffic) by bus from her work in the middle of town, so it was reasonably convenient, and she assured me that it was in a relatively safe area.

~~~~

Six months into her new job, Karina told us she was happy with the work, although she missed her family greatly. She hadn't been able to advance her thesis much as she worked long hours and was often too tired to work on it by the time she arrived home. She also confided in us that she was having trouble covering the costs associated with the thesis. When Michael and I were in Peru in 2010, we had given her enough money for the projected expenses of her thesis, with strict instructions that the money was to remain in her bank account until it was needed for the thesis. However, she told us rather sheepishly over the phone that all the money had been used up. 'Now that I am earning a wage,' she continued, 'my father is constantly asking me for money for medical expenses for my siblings.'

When I suggested to Karina that the thesis must be a priority, so that she could be paid a decent wage which would directly benefit the family, she replied that she knew this but it wasn't so simple. 'I am unable to say no to my father when he asks for money for the health and well-being of my family. My family has to come first.'
~~~~

Although this frustrated Michael and me, we admired Karina's selfless commitment to her family.

Six months later, after she had been working for the Government for a year, Karina's prospects changed again. Her boss, the congressman for Ayacucho, was suspended for two months while under investigation due to allegations of sexual misconduct. For these two months Karina was without work or pay. We gave her enough money to cover her living expenses in Lima and told her that this was a great opportunity to complete her thesis.

However, something else intervened to prevent this happening. Margot's health had rapidly deteriorated during the year. She got to the stage where she couldn't go for more than five minutes without needing to urinate, and she had constant backache and pain in the pelvic area. She had numerous tests in Ayacucho and was given various treatments, none of which helped her. Finally, in desperation, she travelled to Lima for further investigations. Karina spent much of her two month enforced break looking after Margot and taking her to her various appointments.

Karina hadn't been able to devote much time or energy to her thesis by the time she went back to work. Then, when she started back at work, she found that she and many of the other staff had received a fifty percent wage reduction. Her pay would now not even cover her living expenses. At a loss, she travelled to Ayacucho to talk with her old university professors who suggested another way that she could finish off her Law qualification, and together they mapped out a course of action. She would need to spend two months studying various court proceedings and write up her findings. After passing an exam, she would then be a qualified *abogada.* She would continue later with the thesis, which could be incorporated into a Masters qualification. So, with our promised extra support for another two months, Karina left her job to concentrate full-time on her studies.

It did take longer than the promised two months, as everything in Peru seems to, but in October 2013, after over nine years of study, Karina passed her examination and became a fully qualified lawyer. We all breathed a collective sigh of relief. She could now embark on her career and be paid fairly for her work.

~~~~

We are so proud of our *ahijada* and her achievements. She has come from a poor indigenous family without the opportunities we take for granted in Australia. University was a constant struggle: her room lacked adequate lighting by which to study and she had to manage without a computer. She battled her own illnesses and had the constant concern for the health of her father and siblings, yet she persevered and through sheer hard work and against all the odds, she finished a law degree, coming first in her year.

Karina realises how fortunate she is to have had the opportunity to study. Her dream continues to be to work in human rights law to help other less fortunate people to obtain equal rights and a better future and we believe that she will achieve this goal.
~~~~

EPILOGUE

Mariluz left her job at PRONAA in the middle of 2010, stating that her pay was too unreliable, and acquired another six month contract with a different agency. Her new job was still in the *selva* but this time her role was to provide instruction in productive agricultural techniques to 40 small communities. She enjoyed the work but the contract ended in December. Since then she has had several different jobs, all on limited contracts, some of which she has enjoyed while with others she has had to work ridiculously long hours for very little pay.

Mariluz would like to complete a degree as she still feels marginalised and unable to find a well paid job because she 'only has a diploma' rather than a degree. She dreams of setting up her own business – her latest idea is selling boutique organic coffee, grown on the family *chacra*, although she lacks the capital to do this right now. Michael and I talked about whether or not we should give her the money for this, but decided that given we have already supported her to receive her diploma, now she should find her own way to work towards her future. We are confident that with her drive she will eventually succeed.

Wilbur stopped studying to look after Celestino (who had become almost totally blind by the middle of 2011) and Jharol the baby. It was hard for us to imagine Wilbur taking on these responsibilities, but talking and laughing with his sisters about the situation, they said he was doing a marvellous job and that he loves Jharol, who is now five years old, and takes him everywhere. I wanted to know what Wilbur cooked and Mariluz told me he could cook eggs and rice. I don't imagine they are eating a very varied diet when Carmen is down in the *selva*, which is more often than not!

In 2013 Celestino had two operations to remove the cataracts from his eyes and he is happily now able to see again, although he still suffers from his numerous other ailments. He never did have the operation to cure his other ailments.

Wilbur's *tio* Edmundo gave him a beaten up old truck and helped him to fix it into some sort of working order. He has been using it to earn some money, transporting goods to a neighbouring village.

Marleni, meanwhile, continued to suffer with chronic tonsillitis. We forwarded the money for a tonsillectomy and, after two months of recovery time, she was finally free from the sore throat that had plagued her for so long. We had hoped that once she'd recovered physically, she would also recover mentally. Unfortunately this wasn't to be. She spent the next year suffering from significant mental health problems which affected her motivation to make something of her life. She was prescribed medication and is now in a much better state of mind. We've even been able to laugh with her again on the phone. Marleni has been living with Carmen in the *selva* and helping on the *chacra.*

Margot finished school at the end of 2010. She and Nélida attended an institute in Ayacucho to try to qualify for university in 2012. They didn't get accepted into university and blamed the corrupt system. They said that only those who had the money to bribe the officials were granted a place.

~~~~

There have been times, over the years, when I have been annoyed at Mariluz and Karina for not answering my emails for long periods, and then we've found out that they did indeed write, but the emails never got through. As great as the computer age is, it's not infallible and I've written an annoyed email or two, only to be answered with surprise that the emails they sent had never arrived. Surprisingly, every parcel we have sent via snail mail up to this point in time has arrived, even if at times, months later.

In the last few years, contact with the family has become easier now that some of them have mobile phones. Whereas before, we had to go through the difficult and expensive procedure of arranging a time for them to go to the *cabinas* in town and the difficulties of making a connection, now we can phone them direct. With an Australian phone card we can talk for an hour for three dollars, so we phone more regularly. Every time we talk with any of them, they ask us when we are coming back to Peru, a question to which we're not able to give a definitive answer.
~~~~

There was another time, over two years ago now, when we felt that the Carbajal Moreiras were taking us for granted. Apart from a brief email from Karina, we hadn't heard from any of them for a couple of months, previously unheard of. Although we didn't distrust them we were nonetheless annoyed at the lack of response, particularly from the younger family members who we were now supporting. I decided that I wouldn't deposit their monthly stipend, knowing that this would elicit a quick response. Sure enough an email arrived a few days later from Karina asking if I'd forgotten to deposit the money. I wrote straight back explaining that no, I hadn't forgotten, but expressed our feelings of being taken for granted. I told her that we did intend to continue our support for the family but that we needed more contact from them. I also wondered why none of the others had written – we were, after all, supporting the whole family, not just her and Mariluz. Surely Margot, Nélida or Marleni could have written.

Karina emailed straight back with lengthy apologies and explanations. I followed up with a phone call and caught Karina at an after-work social function. She went into the toilet cubicle and then poured out her heart, for over half an hour. I was unable to get a word in.

'I am so sorry,' she sobbed, 'I understand exactly why you feel this way – I would feel the same. Everyone in my family loves you and we are deeply upset that you distrust us. Even if you don't give us one more *centavo*, you are still a part of our family and we love you unconditionally. You will always be welcome in our house.' She was crying into the phone. 'It's really bad of me not to have written and you have every right to be angry with me. I have been so busy at work and we're not allowed to send personal emails. When I finish work, it's late and hard to get to an internet café. Mariluz is in the *selva* and can't always get to an internet and often there is no connection. Margot has been very ill and Nélida doesn't know how to email. I should have taught her. It's my fault. Marleni is with *mamá* in the *selva*, *papá* is ill. I am stressed at work and I don't know how I can ever finish my thesis...'

I was in tears too and felt bad that my email had caused them all so much anguish. But it had to be said and I was glad the air was cleared. From that day onwards, whenever there is a slightly longer break between emails, we don't think anything of it. We understand their feelings and we know they'll be in touch when they can. We know that it is more difficult for them to get to a computer than it is for us.

~~~~

The Carbajal Moreira family continues to struggle on, battling with their daily life. What continues to amaze and impress us is the fact that they are all still working together as a tight family unit. Any money earned is spent as needed for the welfare of the whole family. This is despite the fact that the 'kids' are all grown up and ranging from 20 to 31 years of age.

We had hoped that some of the younger girls would also be able to be educated beyond school but, although they have the motivation and intelligence, their health problems are preventing them from being able to study at the moment. We hope this situation will be remedied in the not too distant future.

~~~~

Margot's dream of studying was dashed when she became very ill again in early 2013 and travelled to Lima for further investigation. She saw several doctors who offered different diagnoses and prescribed a whole range of medications. Eventually she was seen by one of the leading doctors in the field. After numerous treatments and various medication regimes, none of which eased her symptoms, she was diagnosed with Interstitial Cystitis (known as Painful Bladder Syndrome in Australia), an incurable illness. She told us that patients with this illness have to manage their pain and symptoms with various medications. There are some possible surgical interventions, but the result is not always favourable. We have continued to offer our financial support to Margot to cover her medical expenses.

In 2014 Margot went into hospital for an operation to alleviate her symptoms. Unfortunately the operation went badly and one of her intestines was accidently nicked in the procedure. She then contracted an infection which nearly killed her and spent over two months in hospital. Mariluz left her job in the jungle to care for Margot in hospital as the medical care provided by the hospital was inadequate. Mariluz showed incredible sisterly love and devotion and remained by Margot's side 24 hours a day. She was left with a colostomy bag for several months until she was strong enough for another operation, in January 2015, to fix up the doctor's error. At the time of writing, she is recovering from the second operation and her original symptoms continue.

~~~~

Karina finished off her Masters qualification at the end of 2013 and began working towards a doctorate. In early 2014 she began intensive evening English classes but had to stop attending when Margot became so ill. Her doctorate is also on hold. In late 2014 Karina began working for the Ministry of Culture, a job she told me she is really enjoying. Part of her job relates to the linguistic rights of people who speak local languages such as Quechua, Ashaninka, Awajun and others. During her first week in the job she travelled to Huancayo to meet with Quechua speaking justices of peace and she has already travelled to several other regional areas. She's excited about this job and the new opportunities that may arise.

~~~~

Nélida has started a college course in Business Administration. She studies in the morning and works in the afternoons for a local council in Lima, a job Karina procured for her.

~~~~

We hope one day things will be much easier for the Carbajal Moreira family, but until then we will continue to support them financially and emotionally. After all, they are our family too.

February 2015

If you would like updates on the family, please visit
www.laniimhofperuviandream.wordpress.com
~~~~

AFTERWORD

Friends have often asked Michael and me why we chose to support one family rather than spreading our charity further and supporting a whole community. They have asked us if we think the family is milking us 'rich' westerners, considering we have been supporting them for such a long time. They wonder what others in the community feel about the support the Carbajal Moreiras are receiving from us and expect that it must create feelings of inequality and jealousy. Why have they been singled out for support?

In theory, Michael and I like the way agencies which offer child sponsorship programs, such as Plan and World Vision, operate. They don't just support the one child who is 'the sponsor child', but support a whole community.

We don't directly support a community. We support one family, going against our normal view of an effective support mechanism. However, our support for the Carbajal Moreiras was not planned. It just happened and it grew and it continued. Why? Because the bond between our two families grew and flourished until 'we' considered 'them' to be 'our' family and vice versa.

Although by now we feel our support for the Carbajal Moreiras should have finished, we can't just abandon a family we consider to be our own. If the Peruvians had not been beset by so many health problems, we would have been able to withdraw our financial support by now. They certainly don't expect us to continue supporting them, but are very appreciative that we are. Karina has often written of her embarrassment that she is a fully qualified lawyer, yet they are still relying on our support. For example, without our support, Margot would not be able to obtain the health care that she needs.

We also have not taken our roles as godparents lightly. Karina is like a daughter to us, as are the rest of the kids. If our daughter needed health care, we would not think twice about paying for such treatment. This is how we feel about the family.

As for jealousy in the community, this was something that had concerned us and we actually asked the Carbajal Moreiras this same question when we were last with them in 2010. Celestino explained that no-one in the community knows that they are receiving overseas support. Their neighbours, of course, know that they have had *gringo* house guests, but they don't know any more than that. Even the younger Carbajal Moreiras never knew about the financial assistance until they became adults. The family doesn't have more possessions than their neighbours – in fact they have fewer. They don't live substantially differently to their neighbours. At times they still struggle financially like many others in the community. In fact, if Celestino was still able to work and provide for his family, they would be in a much more financially secure state.

Most of Mariluz and Karina's colleagues at college and university had it much easier than they did, not having to scrimp and save to the same extent. They had working parents who were able to provide them with adequate support. We are so proud of all that they achieved.

The children's achievements would not have been possible without Carmen and Celestino, who instilled such wonderful ethics in all of their offspring. Although Celestino is housebound, he continues to be the foundation stone of the family. He is the wits of the family and they all listen to the advice that he continues to provide. He holds the family together.

I believe it was fate that led our two families together. It is love and respect that will keep that bond going. Michael and my lives have certainly been enriched by becoming a part of a large loving indigenous Peruvian family and learning about their culture. It also makes us appreciate just how good we have it in Australia.

Glossary

Abuela/ Abuelita – grandmother
Abuelo – grandfather
Ahijada – goddaughter
Altiplano – the high plains
Artesanía – handicrafts
Aymara – indigenous group of people
Baño – toilet
Bonito/a – beautiful
Cajero Automatico – ATM
Camioneta – ute
Campesino – peasant / farmer, country folk
Carpa – tent
Carretera – highway
Cascada – waterfall
Centavo – cent – 100 centavos = 1 sol
Chacra – plot of land/ small farm/orchard
Chicha – fermented drink made from maize (corn)
– not always alcoholic.
Chifa – Chinese restaurant
Chileno – Chilean person
Colectivo – car, taxi or van used as shared transportation and always running the same route
Combi – van/mini-bus used as a *colectivo*
Come (pronounced comé) – eat
Compañero – companion, colleague, comrade
Cordillera – mountain range
Cuatro por cuatro – (literally four by four) – four-wheel drive
Cuidado! – take care!
Cuy – guinea pig
Está bién? – is it okay? Are you okay?
Familia – family
Fiesta – festival
Garbanzos – chick peas

Gringo/a – what South Americans call white people – originally used more for North Americans, but now for all white tourists.
Helado – ice cream
Hola – a greeting – hello
Hospedaje – accommodation in a family home
Humita – a delicious food parcel made from sweet corn – a Peruvian and Chilean specialty
Inca Cola – a typical Peruvian soft drink, yellow coloured and tasting a bit like Passiona
Isla – island
Jefe – boss
Lago – lake
Laguna – lagoon
Lúcuma – a fruit native to Peru, has a floury consistency and a vanilla like taste
Madrina – godmother
Manta – a square shaped coloured woven cloth with multiple uses ranging from carrying babies, food and firewood to a tablecloth.
Más – more
Media hora más – half an hour more
Moto-taxi – a three wheeled motor bike with a covered cabin behind the driver. It can seat about 3 passengers.
Ojalá – hopefully, God willing
Pacay – an edible bean also known as the ice-cream bean
Pachamanca – feast – the meat and vegies are all roasted in an underground pit.
Padrino – godfather
Padrinos – godparents
Palta – avocado
Pan – bread (usually refers to bread rolls)
Papas fritas – hot chips
Peón – worker, labourer
Plaza de armas – central town square – present in virtually every Peruvian town or city (and throughout South America).
Pronto – quickly, soon
Propina – tip
Pueblo – small town
Quechua – Indigenous people, descendents of the Inca

Ratero – robber
Rico/a – delicious (usually in relation to food)
Río – river
Selva – jungle
Semana Santa – Easter
Sendero Luminoso – Shining Path – a terrorist organisation that wreaked havoc in Peru from 1980 to 2000
Sí – yes
Sol (plural **soles**) – Peruvian currency (also the word for sun) 100 soles = approximately 40 Australian dollars.
Supermercado – supermarket
Taxista – taxi driver
Terremoto – earthquake
Tibia – luke-warm
Tienda – shop
Tío/Tía – uncle/aunt
Tuna (pronounced toona) – fruit from the cactus plant – can be red, yellow or orange
Yuca / **Pituca** – root crops

Mariluz & Abuelita shelling peas

ACKNOWLEGEMENTS

This book has only been possible with the help of many people. I am indebted to all those who gave me advice and tips on my writing and those who corrected my poor grammar.

I have to give a special thank you to my very dear family friend, Yola Center, who edited the entire manuscript not once but twice. She also kept me with a smile on my dial when querying certain aspects, like did I really need that much detail in relation to going to the toilet. I did cut some out! A huge thank you also to my other two key editors, Phil Cocking and Aviva Imhof, who both worked through the entire manuscript.

Thank you very much to Claire Heath from Scribblygum Writing and Editing who edited a few chapters for me and gave me many suggestions on how to improve my writing style. Thanks also go to Maureen Bell who made me think about how and why I was writing the book.

Thank you very much to Simon Hunter who, when asked if he could proof read the manuscript, did so meticulously and with incredible attention to detail and even did some extra editing on the way. He was also responsible for me deleting numerous commas (sorry Yola).

Thank you Kate Matthew and Kathy Thieben who made the initial suggestion that I should write the book and then went on to offer further editing and advice on the manuscript.

Thanks very much Gill Souter for the wonderful cover design and publishing assistance. I couldn't have done it without you.

David Rowe, thank you very much for preparing the map for me at short notice.

Thank you to all other friends and family who read individual chapters to edit, proof-read and offer suggestions including but not limited to Jenny Kubale, Agi Seeman, Anne Holder, George Thieben, Louise Dalton, Sue Hailstone and Tessa. There were many more of you who listened to me talk about the family and offered suggestions along the way and who also read bits and pieces for me. Thank you.

Thanks of course go to my loving husband and travelling companion, Michael Smith, who has lived and continues to live the story with me. He not only had to put up with me spending hours locked away in the office but was also co-opted to read parts of the manuscript more than once.

And finally a huge thank you to the entire Carbajal Moreira family who have agreed for their story to be told and have helped in the process when asked. I'm just sorry that most of the family won't be able to read the story as they don't speak English - yet. Hopefully this will change soon.

Mariluz, Wilbur, Nélida, Margot, Karina, Michael, Marleni with the 'Imhof Smith' *moto-taxi* in Huanta – 2004

Mariluz, Abuelita, Marleni, Nélida, Celestino, Karina, Margot, Wilbur, Carmen – 2004

Margot & Nélida bathing in the *rio* with cousins - 2004

The back of the Carbajal Moreira home in Huanta. You can see the ladder with the new handrail that Michael and Wilbur built. Nélida and Margot are on the veranda behind which are the bedrooms 2010

Michael, Wilbur, Carmen, Karina, Nélida, Margot in front of the fountain in Huanta's plaza de armas - 2010

Back: Marleni, Lani, Wilbur, Celestino
Front: Jharol, Margot, Carmen, Nélida - 2010

Back cover photos

Top: Karina with her mother on graduation day

Bottom: Back row – Celestino, Marleni, Nélida, Carmen, Margot, Karina, Lani
Front row – Michael, Wilbur, Mariluz & Jharol - 2010

www.ingramcontent.com/pod-product-compliance
Lightning Source LLC
Chambersburg PA
CBHW031833090426
42741CB00005B/227

* 9 7 8 1 8 7 6 7 7 9 9 8 6 *